"Ken Bailey is the consummate expert o[n]
here he applies these skills to one mo[re]
ployed in a variety of biblical stories and parables. His interpretations use a variety of
tools unknown to many of us: ancient versions, original languages, cultural anthropology, ancient Middle Eastern writers who shared this ancient culture, and his own
personal career embedded in a crosscultural life in the Middle East. Always insightful,
always fresh, consistently surprising, Bailey has produced yet another book that will
get many of us rethinking beloved passages of Scripture in completely new ways."
Gary Burge, professor of New Testament, Wheaton College

"'The Lord is my shepherd.' There is no more beloved picture of God's relationship
with his people. Jesus' declaration that he is 'the good shepherd' has comforted
Christians for centuries. Using his impressive knowledge of Scripture and his experience living for many years in the Middle East, Bailey deepens and enriches our
understanding of what it means to be members of God's flock."
Tremper Longman III, Robert H. Gundry Professor of Biblical Studies, Westmont College

"Kenneth Bailey refreshes the souls of readers with deep textual insights and helpful
contextual background to safely shepherd readers through the thousand-year story
of Psalm 23. He makes several stops along the way in the Prophets, before settling
into the Gospels where he deftly introduces us to a fresh understanding of the Good
Shepherd. Anyone who loves the 23rd Psalm will love this book."
David Lamb, associate professor of Old Testament, Biblical Theological Seminary; author
of *God Behaving Badly*

"'You prepare a table before me . . . my cup overflows.' What a feast Ken Bailey has
prepared for us in this book, and what an overflowing cupful of insights and illumination. If you ever thought there was nothing more you could ever learn or preach
about the biblical image of the good shepherd, this book has an abundance of surprises. Again and again I thought, 'Why have I never seen that before?'—as Ken
draws on his rich lifetime's experience of Middle Eastern culture to explore biblical
texts, and particularly when he shows eye-opening connections between Old and
New Testament texts around the shepherd theme. This is a book that simultaneously
brings the Bible to life, and exalts the Lord Jesus Christ by deeply enriching our
understanding of his mission and claims as the Good Shepherd."
Christopher J. H. Wright, International Ministries Director, Langham Partnership

"Deftly wielding the tools of biblical scholarship, story-telling, and cultural exegesis,
Ken Bailey has restored to its full color and brilliance one of the most magnificent
images of Scripture—the character and work of the Good Shepherd. This book is a
treasure trove of useable insights for preachers and teachers and a devotional classic
for daily disciples alike."
Daniel Meyer, Christ Church, Oakbrook, Illinois

36 Simile vs metaphor

THE
GOOD
SHEPHERD

A THOUSAND-YEAR JOURNEY FROM
PSALM 23 TO THE NEW TESTAMENT

KENNETH E. BAILEY

IVP Academic

An imprint of InterVarsity Press
Downers Grove, Illinois

InterVarsity Press
P.O. Box 1400, Downers Grove, IL 60515-1426
ivpress.com
email@ivpress.com

InterVarsity Press® is the book-publishing division of InterVarsity Christian Fellowship/USA®, a movement of students and faculty active on campus at hundreds of universities, colleges and schools of nursing in the United States of America, and a member movement of the International Fellowship of Evangelical Students. For information about local and regional activities, visit intervarsity.org.

Scripture quotations, unless otherwise noted, are from The Holy Bible, English Standard Version, *copyright © 2001 by Crossway Bibles, a division of Good News Publishers. Used by permission. All rights reserved.*

Photo credit: Shepherd leading sheep in Judean Hills by Garo, circa 1930. Used by permission.

Cover design: Cindy Kiple
Interior design: Beth McGill
Images: The Good Shepherd by Philippe de Champaigne at Musee des Beaux-Arts, Lille, France / Giraudon / The Bridgeman Art Library
> *sheep on pasture: © Petoo/iStockphoto*

ISBN 978-0-8308-4063-2 (print)
ISBN 978-0-8308-9698-1 (digital)

Printed in the United States of America ∞

Library of Congress Cataloging-in-Publication Data

Bailey, Kenneth E.
 The good shepherd : a thousand-year journey from Psalm 23 to the New
Testament / Kenneth E. Bailey.
     pages cm
 Includes bibliographical references and index.
 ISBN 978-0-8308-4063-2 (pbk. : alk. paper)
 1. Shepherds in the Bible. 2. Metaphor in the Bible. 3. Typology
(Theology) I. Title.
  BS680.P35B35 2014
  220.6'4--dc23

                                                            2014033349

P	23	22	21	20	19	18	17	16	15	14	13	12	11	10	9	8	7	6	5	4	3	2	1
Y	33	32	31	30	29	28	27	26	25	24	23	22	21	20	19	18	17	16	15	14			

to

John and Susan Bailey

and

Tim and Elizabeth Daigle

in gratitude for shared

faith,

family and

friendship

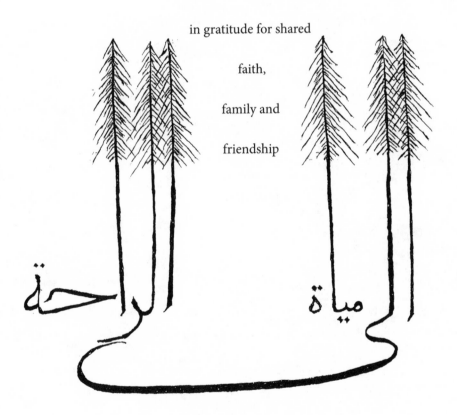

"Beside the still waters."

CONTENTS

ABBREVIATIONS

BAGD   Walter Bauer, W. F. Arndt, F. Wilber Gingrich, Frederick W. Danker, eds., *A Greek-English Lexicon of the New Testament and Other Early Christian Literature* (Chicago: University of Chicago Press, 1979).

Ibrahim Sa'id, *Luqa*

Ibrahim Sa'id, *The Gospel of Luke* (1970; reprint, Cairo: Middle East Council of Churches, 1980).

Ibn al-Salibi, *Tafsir*

Dionesius Ibn al-Salibi, *Kitab al-Durr al-Farid fi Tafsir al-'Ahd al-Jadid* [*The Book of Precious Pearls in the Interpretation of the New Testament*], 2 vols. (Cairo: 'Abd al-Masih Dawlayani, 1914). Ibn al-Salibi wrote in Syriac and died in A.D. 1164. These volumes were translated into Arabic at the Monastery of Za'farani (Southeast Turkey) in 1728. Volume one (*Matthew and Mark*) lists no date or place of publication. However volume two (*Luke and John*) lists "Cairo, 1914" as the place and date of publication.

Ibn al-Tayyib, *Tafsir*

Ibn al-Tayyib, *Tafsir al Mashriqi*, 2 vols. (Cairo: Towfiq Press, 1910).

LVTL, *Lexicon*

Lexicon in Vetris Testamenti Libros, ed. Ludwig Koehler and W. Baumgartner (Leiden: E. J. Brill, 1958).

LSJ, *Greek-English Lexicon*

H. G. Liddell, Robert Scott and H. S. Jones, *A Greek-English Lexicon*, rev. J. S. Jones (Oxford: Clarendon, 1966).

TDNT   *Theological Dictionary of the New Testament*, ed. Gerhard Kittel and G. Friedrich, 10 vols. (Grand Rapids: Eerdmans, 1967-1976).

"Midrash is the hammer

which awakens the slumbering sparks

in the anvil of the Bible."

BABYLONIAN TALMUD,
SANHEDRIM

PREFACE

My journey with the theme of this book began with seven years of my childhood in the late 1930s in the south of Egypt, where my family lived in the village of Edmu in the province of Minya. After some years of absence, that journey continued from the mid 1950s and into the 1960s when I served for ten years with the rural churches of the Egyptian Evangelical Church in the same district. This was followed by twenty years in Lebanon, and finally by a further ten years living and teaching at the edge of Bethlehem in Israel/Palestine at the Tantur Ecumenical Institute, where shepherds grazed their flocks around us. Thus, for nearly fifty years, Middle Eastern shepherds with their flocks were a part of the larger context in which I grew up and then lived and taught the New Testament. It was my privilege to have laymen and clergy in three countries as my students who had herded sheep for extended periods in the Eastern Mediterranean.

Sheep-herding in the Middle East falls into two overlapping categories. First, there are the seminomadic sheep herders who often have large herds and spend months away from their villages following seasonal rains and grazing the open pasture land. Second, there are settled village families, each of whom owns a few sheep. It is customary for a number of families to combine their animals, and for one young man (or two young women) to form them into a herd and take them out each day to graze. This second pattern is widespread and more universal than the first. Some villagers develop large herds and still return to the village each night.

Countless books and articles have been written on the texts selected for this work. Of particular interest are the brief monographs written by Middle Easterners who in their earlier years themselves herded sheep. Each of these shepherds emigrated to the West, and at some point in their lives, using their own personal experience as shepherds, published their perceptions of Psalm 23. I have chosen five such accounts in which these two patterns are observable. The five are as follows:

Rev. M. P. Krikorian grew up in the late nineteenth century in the mountains behind the cities of Tarsus and Adana, which are now in Turkey. While he was in high school his family acquired a herd of a hundred sheep, and his father selected him to herd them. Initially the young man "wept bitterly at the suggestion" because it meant that he was obliged to drop out of school.[1] Yet some years later after becoming a pastor in the Middle East and then surviving the Armenian Genocide, he emigrated to the West and wrote a book on the Twenty-Third Psalm, which he dedicated to "My beloved father who gave me that first chance to become a shepherd."[2] The family had a long tradition of herding sheep, but for Krikorian it was a new experience. He acquired shepherding skills from the family, from other shepherds and from the sheep themselves. In his case, he returned each night to his family home in the village. His book is titled *The Spirit of the Shepherd: An Interpretation of the Psalm Immortal.*[3]

Rev. Faddoul Moghabghab was born in the city of Ain-Zehalta in the mountains of Lebanon. As a young man he herded the family's small flock. As he notes, "My father owned a number of sheep and lambs; it is customary for all the people of Mount Lebanon to keep a few sheep." Later in life he attended university and seminary in Beirut and in time emigrated from Lebanon to America, where he wrote a book about his experiences as a Middle Eastern shepherd.[4]

Moving from north to south across the Middle East, a brief but useful account of the life of a shepherd is available from George M. Lamsa. A

---

[1] M. P. Krikorian, *The Spirit of the Shepherd: An Interpretation of the Psalm Immortal*, 2nd ed. (Grand Rapids: Zondervan, 1939), p. 11.

[2] Ibid., p. 3.

[3] I am indebted to Rev. Avidis Boynerian for bringing this book to my attention and for acquiring a copy of it for my use.

[4] Faddoul Moghabghab, *The Shepherd Song on the Hills of Lebanon: The Twenty-Third Psalm Illustrated and Explained* (New York: E. P. Dutton, 1907).

deacon of the Syrian Orthodox Church, Dr. Lamsa grew up in a community
of seminomadic sheep herders in Syria. He writes,

> My ancestors for untold generations were sheep raising people. My father and
> my mother loved and tended sheep. I was raised in a sheep camp. We lived in
> a tent made of the hair of goats just as Abraham and Isaac did. Like other boys,
> I was taught and disciplined by the shepherds. Since my father was chief
> shepherd, I was taught thru [*sic*] his wisdom.[5]

Lamsa became a Syriac scholar and translated the fourth-century Syriac
Bible (the Peshitta) into English. He also published many other books recording his studies of and reflections on that same Syriac Bible. Along with
these numerous works he published a short study titled *The Shepherd of All:
The Twenty-Third Psalm.*

Stephen A. Haboush grew up in Galilee. In his youth he became the
shepherd of the family flock of sheep. Later in life he immigrated to America
and wrote a book titled *My Shepherd Life in Galilee: With an Exegesis of the
Shepherd Psalm.*[6] His short work is authentic and helpful.

Abrahim Mitri Rahbany was not a shepherd, but he grew up in the mountains of what is now Lebanon, surrounded by farmers and shepherds. He
observed those shepherds with their sheep on a daily basis for all of his early
years. Later in life he wrote a book that covers many aspects of Eastern life
and the Gospels. This book, titled *The Syrian Christ*, includes a helpful
chapter on sheep and shepherds.[7]

In addition to these five Middle Easterners we can note two Westerners,
one American and the other British. William Thompson lived and served
in Lebanon for twenty-five years as a missionary of the American Presbyterian Church. He learned Arabic well and made numerous extensive
journeys on horseback across what is now Lebanon and Israel/Palestine. His
observations and reflections were published originally in 1858 in two
volumes under the title *The Land and the Book*.[8] Eric F. F. Bishop of England
served in Jerusalem with the Church Missionary Society for twenty-eight

[5]George M. Lamsa, *The Shepherd of All: The Twenty-Third Psalm* (Philadelphia: A. J. Holdman, 1939), p. 8.

[6]Stephen A. Haboush, *My Shepherd Life in Galilee: With an Exegesis of the Shepherd Psalm* (Chicago: Merchandise Mart, 1949), pp. 1-8.

[7]Abraham M. Rihbany, *The Syrian Christ* (New York: Houghton Mifflin, 1916), pp. 295-309.

[8]W. M. Thomson, *The Land and the Book* (New York: Harper, 1871), 1:229-305.

years and authored *Jesus of Palestine* and *Prophets of Palestine*, which have valuable information about the biblical text and the world of Middle Eastern shepherds.[9]

Of more limited value are recent accounts by Westerners who were at various times in their lives exposed to shepherds and their sheep. Leslie D. Weatherhead of England gathered data regarding sheep from as far away as India,[10] and Phillip Keller owned and operated a sheep ranch in East Africa and was involved with sheep in the American West.[11] These authors apply experience from sheep-herding in Africa, Asia and America to Psalm 23. Occasionally it fits and is useful.

In addition to these English-language sources, this study has relied heavily on the Arabic writings on the good shepherd texts that are available to us. Much has been lost across the centuries, but a few treasures, ancient and modern, have survived. I have had the following available to me.

ARABIC LANGUAGE COMMENTARIES

Ibn al-Salibi, Dionesius. *Kitab al-Durr al-Farid fi Tafsir al-'Ahd al-Jadid* [The Book of Precious Pearls in the Interpretation of the New Testament]. 2 vols. Cairo: 'Abd al-Masih Dawlayani, 1914.

Ibn al-Salibi was bishop of Amad (Diyarbakr). He wrote in Syriac and died in A.D. 1164. This commentary was translated into Arabic in the Monastery of Za'farani (Southeast Turkey) in 1728.

Ibn al-Tayyib. *Tafsir al-Mashriqi* [A Commentary on the Four Gospels]. 2 vols. Cairo: Tawfiq Press, 1910.

Ibn al-Tayyib was a part of the Church of the East. He was a brilliant scholar, a medical doctor, a translator, an author and secretary to the patriarch of his church. He wrote books on medicine and theology. He produced philosophical works along with a number of high-quality commentaries. These two volumes are among them. He lived in Baghdad and died in 1043.[12]

---

[9]Eric F. F. Bishop, *Jesus of Palestine* (London: Lutterworth, 1955), and *Prophets of Palestine* (London: Lutterworth, 1962).

[10]Leslie D. Weatherhead, *A Shepherd Remembers* (New York: Abingdon, 1938).

[11]Phillip Keller, *A Shepherd Looks at Psalm 23* (Grand Rapids: Zondervan, 1970).

[12]Samir Khalil, "Ibn al-Tayyib, a Polyvalent Thinker," in *Christianity: A History in the Middle East* (Beirut: Middle East Council of Churches, 2005), pp. 518-29.

Matta al-Miskin. *The Gospel According to Luke* [Arabic]. Cairo: Monastery
of Saint Makar, 1998.

————. *The Gospel According to Saint Matthew: Studies, Interpretation and
Explanations* [Arabic]. Cairo: Monastery of Saint Maqar, 1999.

Father Matta al-Miskin (d. 2009) was a monk at the Coptic Orthodox
Monastery of St. Makar in Wadi Natron (between Cairo and Alexandria). He spent most of his life writing extensive commentaries on
the Gospels, which were published by his monastery. His work is little
known outside of the Arabic-speaking Christian world. His monastic
spirituality is deep, and these volumes will no doubt in time be translated into English and bless the worldwide church for many generations
to come.

Sa'id, Ibrahim. *Sharh Bisharit Luqa* [Commentary on the Gospel of Luke].
Cairo: Middle East Council of Churches, 1980.

————. *Sharh Bisharit Yuhanna* [Interpretation of the Gospel of John]. Cairo:
Dar al-Thaqafa, n.d.

Rev. Dr. Ibrahim Sa'id was a pastor and scholar of the Egyptian Evangelical Church in the mid-twentieth century. He was a brilliant preacher
in the finest Classical Arabic, and under his leadership the Qasr al-
Dubara church on the famous Maydan al-Tahrir in central Cairo was
built. He authored extensive commentaries on Luke and John.

ARABIC TRANSLATIONS OF THE BIBLE

Translation is always commentary. The translators must try to understand
the text, and only then can they present it in the receptor language. This
study has made use of a collection of twenty versions of the New Testament
into Arabic and four versions of the Old Testament. I have managed to acquire copies of all the printed Arabic New Testaments that began to appear
at the very end of the sixteenth century. I have also acquired films of many
hand-copied Bibles from before that time that date as far back as the ninth
century. A brief description of these versions is available in my book *Paul
Through Mediterranean Eyes.*[13] How have Eastern Christians understood this
text? This question can often be answered by noting how they translated the

---

[13]Kenneth E. Bailey, *Paul Through Mediterranean Eyes* (Downers Grove, IL: IVP Academic, 2011),
pp. 538-43.

verses in question. An interpretive flow from these centuries of Eastern Bible translation have constantly influenced this study.[14]

ARMENIAN

Nerses the Graceful of Lambron. *On Psalm 23 [22]*. In *Commentary on the Psalms, Manuscript 1526*.

This was translated for me by the Rt. Rev. Anushavan, bishop of the Armenian Orthodox Church of North America, New York. This twelfth-century manuscript is held in the Mesot Nashotots Institute of Ancient Manuscripts, Yerevan, Armenia.

I have also relied on information I was privileged to glean over two decades from several of my students at the Near East School of Theology, Beirut, Lebanon, who herded sheep in their early years. From their living experiences I have gained many insights. Finally, it was my privilege on numerous occasions to observe and question shepherds with their sheep in the south of Egypt (ten years), the mountains of Lebanon (twenty years) and in the West Bank, Israel/Palestine, near Bethlehem (ten years). While writing parts of this book I was able to observe numerous shepherds leading their flocks among the terraced hills around Bethlehem.

My deepest gratitude must be extended to countless friends over a sixty-year period that stretch from the south of Egypt to Armenia who have done their best to keep me on "the paths of righteousness" in my interpretation of this great biblical theme.

Without the help, guidance and support my editor, Andrew Le Peau of InterVarsity Press, this work would never have been written. His wisdom and friendship have sustained me in all stages of the composition of this book. I wish also to express my unending gratitude to my personal secretary and copyeditor, Sara B. Makari, who has been tireless in assisting me on all levels of composition of this study. My thanks go out as well to Dr. Gary Burge, who in spite of his heavy academic schedule of teaching and writing in the field of New Testament graciously agreed to read through the chapters

---

[14]All of the quotations from Arabic are my own translations. It seemed tiresome to clutter up the notes with constant repetition of the phrase *my translation*. I am solely responsible for any errors in this regard.

on the Gospels, and who offered numerous helpful suggestions on many levels. Mr. Tom Finnegan, my computer guru, kept my hardware functioning properly and rescued me from many software glitches. To him I am deeply indebted.

Thanks must be extended also the staff of the library of Pittsburgh Theological Seminary who have graciously allowed me to check out numerous books and keep them on my desk for an embarrassing length of time. I am also grateful to the Rt. Rev. Bishop Anoushavan Tanielian of the Armenian Orthodox Diocese of Eastern America for his translation of the Psalm 23 section of the untranslated and unpublished twelfth-century Armenian commentary on the Psalms by Archbishop Nerses the Graceful of Lambron.[15]

I invite you, gentle reader, to join me on the journey from David's famous psalm through good shepherd texts in the Hebrew Scriptures and in the Gospels to a final word from St. Peter on the subject. A rich biblical feast of ethical, theological and artistic delights awaits us. My goal is to uncover those delights and make them available to the worldwide church.

Kenneth E. Bailey
New Wilmington, PA

---

[15]*Manuscript 1526* (13th cent.), in the Mesot Nashotots Institute of Ancient Manuscripts, Eravan, Armenia.

INTRODUCTION

At the time Philip Schaff was writing his eight-volume *History of the Christian Church*, the Christian catacombs of the first four centuries in and around Rome were being discovered and studied. The Christian art world was intensely interested in the images depicted in those early Christian tombs. Schaff says,

> Roman Catholic cemeteries are easily recognized by crosses, crucifixes and reference to purgatory and prayers for the dead; Protestant cemeteries by the frequency of Scripture passages in the epitaphs, and expressions of hope and joy in prospect of the immediate transition of the pious dead to the presence of Christ. The catacombs have a character of their own, which distinguishes them from Roman Catholic as well as Protestant cemeteries.
>
> Their most characteristic symbols and pictures are the Good Shepherd, the Fish, and the Vine. These symbols almost wholly disappeared after the fourth century, but to the mind of the early Christians they vividly expressed, in childlike simplicity, what is essential to Christians of all creeds, the idea of Christ and his salvation, as the only comfort in life and in death. The Shepherd, whether from the Sabine or the Galilean hills, suggested the recovery of the lost sheep, the tender care and protection, the green pasture and fresh fountain, the sacrifice of life: in a word, the whole picture of a Saviour.[1]

To this Schaff adds a footnote from A. P. Stanley's *Lectures on the History of the Eastern Church*:

> What was the popular Religion of the first Christians? It was, in one word, the

---

[1]Philip Schaff, *History of the Christian Church* (1859; repr., Peabody, MA: Hendrickson, 2002), 2:308.

Religion of the Good Shepherd. The kindness, the courage, the grace, the love, the beauty of the Good Shepherd was to them, if we may so say, Prayer Book and Articles, Creeds and Canons, all in one. They looked on that figure, and it conveyed to them all that they wanted. As ages passed on, the Good Shepherd faded away from the mind of the Christian world, and other emblems of the Christian faith have taken his place. Instead of the gracious and gentle Pastor there came the Omnipotent Judge or the Crucified Sufferer, or the Infant in His Mother's arms, or the Master in His Parting Supper, or the figures of innumerable saints and angels, or the elaborate expositions of the various forms of theological controversy.[2]

The author of this remarkable quote was the dean of Westminster Abbey and canon of Canterbury Cathedral.

Another indication of the intense early focus on this image appears in a study of the parables by Richard C. Trench, who writes,

On no image does the early Church seem to have dwelt with greater delight than this of Christ as the good Shepherd bringing home his lost sheep. Proofs of this are the very many gems, seals, fragments of glass, and other early Christian relics which have reached us, on which Christ is thus portrayed as bringing back a lost sheep to the fold upon his shoulders. From a passing allusion in Tertullian (*De Pudicitia* vii 10) we learn that it was in his time painted on the chalice of the Holy Communion. Christ appears in the same character of the Good Shepherd in bas-reliefs on sarcophagi, and paintings in the catacombs—one of which last is believed to be as early as the third century. . . . And it is observable that this representation always occupies the place of honour, the centre of the vault or tomb.[3]

Regarding the good shepherd, the Bible invites its readers on a thousand-year theological journey that can be likened to a movie consisting of nine major episodes. Anyone who enters the movie theater in the middle of the showing of a film may find the scene on display of interest—like watching a preview of some "coming attraction." Yet the viewer knows that the full story can only be understood when one views the film from the beginning to the

---

[2]Arthur P. Stanley, "Study of Ecclesiastical History," in *Lectures on the History of the Eastern Church* (n.d.), p. 283; quoted in Philip Schaff, *History of the Christian Church* (1859; repr., Peabody, MA: Hendrickson, 2002), 2:308, n. 1.
[3]Richard C. Trench, *Notes on the Parables of Our Lord*, 7th ed. (London: John W. Parker, 1857), p. 380 (second note on page).

end. Or, when viewing a film at home, a friend may enter the room in the middle of the showing and ask, "What is going on?" Someone in the circle who was there from the beginning will then offer a quick explanation as the entire room settles down to enjoy the rest of the film. Something of the same dynamic should function when one examines any of the nine major biblical texts on the good shepherd that begin with Psalm 23. Each of the "episodes" of the good shepherd story needs to be studied in the light of what has come before on the same topic. But generally each scene is read in isolation from the long tradition of which it is a part. This study focuses on the nine major episodes, but makes no attempt to include all the casual good shepherd biblical references.

The Bible has hundreds of verses that mention sheep, shepherds, flocks and sheepfolds. My focus in this work is on those major texts where the following cluster of themes appears:

1. the *good shepherd* (in the Old Testament always identified as God)

2. the *lost sheep* (or lost flock)

3. the opponents of the shepherd

4. the *good host(ess?)*

5. the *incarnation* (promised or realized)

6. the *high cost* the shepherd sustains to find and restore the lost

7. the theme of *repentance/return*

8. *bad sheep*

9. a *celebration*

10. the *end* of the story (in the house, in the land or with God?)

Nine times in Scripture nearly all of these dramatic elements appear: four times in the Old Testament (Ps 23; Jer 23; Ezek 34; Zech 10) and five times in the New (Mt 18; Mk 6; Lk 15; Jn 10; 1 Pet 5).

The inclusion of Mark 6:1-52 is because in Mark's Gospel the account of the feeding of the five thousand has Psalm 23 as "music in the background" all through the text, as we will see.

I have presented the four discussions of the good shepherd in the Gospels in a special order for the following reasons.

- Luke 15: Through a parable *Jesus defines himself* as the good shepherd.

- Mark 6: Jesus *acts out this identity* in a *dramatic action.*

- Matthew: The *disciples* are called to be *good shepherds.*

- John: The good shepherd texts come to their *climax at* the *cross* and in the *resurrection.*

- Peter: The *elders* are *shepherds,* Peter is *the fellow shepherd,* and *Jesus* is the *chief Shepherd.*

In short, it seems appropriate to reflect first how *Jesus identifies* himself as the good shepherd (Lk 15) and then to look at *how he lived out that identity* (Mk 6). Continuing on, the title of "shepherd" is also applied by Jesus to the *disciples* (Mt 18), and in John 10 the entire good shepherd tradition comes to its *climax* as it reflects on the *cross and the resurrection.* Perhaps three decades after the resurrection we see Peter using the good shepherd as a *model for the elders/pastors* of the church. In our reflections on the nine texts we will pay close attention to what remains the same and to what is added, along with what is revised or omitted.

In the texts under examination, the authors usually organize their material into small units that I have chosen to call *cameos.*[4] Sometimes these cameos flow in a *straight-line sequence* with the conclusion at the end. On other occasions an A-B-C, A-B-C pattern appears, where a series of ideas is presented and then repeated in the same order. This artistic style I have called *step parallelism.* Finally, the common pattern of 1-2-3-4-3-2-1 also appears. This style has been called "chiasm" and "inverted parallelism." I prefer the less technical phrase *ring composition* because the author presents a series of ideas and then circles back to the starting point, creating a literary ring.[5] One brilliant example where all three of these techniques appear in a single passage is Isaiah 28:14-18 (see fig. 0.1).

---

[4]They could be called "stanzas," but I am not suggesting that the material is poetry. I prefer the word *cameo* in the sense of a "cameo appearance" of a particular actor in a film. The cameo has its own inner integrity while being a part of a larger whole.

[5]For a more detailed description of these three styles of writing as they appear in the Bible see Kenneth E. Bailey, *Jesus Through Middle Eastern Eyes* (Downers Grove, IL: IVP Academic, 2008), pp. 13-18; and Kenneth E. Bailey, "Prelude: The Prophetic Homily Rhetorical Style and Its Interpretation," in *Paul Through Mediterranean Eyes* (Downers Grove, IL: IVP Academic, 2011), pp. 33-53.

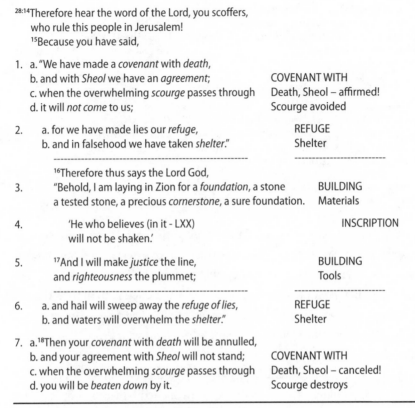

28:14Therefore hear the word of the Lord, you scoffers,
who rule this people in Jerusalem!
15Because you have said,

1. a. "We have made a *covenant* with *death*,
    b. and with *Sheol* we have an *agreement*;   COVENANT WITH
    c. when the overwhelming *scourge* passes through   Death, Sheol – affirmed!
    d. it will *not come* to us;   Scourge avoided

2. a. for we have made lies our *refuge*,   REFUGE
    b. and in falsehood we have taken *shelter*."   Shelter

    16Therefore thus says the Lord God,
3. "Behold, I am laying in Zion for a *foundation*, a stone   BUILDING
    a tested stone, a precious *cornerstone*, a sure foundation.   Materials

4. 'He who believes (in it - LXX)   INSCRIPTION
    will not be shaken.'

5. 17And I will make *justice* the line,   BUILDING
    and *righteousness* the plummet;   Tools

---

6. a. and hail will sweep away the *refuge of lies*,   REFUGE
    b. and waters will overwhelm the *shelter*."   Shelter

7. a. 18Then your *covenant* with *death* will be annulled,
    b. and your agreement with *Sheol* will not stand;   COVENANT WITH
    c. when the overwhelming *scourge* passes through   Death, Sheol – canceled!
    d. you will be *beaten down* by it.   Scourge destroys

Figure 0.1. Isaiah and the coming storm (Is 28:14-18)

The entire text flows in a *straight-line sequence* that makes sense. At the same time the seven cameos demonstrate *inverted parallelism*. (Note the summary words on the right.) Furthermore, when the *first* cameo is compared with the *seventh*, the ideas *within* each cameo repeat using the A-B-C-D, A-B-C-D pattern (noted earlier) that I have named *step parallelism*. The entire prophetic homily is composed of three sections. The beginning and the end are in the present, while the center presents a vision of hope for the future. Also the cameos on the outside are longer than those that appear in the center.

These rhetorical features are used again and again throughout the Bible. I will note them when they appear in the texts under study. One final feature of this amazing passage is worth noting in passing because it will appear in Psalm 23 and in John 10. Figure 0.2 highlights these rhetorical features at the beginning (1), the center (4) and the end (7) of Isaiah 28:14-18.

1. a. "We have made a *covenant* with *death*,
    b. and with *Sheol* we have an *agreement*;   COVENANT WITH
    c. when the overwhelming *scourge* passes through   Death, Sheol – affirmed!
    d. it will *not come* to us;   Scourge avoided

----

    4. 'He who believes (in it - LXX)   INSCRIPTION
       will not be shaken.'

----

7. a. [18]Then your *covenant* with *death* will be annulled,
    b. and your agreement with *Sheol* will not stand;   COVENANT WITH
    c. when the overwhelming *scourge* passes throug   Death, Sheol – canceled!
    d. you will be *beaten down* by it.   Scourge destroys

Figure 0.2. The outside and the center of Isaiah 28:14-18

The first cameo (1a) tells of "a *covenant* with death." However, Israel already had a covenant, so why did the rulers make a new one? Connected to this is the first line in the center (4a) that focuses on "He who believes." The topic of believing for ancient Israel inevitably included faith in their unique covenant with the God of Israel. This theme joins 1a to 4a. The reader is prompted to ask, how can Israel make a *"covenant with death"* (1a) when it already believes in a *covenant with the God of Israel*? This should be impossible! Isaiah is criticizing the leadership in Jerusalem for making a covenant with the Egyptians when the Assyrians threatened Israel in about 701 B.C. The Egyptians worshiped gods of death. A "covenant with death" is code language for "a covenant with the Egyptians." Then the second line in the center cameo (4b), "will not be shaken," relates to the last line in cameo 7d that says "will be beaten down by it." Those who place their confidence in the "covenant with death/Egypt" will not only be "shaken" (cameo 4b) they will be "beaten down" (cameo 7d). In this way with great skill Isaiah relates the *center* to the *beginning* and the *end* of this rhetorical piece. This rhetorical style will appear, as noted, in Psalm 23 and in John 10.

A further focus of this study has to do with the Syriac, Arabic and Hebrew translations of the texts under study. To translate is to interpret. No person or persons can translate any text from one language to another without deciding what the original text means. This truism is obvious to all. Thus modern English language commentators often note how a particular word or phrase appears in the King James Bible (Authorized Version) or the NIV or the RSV or the NRSV and so forth. The point being that learned scholars have made these translations, and their views are worthy of note. At times a commentator will reach back to Luther's German Bible or perhaps note the fifth-century Latin Vulgate. All of this is well and good. But what of the versions made (with similar care and careful scholarship) in the East? In the early centuries of the life of the church it was accepted that Latin, Greek and Syriac were the major languages of the faithful. John Meyendorff has written,

> The idea that the early Christian tradition was limited to its Greek and Latin expressions is still widespread. This assumption distorts historical reality and weakens greatly our understanding of the roots of Christian theology and spirituality. In the third and fourth centuries, Syriac was the third international language of the church. It was the vehicle of Christian missionary expansion on Persia, Armenia, Georgia, India and even in Ethiopia.[6]

If it is valuable to note Jerome, the King James translators and the work of the scholars who produced the NRSV or the ESV, then surely it is also worth the effort to contemplate the work of the ancient translators of the Syriac, Arabic and Hebrew versions of the text. Such notations will occasionally appear throughout the study.

The scope of the texts involved in this study has been for me quite daunting. Psalms, three different prophets, Jesus, the Four Evangelists and Peter are all a part of the journey before us. My intent in this work is not a fully documented technical commentary on the passages involved. Rather, our focus is on the unfolding of the extraordinary story that is created in Psalm 23 and repeated (with changes) across a thousand years down to the penning of 1 Peter. Furthermore, biblically speaking, with 1 Peter this process of retelling the story of the good shepherd and his lost sheep naturally stops. The canon is closed, and as we are not prophets of Israel or apostles of the early church, we cannot presume to write in their names. Surely our task is to understand as best we can the original intent of various accounts of the good shepherd and to strive to faithfully apply those meanings when applicable to the church and to the world in our day.

As noted, the image of the good shepherd had great weight in early Christianity. My prayer is that the significance of this great classical image will

---

[6]John Meyendorff, preface to *Ephrem the Syrian: Hymns,* by Kathleen McVey (New York: Paulist Press, 1989), p. 1.

one day be restored to its original power and splendor, and that this modest effort may make some contribution to that restoration.

In a television interview about her book *Team of Rivals: The Political Genius of Abraham Lincoln*, Doris K. Goodwin described the fact that there have been more than fourteen thousand books written about Abraham Lincoln. Naturally, she found that fact intimidating. Yet she pressed on boldly in the writing of her book with the fond hope of uncovering new insights into the person of Abraham Lincoln. I face a similar intimidating dilemma and can only hope that the chosen lens for this study will shed new light on the well-known biblical texts about the good shepherd, and prove to be of value to you, gentle reader, and to the worldwide Christian church.

1

THE GOOD SHEPHERD
IN PSALM 23

The challenge before us in this chapter is particularly intimidating because of the richness of Psalm 23. This famous text has invoked centuries of awed devotion to the Lord, who "is my shepherd" and who is "with me/us" even in the deep shadows of death. Added to that is the two millennia of loyalty to Jesus the good shepherd, who lays down his life for his sheep. Thus I begin this journey with the prayer that I will be found faithful to what I have been given and in what I have discovered across decades of study and reflection on this topic.

In the Old Testament the good shepherd image is used in three ways. The *first* is where God is described as the shepherd of Israel. Psalm 78:52 reads,

> Then he led forth his people like sheep,
>> And guided them in the wilderness like a flock.

The same theme occurs again in Psalm 79:13 where the people affirm:

> Then we your people, the sheep of your pasture,
>> Will give thanks to you forever.

Repeating the same image, Isaiah 40:11 reads,

> He will tend his flock like a shepherd;
>> He will gather the lambs in his arms;
> He will carry them in his bosom,
>> And gently lead those what are with young.

Second, the leaders of Israel are also referred to as shepherds. In Psalm

78:70-71, *David* is chosen by God to be the shepherd of his people. The text says,

> He chose David his servant
>   and took him from the sheepfolds;
> from following the nursing ewes he brought him
>   to be the shepherd of Jacob his people,
>   Israel his inheritance.

Moses is also referred to as a shepherd. Isaiah wrote of God (Is 63:11):

> Then he remembered the days of old,
>   Of Moses his servant.
> Where is he who brought up out of the sea
>   The shepherd[1] of his flock?

Third, the Old Testament also includes a promise of a new leader in Israel who will come forth from Bethlehem. Of this ruler the prophet Micah (Mic 5:4) writes,

> And he shall stand and shepherd his flock in the strength of the LORD,
>   in the majesty of the name of the LORD his God.

These three uses of the image of the shepherd are important and provide a general background for the image of the shepherd in the Old Testament. With these texts in mind, we can note that the nine major texts that appear in this study were selected because each of them comprises a series of themes that are like notes in a tune that is known to the various singers of the biblical song of the good shepherd. As observed in the introduction, these "notes" are

1. the *good shepherd and his identity*

2. the bad shepherd

3. a *lost sheep*/a lost flock

4. the *good host(ess?)*

5. the *incarnation of the shepherd*

6. the *shepherd pays a high price to find and restore the lost*

---

[1]The Hebrew text here uses a singular, which appears in the KJV and the NIV. The singular is also used in the Arabic and Syriac versions. RSV and ESV list a plural.

7. *repentance/return* (and the use of the verb *shuv*)

8. the bad sheep

9. a *celebratory* meal

10. the *ending* of the story (in the *house*, in the *land* or *with God*)

1. [23:1]The Lord is my shepherd;   LORD - SHEPHERD
     I shall not want.   No Wants

2.   [2]He settles me[a] down
         in green pastures.   FOOD &
         He leads me beside still waters.   Drink

3.   [3]He brings me back/he causes me to repent.[b]   RESCUE
             He leads me in paths of righteousness   Security
             for his name's sake.

4.   [4]Even though I walk through the valley
                 of the shadow of death,[c]   DEATH/EVIL
                 I will fear no evil,   No Fear

5.   for you are with me;
                 Your rod and your staff,   SECURITY
                 they comfort me.   Comfort

6.   [5]You prepare a table before me
         in the presence of my enemies;[d]   FOOD &
         You anoint my head with oil;   Drink
         my cup overflows

7. [6]Surely goodness and mercy
     shall follow me all the days of my life,   GOODNESS AND MERCY
     and I will dwell in the house of the LORD   LORD - House all the Days
     for the length of the days.[e]

---

[a]William Holladay translated ירביצני / (Hiphil) as "he lets me down" rather than the traditional "he makes me lie down." See William L. Holladay, *A Concise Hebrew and Aramaic Lexicon of the Old Testament Based upon the Lexical Work of Ludwig Koehler and Walter Baumgartner* (Grand Rapids: Eerdmans, 1971), p. 332. The Arabic text in the *London Polyglot* (1657) reads: *ahallani,* which means "he settles me down." The 1993 Arabic Bible translates it "He lets me rests." Jeremiah 33:12 (RSV) translates the same verb as "resting their flocks."

[b]The Hebrew reads *nafshi yeshobeb,* which literally translated allows for the two options I have listed in the text. The Arabic and Syriac versions read "He brings me back." The Syriac mirrors the Hebrew and can also mean "He causes me to repent."

[c]The Hebrew allows for both the "shadow of death" and the "shadow of deep darkness."

[d]The Hebrew here is צרר, which can also be translated "adversaries" as in Ps 31:11. The root meaning has to do with tying something down or restricting someone.

[e]The Hebrew is *leorek yamim* (literally, "the length of the days"). This translation is used by Arthur Weiser, *The Psalms* (Philadelphia: Westminster Press, 1962), p. 227.

Figure 1.1. The good shepherd and Psalm 23

The eight italicized items on the above list appear in Psalm 23, only *bad sheep* and *bad shepherds* are missing. At the same time the psalm is composed using what I have called the "prophetic rhetorical template" (see fig. 1.1).[2]

THE RHETORIC

Using the previously mentioned style, the good shepherd psalm is made up of seven semantic units which I prefer to call "cameos." They are the building blocks of the psalm. I have added summaries to the right of each cameo in order to highlight the major ideas that appear and then repeat elsewhere in the piece.

An important part of the overall structure of the psalm has to do with the use of first, second and third persons (see fig. 1.2).

1.   *First* person ("*I* shall not want")
2.   Third person ("*He* settled me down/leads me")
3.   Third person ("*He* brings/leads")
4.   *First* person ("*I* walk/*I* do not fear")
5.   Second person ("*You* - with me/ *Your* rod/staff comfort me")
6.   Second person ("*You* prepare/anoint")
7.   *First* Person ("*I* will dwell")

Figure 1.2. The use of first, second and third person in Psalm 23

This use of "person" is not random. As noted earlier, the author of ring composition often connects the beginning, the center and the end of the text. The use of the first person *I* makes that connection in this text.[3] The shift to the third person *he* appears in the second and third cameos. In cameos five and six, God "walks on stage" and the conversation between God and David becomes highly personal. Cameos 1, 4 and 7 are so closely connected that if the psalm were composed of those three cameos alone, it would still make sense.

A second feature of ring composition is that there is often a point of

---

[2]Kenneth E. Bailey, *Paul Through Mediterranean Eyes* (Downers Grove, IL: IVP Academic, 2011), pp. 39-41. I have chosen the designation "prophetic rhetorical template" to refer to seven short literary *cameos* (units) that move to a climax in number 4 and then repeat backwards. This style has been called "chiasm." I prefer to call it "ring composition." The small raised numbers at the beginnings of some of the lines refer to the traditional verse numbers.

[3]This feature was observed generally in ring composition by N. W. Lund, *Chiasmus in the New Testament* (1942; repr., Peabody, MA: Hendrickson, 1992), p. 41.

turning just past the center, where the text begins to repeat ideas backwards.[4]
At that spot something critical to the entire passage can appear. This particular feature occurs here. The phrase "you are with me" (incarnation) is placed at this pivotal point in the psalm and stands out as a result.

COMMENTARY

The images for God used throughout the Psalter have a distinctive "homeland security" ring to them.[5] Dominant metaphors that describe God include:

- Shield
- High tower
- Fortress
- High place
- Refuge
- Rock
- Stronghold
- Horn of salvation

At times these images are presented together and have a powerful cumulative effect. Psalm 18:1-3 includes most of the list and reads,

> [18:1]I love you, O LORD, my *strength*.
> [2]The LORD is my *rock*
>   and my *fortress* and my *deliverer*,
> my God, my *rock*,
>   in whom I take *refuge*,
> my *shield*, and the *horn of my salvation*,
>   my *stronghold*.
> [3]I call upon the LORD,
>   who is worthy to be praised,
> and I am saved from my enemies.

After the generic phrase "O LORD, my strength" seven images explain the

---

[4]Lund refers to "the law of the shift at the centre." I have found that the point of turning is more often just past the center, where the ideas begin to repeat. See ibid., pp. 40-41.
[5]For ease of reference the cameo under discussion will be reprinted.

nature of that strength. The list (in order) includes rock, fortress, deliverer, refuge, shield, horn of salvation and stronghold. At the end there is a second nonmetaphorical affirmation using the words "I call upon the LORD . . ." For security reasons, in the ancient Middle East people naturally felt a compelling need to reside in a well-fortified enclosure on the top of a hill.

For the authors and the original readers of the psalms this made perfect sense. When a town was attacked by Bedouin raiders or an invading army, the people needed fortified space on high ground in which they could live or take refuge.[6] Yet overuse of such language could produce paranoia and a siege mentality. Perhaps aware of the danger of these unintended possibilities, the Psalms offer three countercultural options for understanding the nature of God. These are:

1. God is a *Shepherd.* "The LORD is my shepherd" (Ps 23).

2. The Lord is like a *mother,* (Psalm 131:2 reads, "I have calmed and quieted my soul, / like a weaned child with its mother, / like a weaned child is my soul within me." Here the language is somewhat ambiguous. But in Isaiah 66:12-13 God promises the returning refugees that he will "extend peace to her [Jerusalem] like a river," and also affirms "as one whom his mother comforts / so I will comfort you; / you shall be comforted in Jerusalem." Isaiah 42:13 records, "The LORD goes forth *like a mighty man."* Then in the following verse God says, "now I will cry out *like a woman in travail,* / I will gasp and pant" (Is 42:14). All three of these texts use similes rather than metaphors. God is not called "mother," but rather he at times acts with tender compassion *like a* mother.

3. God is like a *father.* Psalm 103:13: "*As a father* shows compassion to his children, / so the LORD shows compassion to those who fear him." In Isaiah 63:16 and Isaiah 64:8 the prophet uses the same image but shifts from a simile to a metaphor and addresses God saying, "O LORD, You are our Father."[7]

The Psalms thus offer a "minority point of view" regarding the nature of God. Yes, God can be likened to a high tower, a fortress and a rock. Yet he can also be understood to be like a *good shepherd,* a *good woman* and a *good father.*

---

[6]This need for a town that was also a fortress was common across the ancient Middle East.
[7]God is likened to a father (using a simile) and also affirmed to be a father (using a metaphor).

It is no accident that the trilogy of parables in Luke 15:1-31 centers on a *good shepherd*, a *good woman* and a *good father*.[8] It appears that Jesus observed the two kinds of images for God in the Psalms and opted for the three countercultural images already noted. At the same time, the dominant list of "homeland security" images does *not appear* in the New Testament, where God is never described as a fortress, a rock or a high place. Indeed, with Martin Luther, I happily sing, "A mighty fortress is our God." It is right to preserve and rejoice in the biblical imagery it affirms. But the new trilogy is also important, and its concrete word pictures have special prominence in the New Testament.[9] At the beginning of that list is *the good shepherd*, to which we now turn (see fig. 1.3).

Psalm 23 opens with a famous line (see fig. 1.3).

1. The Lord is my shepherd,	LORD - SHEPHERD
I shall not want;	No Wants

Figure 1.3. The Lord is my shepherd (Ps 23:1)

The open pastureland of Samaria and Judea stretches from the Eastern part of Samaria down to the Negev south of Beersheba. Before modern times and cell phones, the moment the lone traveller and the shepherd left the shelter and protection of the villages along the north-south ridge, they were on their own. Having tramped across those open hills for years and having taken extended trips by camel deep into the Sahara Desert I am aware of the special experience of surrendering to the to the mercies of the wilderness or the desert.

"The Lord is my shepherd," among other things, means "I have no police protection." In those open trackless spaces the traveler and his companions are alone. Thieves, wild animals, snakes, sudden blinding dust storms, water shortages, loose rocks and furnace-like heat are all potential threats to any traveler. All of this was affirmed in the twelfth century in the Armenian Orthodox tradition through the extensive commentary on the Psalms composed by Archbishop Nerses of Lambron in Armenia. He wrote:

---

[8]Luke writes, "He told them this *parable* saying . . ." That is, Luke clearly understood the three stories to be parts of a single parable.

[9]I quickly grant that "father" is a name and thereby more than a metaphor. See Is 63:16; 64:8.

"The Lord is my shepherd."

In other words, I wandered in the midst of beasts, dogs and bulls (that) surrounded me; lions opened their mouths and wished to ravish me. I was terrified, and because of fear I made a treaty with the Savior. Therefore, do not be afraid, O my soul, for He is my shepherd, and "I shall not want."[10]

The good archbishop knew full well that the opening verse of this psalm is a profound commitment to the Lord as the source of security in the midst of many dangers where no other help is available.

Without hesitation, the sheep confidently follow the shepherd, knowing that with him in the lead all will be well. The rest of the psalm expounds the meaning of this freighted first line.

Furthermore, this psalm has a feature unique to the list of nine texts under discussion. No sheep is ever taken out to pasture alone. The cost of the labor involved would be prohibitive. A flock is thereby always assumed. But in this famous psalm, the focus is on the individual. David is describing his own spiritual journey. In the highly individualized Western world, the importance of community is too easily forgotten when matters of faith are under discussion. In the East, the sense of community is so strong that the importance of the individual within that community can be neglected. Both are indispensable. When one is "on stage," the other is nearby, just "off stage."

The celebrated Lebanese poet Khalil Gibran reflects on the deep interconnectedness between joy and sorrow. He writes, "When you are sorrowful, look again in your heart, and you shall see that in truth you are weeping for that which has been your delight." He continues, "Together they come, and when one sits alone with you at your board, remember that the other is asleep upon your bed."[11] A deep interconnectedness also appears when we note the importance of the individual and the community in the family of faith. In Psalm 23 the individual eats with us "at our board," and the community is asleep "on our bed." Recognizing the importance of each, it is clear that in this text David is reflecting on his personal journey with his shepherd.

"I shall not want" carries special nuances in a capitalistic society. Our entire economic system is built on creating and then satisfying as many

---

[10]Nerses the Graceful of Lambron, *On Psalm 23 [22]*, in *Commentary on the Psalms, Manuscript 1526.*

[11]Kahlil Gibran, *The Prophet* (1926; repr., West Molesey, UK: Merchant, 2004), pp. 36-37.

perceived wants as possible. Television advertising is deliberately fashioned to catch the viewer's attention and create a sense of "I must have this medication or that electronic gadget" in order to be healthy, entertained, happy, and successful. The goal appears to be: Create *wants* and turn them into *felt needs*. If we can do enough of this we will all become richer and live happily ever after.

The psalmist has a very basic set of wants that the shepherd provides for his sheep. That list includes food, drink, tranquility, rescue when lost, freedom from the fear of evil and death, a sense of being surrounded by the grace of the Lord, and a permanent dwelling place in the house of God. An ever-rising mountain of material possessions is not on the list. There is no hint of any need for power or control. An externally generated set of compulsive desires and the need to be constantly entertained are also absent. The sheep knows that only with the shepherd's help can they secure the above limited list of basic wants.

When ring composition is used in the construction of a biblical text, the matching cameos must be taken into account. The first and the seventh cameos form a pair, and thus in cameo 7 (at the end) the psalm affirms that the deepest needs of the singer of the psalm have to do with the goodness (*tov*) and the grace (*khesed*) of God (cameo 7). "The Lord" is only directly mentioned at the beginning and at the end of the psalm. The shepherd (of course), as my leader, sees to my wants each day (cameo 1), and on returning home each evening *I am followed* by "goodness and mercy" (cameo 7). More on this follows.

With this introduction, the psalmist begins to list the wondrous ways the good shepherd cares for his deepest needs. The author begins with food and drink (see fig. 1.4).

2.   He settles me down
       in green pastures.   FOOD &
       He leads me beside still waters.   Drink

Figure 1.4. The pasture and the still waters (Ps 23:2)

A dog can be trained to sit and to lie down. Not so a sheep. A well-known proverb affirms, "You can lead a horse to water, but you cannot make him drink." In like manner, no one can *make* a sheep lie down. Sheep will only lie down when they have had plenty to eat, have quenched their thirst and are not threatened by any wild animal or disturbed by biting insects.[12] The barking of one stray dog can cause an entire herd to jump up and even run off if not stopped by an alert shepherd. The traditional language "He makes me to lie down" sounds as if some kind of force is involved. Such a reading creates unnecessary problems. The Greek Old Testament uses the word *kataskēnoō*, which the LJS *Greek-English Lexicon* translates "settle down" or "rest."[13] Lamsa notes, "Where grass is abundant, sheep are quickly satisfied. Then they lie down and the food digests."[14] As discussed in footnote 4 I have chosen "he settles me down."

In a good year in the Holy Land, rains begin in November and usually conclude by the end of February. It takes some time for the parched earth to produce "green pastures." Having watched this cycle for thirty winters in Lebanon and in Bethlehem, I know that green pastures are available for not more than three months a year. For the other nine to ten months all pastures are brown. During ten of those years, I was teaching at the Tantur Ecumenical Institute at the edge of Bethlehem. Each morning the gardener for the institute came to work riding his donkey, which he tethered to a tree just under my study window. Each year during December and January I had the special pleasure of watching the happy animal nibble the fresh green grass around his tree. For the following nine months of the year I felt sorry for him as he stood quietly each day, staring patiently off into the distance, enduring the heat with nothing but a few wisps of brown straw on which to chew. Green succulent pastures—what a rare delight!

There are no fenced fields in the open wilderness in the Holy Land, and no cultivated hay fields. Sheep are led out of the village each day to graze in the wilderness. In Lebanon I have passed shepherds with their herds near the top of the 8,560-foot mountain of Jabal Sannin towering behind the city of Beirut. On one occasion, near the summit of the mountain, I had an interesting conversation with an experienced shepherd (with his large flock) who described to me in fascinating detail the various options and the nu-

---

[12]W. Phillip Keller, *A Shepherd Looks at Psalm 23* (Grand Rapids: Zondervan, 1970), pp. 23-48.
[13]LSJ, *Greek-English Lexicon*, p. 912.
[14]George Lamsa, *The Shepherd of All: The Twenty-Third Psalm* (Philadelphia: Holman, 1930), p. 36.

merous decisions he was obliged to make each day as he sought forage and water for his more than one hundred sheep, which he led without an assistant or dog. But what are the "green pastures" to which David is referring?

Turning again to Archbishop Nerses we find him interpreting this verse as follows:

> Whenever someone opens the mouth of his faith to drink, Scripture nourishes and grows multiple trees in the field of the church. It adorns one person with virginity, another one is made fruitful with acts of mercy, some are given martyrdom, and others flourish with meekness. Indeed these are the still waters which nourish human souls, anchor them in hope, raise them from hopelessness, command them to work [in ministry], establish them in love and foremost give them stored up nourishment [to produce] all the fruit of the heavenly kingdom.[15]

Such is but a sample of the spiritual richness that the 23rd Psalm has inspired across the centuries in the East. Returning to the shepherd with his sheep on the hillside, after a morning of grazing the sheep need to drink.

The shepherd must plan his day around the availability of water in the middle of the day. In winter the lower, warmer pastures will be grazed while the higher, cooler slopes are reserved for the heat of summer. Traditional grazing rights, relationships between shepherds and the power of the shepherd's village or tribe are all involved in the selection of where to graze and where to water the flock. A morning of grazing in "green pastures" beside a reliable source of still water is the much-longed-for ideal.

The shepherd knows that the sheep need grass, water and tranquility in order to lie down and digest their newly filled stomachs.

The good shepherd "leads me"; he does not "drive me." There is a marked difference. In Egypt where there is no open pasture land I have often seen shepherds driving their sheep from behind with sticks. But in the open wilderness of the Holy Land the shepherd walks slowly ahead of his sheep and either plays his own ten-second tune on a pipe or (more often) sings his own unique "call." The sheep appear to be attracted primarily by the voice of the shepherd, which they know and are eager to follow. It is common practice for a number of shepherds to gather at

---

[15]Nerses of Lambron, *Psalm 23.*

midday around a spring or well, where the sheep mingle, drink and rest. At any time one of the shepherds can decide to leave, and on giving his call all his sheep will immediately separate themselves from the mixed flocks and follow their shepherd wherever he leads them. E. E. F. Bishop documents the following incident.

> During the riots in Palestine in the middle thirties a village near Haifa was condemned to collective punishment by having its sheep and cattle sequestrated by the Government. The inhabitants however were permitted to redeem their possessions at a fixed price. Among them was an orphan shepherd boy, whose six or eight sheep and goats were all he had in the world for life and work. Somehow he obtained the money for their redemption. He went to the big enclosure where the animals were penned, offering his money to the British sergeant in charge. The N.C.O. told him he was welcome to the requisite number of animals, but ridiculed the idea that he could possibly pick out his "little flock" from among the confiscated hundreds. The little shepherd thought differently, because he knew better; and giving his own "call", for he had his *nai* (shepherd's pipe) with him, "his own" separated from the rest of the animals and trotted out after him. "I am the Good Shepherd and know my sheep—and am known of mine."[16]

As noted, watering the flock is also an important part of each day. Sheep are afraid to drink from moving water even if it is shallow. Lamsa writes, "Sheep cannot be watered at places where the water is swift."[17] If a stream is available, at times Middle Eastern shepherds dig a short, dead-end channel that leads away from the stream. Lamsa says, "In certain places, where the water is swift, shepherds construct nooks near the edge of the stream to make it easier for the sheep to drink."[18] The sheep quickly line up along such a channel of "still water" and quench their thirst. A small natural pool along a stream is fine, but if a well or cistern is the only source of water, a stone watering trough must be built, cut or dug beside the well into which the shepherd can pour the water he draws out of the well or cistern. Isaiah 8:6 compares "the waters of Shiloah that flow gently" (and thereby the sheep can drink) to the swift flowing waters of "the River" (Euphrates) that can

---

[16]Eric F. F. Bishop, *Jesus of Palestine* (London: Lutterworth, 1955), pp. 297-98.
[17]Lamsa, *Shepherd of All*, p. 43.
[18]Ibid., p. 42.

overflow its banks (Is 8:7-8). David knows that *still waters* are a must if the sheep are to drink.

M. P. Krikorian grew up in a village near Tarsus in southeast Turkey. Born into a family of builders, his father took him out of school to herd a flock of more than a hundred sheep. Later in life, after becoming an Armenian Methodist pastor in America, he wrote a book about his experiences as a shepherd. In that book he records his surprise on discovering that his sheep would not drink from moving water. He writes,

> Within sound and sight of water they (the sheep) would all begin to run toward it, showing that they were very thirsty. Yet, at their arrival, as I watched them, only a few would be drinking, while others all along the edge of the water, like the pedestrians on a fashionable street in a great metropolis, keep passing each other up and down the stream. . . . I learned the valuable lesson that they do not drink from rippling waters. They continue until every last one of them had found a quiet little pool between stones showing up above the ripples. . . . No turbid streams or ruffled rivulets will tempt them. . . . They want waters that move quietly.[19]

The shepherd, knowing all of this, provides "still water" whatever the cost.[20] The imagery is worthy of much reflection.

With the finest food (green pastures) and water that the sheep can confidently drink (still waters), along with the assumed freedom from any exterior threat, the sheep will lie down to digest their freshly eaten food. A shady place near quiet waters in the midst of green succulent grass is the best of all worlds for any sheep. David affirms that the Lord, his Shepherd, provides all of these for him.

We know a great deal about the turbulent life that David led and can only assume that he found rest, refreshment and tranquility *in the midst* of all his troubles. Murder, incest, betrayal, adultery, treachery, civil war, the killing of his son—David knew them all. Yet he found himself beside quiet waters. Each day the shepherd leads the flock to where it *can rest*. Rest and tranquility are a part of the daily routine.

---

[19]M. P. Krikorian, *The Spirit of the Shepherd: An Interpretation of the Psalm Immortal*, 2nd ed. (Grand Rapids: Zondervan, 1939), p. 45.

[20]Krikorian's suggestion that the sheep will only drink clean water is not supported by Ezekiel 34:19, where the weaker sheep are obliged to drink dirty water fouled by other sheep.

The psalmist continues (see fig. 1.5).

3.	He brings me back / he causes me to repent.	RESCUE
	He leads me in paths of righteousness	Security
	for his name's sake.	

Figure 1.5. The return to righteousness—for his name's sake (Ps 23:3)

The venerated King James Version gave to the English-speaking world the revered phrase "He restoreth my soul." In the English language this has often meant some form of "I was depressed and the Lord 'restored my soul' and helped me to feel better about myself and my world." On numerous occasions our English versions reshape a concrete biblical image into a concept. As Anthony Thiselton astutely observes, "Most English translations, especially NRSV and often NIV, simply abstract the conceptual content of the metaphor from its forceful emotive imagery."[21] I submit that this text is a prime example of this tendency. The literal translation "he brings me back" makes clear that the sheep is lost and the good shepherd is obliged to go after it, find it and carry it back.

Shepherds in Lebanon, and in the Holy Land (in addition to some of my students), have told me that once a sheep knows that it is lost, it tries to hide under a bush or rock and begins quivering and bleating. The shepherd must locate it quickly lest it be heard and killed by a wild animal. On being found it is usually too traumatized to walk and must be carried back to the flock or to the village. When this concrete image is replaced with an abstract idea, "the lost sheep" embedded in Psalm 23 evaporates and the connection between this psalm and the long list of biblical stories about "a good shepherd and a lost sheep" evaporates. Eastern Christianity has not made this mistake. The Septuagint uses the word *epistrepho*, which means "to bring back" or "to return." The Arabic versions translate *yaruddu nafsi* (he brings me back) as does the Syriac Peshitta.[22] The classical Armenian translation from the early fifth century reads, "He brings me from the wrong path to the right path."[23]

---

[21] Anthony Thiselton, *The First Epistle to the Corinthians* (Grand Rapids: Eerdmans, 2000), p. 1053.

[22] The one Arabic exception is the new United Arabic Bible Society version, which accommodates the text to the Western tradition.

[23] I am indebted to Dr. Avadis Boynerian of Watertown, Massachusetts, for checking and translating this reference for me.

This venerated early translation clearly affirms that the sheep in question is lost and that the shepherd must find it and restore it to the "right path."

Sadly, we in the West have lost the image of a lost sheep that is at the heart of Psalm 23. Restoring this image to the psalm opens the door to reconnect the psalm with the rest of the good shepherd-lost sheep biblical stories. The verb *shuv* (return/repent) affirms that connection.

The Hebrew verb *shuv* appears again and again in the collection of good shepherd stories under discussion. On the story line the shepherd is "bringing me back." On the theological line, I am "caused to repent." Psalm 23 uses a causative (polel) form of the verb, which makes clear that this is an action done for me. He (the good shepherd) *brings me back*. Unaided, the lost sheep cannot find its way home. As a lost sheep my only hope is in the good shepherd who will come after me and hopefully find me, pick me up and carry me back to safety. Noting the repetition of this key verb is an important part of the series of texts under examination in this study.

Fortunately the Western tradition has not totally lost this important part of the story, but one must reach some distance back in history to find it. The third verse of the well-known hymn "The King of Love My Shepherd Is" reads,

> Perverse and foolish oft I strayed,
>> But yet in love He sought me,
> And on his shoulder gently laid,
>> And home rejoicing, brought me.[24]

In the eighteenth century Isaac Watts set Psalm 23 to verse and wrote,

> He brings my wandering spirit back,
> When I forsake his ways;
> And leads me, for his mercy's sake,
> In paths of truth and grace.[25]

Two actions are involved. The shepherd must *come after me*, which in itself is a costly endeavor. Having found the lost sheep, a price must be paid by the shepherd to *restore the lost sheep* to the flock. The psalm before us *only mentions the second* (he brings me back). The first is assumed but not

---

[24]Henry Baker, "The King of Love My Shepherd Is," 1868.
[25]Isaac Watts, "My Shepherd Will Supply My Need," 1719.

stated. Reflection on the effort required for the search evolves as the good shepherd tradition moves through its own special history.

The text continues with "He leads me in the paths of righteousness." The clear assumption (affirmed by the Classical Armenian translation, noted earlier) is that I was lost while straying in the *paths of unrighteousness* and the good shepherd brings me back to the *right paths* and leads me on. The open wilderness in the Holy Land often exhibits a maze of faint trails worn by countless flocks of sheep. The shepherd alone knows which of them leads out of that valley to the next stage in the day's journey, rather than abruptly ending in some dead end or at a cliff edge. Regarding the theological implications of the story, the "paths of righteousness" are those that imitate the "righteousness of God" who, out of that righteousness, acts in history to save. His righteousness is a model for my righteousness.

The good shepherd leads his flock in these righteous paths "for his own name's sake." Lamsa writes, "the shepherd is very careful about the paths, because he loves the sheep, and for his own name's sake he would do anything to prevent accidents and attacks by animals. He has to keep his reputation as a good shepherd."[26] He acts out of his own integrity, which he will not violate. He is a *good* shepherd, and a good shepherd *does not* lose his sheep. This theme is repeated and expanded in Ezekiel 36:22-32, as we will observe. Archbishop Nerses astutely comments, "And why did He take such providential care? Not for any bribe, not because He needed to add me to his flock, but only for His name's glory."[27] Thus in the opening cameos of the psalm the shepherd is seen to provide, food, drink, tranquility, rescue and restoration.

Because of its inverted structure the ancient reader of the psalm knew that the center is the climax not the end (see fig. 1.6).

4.	Even though I walk through the valley	
	of the shadow of death,	DEATH/EVIL
	I will fear no evil,	No Fear

Figure 1.6. Passage through the valley of death (Ps 23:4)

The Hebrew text of this cameo can be translated "the valley of the shadow

[26]Lamsa, *Shepherd of All*, p. 52.
[27]Nerses of Lambron, *On Psalm 23*.

of death" (KJV, RSV, ESV) or "the valley of deepest darkness" (NRSV). In a number of places in the Holy Land, at the bottom of a valley, winter streams have cut long, deep crevices in the rock. One such valley is the entrance to the city of Petra in southern Jordan. I first visited that famous city the summer of 1957, a few months after a flash flood had thundered without warning through the long, narrow, thirty-foot high defile that is the entrance to the city. The wall of water had killed some fifty French tourists who were at that time walking through the pass. I recall the trauma that still gripped the Jordanian service personnel who worked at the site. They pointed out to us where two women who were walking ahead of the group heard the screams of their friends and managed to clamber up into the protection of a narrow side crevice, and who seconds later observed the crashing boulders and mangled bodies of their fellow travelers who were swept to their deaths a few feet away in the defile itself. It was indeed "a valley of death." We were told that the late King Hussein visited the site by helicopter the following day to show his solidarity with the living and his compassion for the dead. I have visited a similar narrow defile in Wadi Qelt just above the Orthodox Saint George's Monastery in the mountains near New Testament Jericho. Such water-cut defiles would have been known by a shepherd like David, and could well have been in his mind as he composed this famous psalm. The former shepherd Krikorian describes such a valley that is just south of the Jerusalem-Jericho road. He writes,

> There is an actual valley of the shadow of death in Palestine, and every shepherd knows of it. . . . I had the good fortune of having at least a passing view of this valley. . . . It is a very narrow defile through a mountain range where the water often foams and roars, torn by jagged rocks. . . . The path plunges downward . . . into a deep and narrow gorge of sheer precipices overhung by frowning Sphinx-like battlements of rocks, which almost touch overhead. Its side walls rise like the stone walls of a great cathedral. . . . The valley is about five miles long, yet it is not more than twelve feet at the widest section of the base. . . . The actual path, on the solid rock, is so narrow that in places the sheep can hardly turn around in case of danger. . . . In places gullies seven and eight feet have been washed.[28]

---

[28]Krikorian, *Spirit of the Shepherd*, pp. 68-69.

Lamsa notes,

> Valleys of the shadow of death are paths which wind in between mountains
> where there are dark shadows and deep gorges. Travelers march slowly and
> silently in order to avoid being seen or heard by bandits. The fear of death is
> constantly in their minds. They tremble, they expect trouble or death at any
> time while they are passing through.[29]

The valley of death/deep darkness is a section of the trail that cannot be
avoided. There is no bypass road and no magical escape. The only way
forward is *through* the valley of sin and death.

But the psalm does not say "This valley is where the trail ends, get used
to it!" Rather it is a valley through which the singer of the psalm may need
to pass. But the psalmist knows that his journey does not end there. Certain
types of people endure loss and allow themselves to imagine that they are
trapped in the middle of that dark valley. Often the major problem in relation to the valley is the *fear* that it can generate. Such fear can cripple the
traveler long before a valley appears on the journey. The journey itself
through such a valley does not destroy joy as much as the fear generated by
the anticipation of the valley. Not so for the psalmist, who knows that the
dark valley is a defile through which he must *one day pass*, but he never
contemplates *dwelling* in that fearful gloom. The way through it is open. To
shift metaphors, the psalmist is willing to "cross that bridge when he comes
to it," knowing that the bridge is intact and that it will lead to safety on the
other side.

The reality of fear is specifically mentioned in three of the nine texts
chosen for this study. In most of the others it is assumed. Here in Psalm 23
fear surfaces twice. First is the unspoken fear experienced by the lost sheep.
Once the sheep senses that it is lost, it is paralyzed by fear as noted. This is
why the shepherd must "bring me back" to safety. Second is the fear experienced in the valley of death itself. In this case the sheep is not lost; it is simply
afraid as it moves through the valley. "I will fear no evil" affirms the psalmist.[30]

---

[29]Lamsa, *Shepherd of All*, p. 53.

[30]A brief tangential reflection may be appropriate. Historical interpretation has been the foundation of serious reflection on Scripture at least since the days of John Chrysostom in the fourth
century. What did the original speaker/author intend to say to his original listeners/readers?
is a question that must always be asked. Yet the Christian reading Psalm 23 surely has the
freedom to go beyond what David was thinking and experiencing and reflect on these words

At this point in the psalm God dramatically "walks on stage" and the psalmist addresses him directly (see fig. 1.7).

5.	for you are with me;	
	Your rod and your staff,	SECURITY
	they comfort me.	Comfort

Figure 1.7. The rod and the staff (Ps 23:4)

Here is the "point of turning," in the rhetorically constructed psalm. In this cameo, for the first time in this text, David addresses God directly with the stunning statement, *for you are with me!* If my deepest sense of security is in the efficiency of the police force in my community or the power of the military might of my country, then when they stumble, my fears can easily overwhelm me. But if *the Lord is my shepherd*, I know that he will lead me through the darkest valley and I am delivered from my anticipatory anxiety.[31] What then brings this assurance and confidence?

Sheep have a special problem. They have no defenses. Cats have teeth, claws and speed. Dogs have their teeth and their speed. Horses can kick, bite and run. Bears can claw, bite and crush. Deer can run. But the sheep have no bite or claws and cannot outrun any serious predator. They can butt other sheep, but that ability will not protect them from a wolf or a bear. The sheep's *only security* is the shepherd. Indeed, "you are with me."

Israel was proud of God's constant presence. Deuteronomy 4:7 says, "What great nation is there that has a god so near to it as the LORD our God is to us, whenever we call upon him?" The gods of the nations around Israel lived in temples built for them to inhabit. To talk to the god the worshiper was obliged to visit his "house" where he could be found. An idol was fashioned, and that idol *was* the god. Not so in Israel. They also had "the house of the Lord," the temple, yet at the same time the psalmist (Ps 139:7-10) could ask,

---

in the light of Christ. Why is the believer not afraid of sin and death? Answer: We are *in Christ*, and being in Christ means that through our union with him we have died with him and arisen with him (Col 3:1-3). Thus victory over sin and death is a reality we have already experienced. Because of this, the one who is "in Christ" can face sin and death with a deep sense of "been there, done that!"

[31]Each reader can fill in the details (e.g., 9/11?). As a family we survived ten years of the Lebanese civil war when both the police and the army virtually disappeared.

Where shall I go from your Spirit?
> Or where shall I flee from your presence?

If I ascend to heaven, you are there!
> If I make my bed in Sheol, you are there!

If I take the wings of the morning
> And dwell in the uttermost parts of the sea,

even there your hand shall lead me,
> And your right hand shall hold me.

In Psalm 23:4 that same theology appears. Incarnation is clearly implied even though the details are missing. How and where God is uniquely with us is not discussed. More details will appear later in the tradition with the great affirmation "Emmanuel, God with us" (Mt 1:23). The two texts are profoundly related.

Here in the psalm David continues by explaining how the presence of the Shepherd delivers him from fear. He writes, "Your rod and your staff, they comfort me." These two instruments need to be understood precisely.

The Hebrew word here translated "rod" (*shbt*) has a long history. Its meanings include rod, scepter and weapon.[32] It does not refer to a "walking stick." Rather it is the shepherd's primary offensive weapon for protecting the flock from enemies, be they wild animals or human thieves. The instrument itself is about two and a half feet long with a mace-like end into which heavy pieces of iron are often embedded.[33] It becomes a formidable weapon.

The original people who settled the Nile Valley were shepherds. A twenty-five inch high slate pallet discovered in Egypt dating from about 3000 B.C. depicts a king named Narmer standing over a kneeling captive. The king grasps the captive's hair with his left hand and holds high a mace in his right hand. The king is at the point of bringing the mace down on the head of the helpless captive, and the instrument in the upraised hand of King Narmer is the identical shape and size of the shepherd's rod we are describing.[34] Fur-

---

[32]LVTL, *Lexicon*, p. 941.

[33]Krikorian writes, "Sometimes metals and nails are driven in the end to make the instrument more menacing. One good blow from it will kill or cripple to utter disability almost any ferocious animal" (Krikorian, *Spirit of the Shepherd*, p. 84).

[34]William H. Peck, "The Constant Lure," in *Ancient Egypt: Discovering Its Splendors*, ed. Jules B. Billard (Washington, DC: National Geographic Society, 1978), pp. 34-35.

thermore, the mace was one of the phonograms in the hieroglyphic writing system.[35] This same "rod" (mace) continued in use among shepherds in the holy land well into the twentieth century.

The various uses for this rod/mace mentioned in the Bible include the following:

1. To count sheep (Lev 27:32). When the shepherd wants to count his sheep, as he returns to the sheepfold in the evening, he holds his rod horizontally across the entrance just high enough for the sheep to pass under it one at a time.[36] That way they can be counted. If a sheep is missing, the shepherd will immediately begin a search. Thus the sheep (in the flock of God) can note the shepherd's rod and remember that it is an "alarm system" used to assure everyone's safety. If any sheep is lost, the shepherd will be alerted during the "evening count." Thanks to the rod in the shepherd's hand, if a sheep is lost, a rescue party of some kind will be on its way at once. This entire picture is invoked in Leviticus 27:32, where the sheep are counted by means of the herdsman's rod.

2. To protect the sheep from wild animals and thieves. As noted, before the twentieth century this rod (mace) was the standard weapon in the hand of the shepherd to fight off wild animals and thieves. David defended his ability to fight Goliath by telling Saul,

> Your servant used to keep sheep for his father. And when there came a lion, or a bear, and took a lamb from the flock, I went after him and struck him and delivered it out of his mouth. And if he arose against me, I caught him by his beard and struck him and killed him. (1 Sam 17:34-35)

Clearly David was talking about an instrument in his hand that he could use to kill a lion at close range. That instrument was his rod (mace). The sheep/psalmist can meditate on the shepherd's rod and say to himself, "I am safe *from exterior harm*. My shepherd has his rod and I know he is skilled in using it, when necessary, to protect me."

The Greek equivalent (LXX) is *rhabdos*, which is the word Paul uses in 1 Corinthians 4:21, where he asks "Shall I come to you with a rod or with love?"

---

[35]William K. Simpson, "The Gift of Writing," in Billard, *Ancient Egypt*, p. 147.

[36]The ESV and RSV use "staff" in this verse. The Hebrew word under discussion here is the "rod" (שֵׁבֶט).

In its verb form Paul uses the same word when he affirms in 2 Corinthians 11:25, "three times I have been beaten with rods."

Most certainly the phrase "a rod of iron" (Ps 2:9; Rev 2:27; 12:5) refers to this shepherd's rod/mace with heavy pieces of iron driven into its head. The language does not refer to a crow bar. The usage is like the term *stone ax*. The word *stone* applies to the head of the ax, not its handle. A "flint knife" is the same. The handle is of wood, and only the blade is flint (cf. Josh 5:2-3). The same is most certainly the case with the "rod of iron."

What then of the shepherd's sling? Indeed, the traditional shepherd had a sling that was used to scare away predators (if possible) and to help guide the flock. With skill in operating a sling, the shepherd could bounce a stone off a boulder or tree and keep the sheep on the desired path. But, as noted earlier, the rod/mace was the weapon of choice, even for a lion. In any case, in spite of his famous fight with Goliath, here David makes no mention of a sling.

The other important instrument in the hand of the shepherd that is mentioned in the psalm is the "staff." The traditional shepherd's staff is lighter and longer than the rod. The shepherd leans on his staff, climbs with it and often directs his sheep with it. It is long enough that he can reach some distance and guide the edges of the flock in the right direction. The Hebrew word is *sh'n*, which means "press down" and "lean on," along with "support oneself on."[37] The Arabic Bibles translate with the word as *'uqqaz*, which carries this precise meaning. The shepherd leans on his staff while standing, walking or climbing. It is usually about five feet long, and the shepherd is never without it.[38] Almost always one end has a crook on it. When a lamb cannot scramble down from a ledge or falls into a crevice or down a bank into a stream, the shepherd is able, with the crook in his staff, to catch the lamb by a leg or a shoulder and gently lift it back onto the path.[39] A ceiling fresco in an early Christian catacomb in Bosio (northern Italy) depicts Jesus as the good shepherd with a sheep over his shoulders while holding a staff. With his left hand he holds the four legs of the sheep over his chest, while

---

[37]LVTL, *Lexicon*, p. 1000.

[38]The Arabic versions consistently translate the word as *'uqqaz*. The root of this word has to do with leaning on something. A walking stick is an *'uqqaz*.

[39]Tutankhamen was buried holding such a staff across his chest. He was the shepherd of his people.

with his right hand he leans on just such a staff with a crook at its top.[40] The shepherd's staff is not for defending the flock from any external threat, but for caring for the sheep as he leads them daily in search of food, drink, tranquility and rest.

These two instruments are a pair. The first (the rod) is used to protect the flock from *external threats*. The second (the staff) serves to *gently assist the flock* in its daily grazing. The sight of these two instruments *comfort* the sheep.

The psalm continues with cameo six (see fig. 1.8).

6.   ⁵You prepare a table before me
        in the presence of my enemies;   FOOD &
        You anoint my head with oil;   Drink
        my cup overflows.

Figure 1.8. The table and the cup (Ps 23:5)

Here, the reader is obliged to make an important decision. Is the psalmist still talking about a shepherd and his sheep, or does the imagery shift to a festive meal with a host and a guest? Biblical truth cannot not discovered by majority vote, but there is a strong consensus among commentators around the second option.

Some interpreters have argued that "preparing a table" refers to a diligent shepherd who finds some flat pasture land and before leading his sheep to that place he goes ahead of them, digs up the poisonous plants and kills the snakes.[41] The "enemies" are then the wild animals. This view does not fit the geography of the Holy Land, where there is no high "table land" such as is available in Switzerland and Kenya. Furthermore, the arguments that the words *anointing* and *overflowing cup* refer to a shepherd's care for his sheep

---

[40]This fresco is reproduced in Philip Schaff, *History of the Christian Church* (1859; repr., Peabody, MA: Hendrickson, 2002), 2:867. Schaff also notes, "Most of the catacombs were constructed during the first three centuries; a few may be traced almost to the apostolic age" (ibid., p. 291).

[41]The Hebrew word *table* (*shulhan*) is defined by Koehler and Baumgartner as a hide placed on the ground (LVTL, *Lexicon*, pp. 976-77). This definition is vigorously opposed by Mitchell Dahood, *Psalms I, 1-50*, Anchor Bible (New York: Doubleday, 1965), p. 146. Later Koehler and Baumgartner withdrew their previous translation (see Ludwig Koehler and W. Baumgartner, *Supplementum ad Lexicon in Verteris Testamenti Libros* [Leiden: Brill, 1958], p. 190). Dahood offers no alternative. Most probably some form of the low, round table such as is still in use in traditional villages across the Middle East is assumed. People eat their meals while seated cross-legged on the floor around such a table. The common dish in the center is thereby easily available to all diners.

are not convincing.[42] Granted, the shepherd treats scratches on his sheep with olive oil, but "the overflowing cup" does not fit into the world of a shepherd and his sheep. The text is better understood, and is uniquely enriched, when it is understood to refer to a generous host with his guests. How then are we to understand this cameo?

In cameo 2 the psalmist speaks of food and drink *for animals*. Here in the corresponding cameo, the subject is food and drink *for people*. This shift in a single discussion between animals and people is well known in the recorded stories about Jesus. In Luke 13:15-16 (the "ox and the ass" versus the woman with a bad back), and again in Luke 14:1-5 (the man with dropsy versus the ass and ox), Jesus makes such a move as he defends himself against his critics. The psalmist has a similar progression. In cameos 1-5 the metaphorical use of the shepherd and his sheep is rich and meaningful. As we will see, in Luke 15 Jesus starts with parables of a lost sheep (and a lost coin) and moves on to a discussion of two lost sons (Lk 15:1-32). The move is from animals and coins to people. Then the psalmist's presentation of the nature of God is further enhanced through the use of the image of a host and his guests.

Returning to the psalm, the language is freighted with meaning. Hospitality at meals is a critical aspect of traditional Middle Eastern culture. Lamsa is again helpful when he writes,

> In the East, a man's fame is spread by means of his table and lavish hospitality rather than by his possessions. Strangers and neighbors alike discuss tables where they have been guests. Such tales spread from one town to another and are handed down from one generation to another. There is considerable gossip as to how guests and strangers are entertained.[43]

In traditional Middle Eastern culture, when you want the community to know that you have acquired wealth, you do not buy an expensive car or a large house with acres of grass around it.[44] Rather, you host meals with three times as much food on the table as the numerous guests can eat. The modern Western way of showing off possessions assumes isolation and distance from

---

[42]See Faddoul Moghabghab, *The Shepherd Song on the Hills of Lebanon: The Twenty-Third Psalm Illustrated and Explained* (New York: E. P. Dutton, 1907), pp. 99-115. Lamsa agrees that this verse refers to people, not sheep (Lamsa, *Shepherd of All*, pp. 76-78).

[43]Lamsa, *Shepherd of All*, pp. 65-66.

[44]When astronomical wealth is suddenly available, these traditional values are deeply corroded, as can be seen in the contemporary Arabian Gulf.

the community. It is enough that you drive by, note my palatial house and see my expensive car parked beside it. The psalmist's imagery has to do with community life that is strengthened and solidified by shared meals. But there is more.

To "prepare a table" means to "prepare a meal" (Ps 78:19; Prov 9:2; Is 21:5; 65:11; Ezek 23:41). This phrase cannot mean "set the table," because in traditional Middle Eastern society people eat without using individual plates or eating utensils. Eating is carried out by tearing off a small piece of flat bread and using it to lift food from the common dish to the mouth. Each bite starts with a fresh piece of bread. There is nothing to do to "set the table" except perhaps "spread the rugs" (Is 21:5). As regards the food, servants and women prepare it. The master of the house *provides* the food, he does not *prepare* it. Female involvement in food preparation is particularly clear in Proverbs 9:1-5:

Wisdom has built her house, . . .
   She has slaughtered her beasts, she has mixed her wine,
She has also *prepared her table* . . . she says,
   'Come, eat of my bread
and drink of the wine I have mixed.'

The same scene is clearly depicted in the story of Abraham and his angelic visitors (Gen 18:1-8). The guests arrive and Abraham insists that they rest and eat. The angels accept, whereon Abraham hurries to his tent and tells Sarah to take some fine meal and "make cakes." He then selects a calf, which he at once gives to a servant with orders to "prepare it." Abraham, in good Middle Eastern style, offers the food, prepared by Sarah and his servant, to his guests. In a gesture of high respect, Abraham, *stands* while his guests eat, but Abraham does not *prepare the food.*[45] The father in the parable of the prodigal son orders a banquet. He naturally orders the servants to do the work (Lk 15:22-23). No one would imagine that the father will participate in preparing the food. The Mishnah reflects the same social scene where it reads:

5. If a man gave [food to be cooked] to the mistress of the inn he must tithe

---

[45]In Ps 78:19 the phrase "prepare/spread a table" is used, and its meaning is defined in the text as "give bread or provide meat" (rsv). Again, God is not "in the kitchen" preparing the food.

what he gives to her and also what he receives back from her. . . . 6. If a man gave [food to be cooked] to his mother-in-law he must tithe what he gives her and also what he receives back from her.[46]

Naturally the man himself will not cook his own food. He gives it to a woman that she might prepare it. In the Middle East, as in many cultures around the world, the important task of preparing meals has traditionally been carried out by women and servants. In Psalm 23 God is a shepherd (who leads his flock) not a servant, and thus the text in verse 5 most naturally refers to the work of a woman. In the light of related biblical texts, this is not surprising. Genesis 1:27 reads:

> So God created mankind in his own image,[47]
> In the image of God he create him [singular],
> Male and female he created them [plural].

Clearly, male and female are both created in the image of God. God is spirit and is neither male nor female, but the characteristics of both come from God, who created both genders "in his image." Thus, for God to act like a woman in Psalm 23:5, is in harmony with the biblical tradition.

This same idea recurs in Isaiah 42:13 where God acts "like a mighty man," and then in Isaiah 43:14 God acts "like a woman." Even so here in the psalm God is described as a *good shepherd* who cares for his sheep. He is also acts *like a woman* by preparing a meal for the guest at his table.[48] That is, Psalm 23 is a story of a *good shepherd* and a *good host*. Granted, the Hebrew verb "you prepare" in this text is masculine.[49] But it is a male who engages in activities traditionally seen as the work of females. The phrase *prepare a table* is clearly attached to the work of a female in Proverbs 9:2-5, as previously noted.[50]

---

[46]Mishnah *Demai* 3.5, in Herbert Danby, *The Mishnah* (Oxford: Oxford University Press,1933), p. 23.

[47]The Hebrew here is *ha-'adam*, which ESV notes in the margin as meaning *mankind*.

[48]Peter and John are told to "prepare the Passover" for Jesus and the disciples (Lk 22:7-13), but this task involved the buying and arranging for the sacrifice of a Passover lamb, not just food preparation. At the same time they were responding to a command and acting appropriately as servants of their master.

[49]To use male and female pronouns for God would suggest some form of return to the Canaanites with their male and female gods.

[50]The parable of the two lost sons (Lk 15:11-32) opens with a picture of a generous father who gives the requested inheritance to the younger son. Later in the parable that same father runs down the road and showers his wayward son with kisses. This extraordinary welcome is what

This inclusion of both male and female components in the "good shepherd psalm" disappears for a thousand years and then dramatically reappears in Jesus' matching parables of the good shepherd and the good woman (Lk 15:3-10). In passing we can note that a number of themes are introduced in the psalm, ignored in the subsequent prophetic discussions of the good shepherd and then resurrected by Jesus. More of this later.

Returning to the text before us, the difficult phrase "in the presence of my enemies" needs examination. The central core of what is here affirmed can best be understood to mean: He demonstrates costly love to me irrespective of who is watching. People hostile to me will observe what he is doing and he knows that their hostility against me will be extended to him as a result. He doesn't care. He offers that love anyway.

In the old American South (and in many places in the American North) a European American who invited an African American as a guest to an expensive restaurant in a white section of town would subject himself to intense hostility from the community by doing so. In the parable of the prodigal son (Lk 15:11-32) the community hates the prodigal, and on his return would have thrashed him were it not for the costly intervention of the father in public on the road (v. 20). The celebratory party that evening is *not a gesture of welcome to the return of the prodigal*. It is a celebration of the success of the costly efforts of the father in reconciling his son to himself.[51] The community despises the prodigal because he offended and shamed the family on his departure and now has come back in rags after losing the family's money. The community *will come* to the banquet to show honor to the father for his costly efforts at restoring his son. They *will not attend a banquet* in honor of the prodigal.[52] Thus the son could say to himself that evening, "My father has ordered a banquet [as a gesture of restoration] in the presence of my enemies. The village does not like me. My brother hates me. My father, on the road, in full view of the village, demonstrated great love for me in spite of the hatred of family and community against me."

Important parts of the same scene are present in the story of Zacchaeus

---

traditional Middle Eastern culture allows for the mother, not the father. That is, Jesus creates a scene where *the father acts like a compassionate mother*. Thus David's presentation of a man (shepherd) who acts like a woman and prepares a meal is picked up and repeated by Jesus.

[51]See Kenneth E. Bailey, *The Cross and the Prodigal* (Downers Grove, IL: IVP Books, 2005), pp. 63-74.

[52]Kenneth E. Bailey, *Finding the Lost* (St. Louis: Concordia Press, 1992), p. 156ff.

(Lk 19:1-10), where Jesus spends the night in the house of Zacchaeus the tax collector. The crowd is angry and murmurs, "He has gone in [i.e., for the night] to be the guest of a man who is a sinner." Again and again Jesus engenders hostility because of the people with whom he chooses to eat his meals. He demonstrates costly love to his table companions by eating with them "in the presence of their enemies." Jesus provided a banquet for five thousand people in the presence of their enemy (Herod) in Mark 6 (as we will see). David would have understood.

Anointing in Scripture took place for a variety of reasons. Consecration and inauguration were among them (Is 61:1). Wounds and sores were anointed with oil (Lk 10:34), along with the sick in general (Jas 5:14), but here the reference is to anointing as an act of hospitality. Psalm 23:5 focuses on anointing at a banquet where *the host* anoints the *head of the guest*. In the Middle East, oil used for such anointing is usually perfumed.[53] Once again the clearest biblical example of this custom is in Luke 7:35-50, but the practice is of great antiquity.

From Egypt, during the reign of Thutmose III (d. 1426 B.C.), we have a stunning tomb painting of eight young women at a banquet where each has a cone of scented oil on her head. The point is that the body heat of the guest slowly melts the perfumed cone and the oil thus gradually runs down over her body, anointing her continuously all evening long. The servant girl sports a cone on her head as well.[54]

Returning to Psalm 23, we remember that David is describing a public meal where his enemies are observing the festivities. This particular gesture is bound to infuriate those enemies. The host is "pulling out all the stops." To change the metaphor, "no stone is left unturned" in the host's efforts to assure the guest that he or she is welcome, honored and beloved. Furthermore, the waiters are "hovering." Every time David takes a sip, one of them quickly rushes over to fill his cup. Actually, they are so eager to "do things right" that his cup overflows.[55] David knows full well that this treatment is extraordinary. In Psalm 31:11 he writes,

---

[53]It has been my delight to have enjoyed this particular courtesy for years, on various occasions across the Middle East.

[54]Barbara Mertz, "The Pleasures of Life," in Billard, *Ancient Egypt*, pp. 132-33.

[55]Another option is that the host himself is pouring the wine.

I am the scorn of all my adversaries/enemies
    A horror to my neighbors,
  An object of dread to my acquaintances;
      Those who see me in the street flee from me.

These enemies/adversaries see him as an object of dread, and this causes the neighbors to flee from him in the street. Amazingly, these adversaries/enemies are the same people that the good shepherd ignores as he hosts the psalmist at a banquet in Psalm 23:5.

Finally, this cameo has a further important New Testament connection when compared with 1 Corinthians 10:16-21, where the "table" and the "cup" are prominent (see fig. 1.9).

a. [21]You *cannot drink the cup of the Lord*	THE CUP
b. and the *cup of demons.*	Of The Lord & Demons?
c. You *cannot partake of the table of the Lord*	THE TABLE
d. and the *table of demons.*[a]	Of The Lord & Demons?

[a]Bailey, *Paul Through Mediterranean Eyes*, p. 275.

Figure 1.9. The Cup and the Table in Paul (1 Cor 10:21)

Paul is discussing the Eucharist and the Corinthian assumption that they can participate in the sacraments related to the idols *and* in the sacrament of Holy Communion. To discuss this critical topic, he invokes the language of Psalm 23:5 with its reference to the "cup" and the "table." Apparently Paul looks at Psalm 23:5 and asks himself, *What is the "table" that the Lord prepares for me at great cost, and what is the "cup" that he offers?* Paul's conclusion is that this language finds its fullest expression in the "table and the cup" of the Eucharist.[56] The psalm continues with its final cameo (see fig. 1.10).

7. [6]Surely goodness and mercy	
shall follow me all the days of my life,	GOODNESS AND MERCY
and I will dwell in the house of the Lord	LORD - House all the Days
for the length of the days.	

Figure 1.10. Followed all the way home (Ps 23:6)

---

[56]Ps 69:22 reinforces these connections by linking the "table" with "sacrificial feasts."

This cameo can be understood to have echoes of shepherd imagery. On the way home at the end of each day, the shepherd knows that there is the danger of a wolf or some other predator following the returning herd in the hope that a young or injured sheep might lag behind and become easy prey. If the shepherd has an assistant, one of them will naturally follow closely behind the herd for the specific purpose of preventing such an eventuality. If the shepherd has a dog that animal can take up the "rear guard" position. Sheep, when they aren't lost, know their way home. If there is no assistant shepherd and no dog, the shepherd himself can be the "rear guard."

While visiting Greece in the late 1990s, I was privileged to have an informative chat with a Greek taxi driver who had worked as a shepherd in his youth. He told me of how on one occasion he fell asleep in the field with his sheep during the afternoon siesta and awoke some time later only to discover that the flock was gone. Terrified, he rushed back to the village and to his delight discovered that the flock had, on their own, wandered home. The homeward path from the "still waters" was familiar to them, and when the time came they followed it, much to the relief of the shepherd.

David can be understood to be assuming this larger picture in his final cameo. But rather than a wolf or a lion following the flock on their homeward way, the psalmist senses that the "goodness" (*tov*) and mercy (*khesed*) of God are following him all the days of his life.

The language assumes movement. You cannot follow someone unless they are on the move, and the idea of being followed is not generally a pleasant thought. The phrase *We are being followed* is generally a fearful thought for any traveling band, large or small, and can be terrifying if one is alone. Naturally this depends on who is doing the following. Long-distance runners who are followed by an emergency van are naturally encouraged and reassured by the van's presence. If anyone falls ill or there is an accident, help is near.

The language in the psalm involves personification. *Goodness* and *mercy* become people who follow the psalmist. That is, God "walks on stage" and becomes an actor in the drama.

The first word, *goodness* (*tov*) is a general word in Hebrew for "good." Koehler and Baumgartner list "pleasant, useful, efficient, beautiful, kind, right, (and) morally good."[57] Thus David first notes that he is not surrounded by or followed by evil but by good. This in itself cries out for much reflection.

As a survivor of seven Middle Eastern wars, I can remember days when an atmosphere of evil seemed palpable. As noted, David also passed through many troubles, many of which he brought on himself. There was his sordid affair with Bathsheba (2 Sam 11), not to mention incest and murder among his children (2 Sam 13). To this we can add the civil war that climaxed with the killing of his son Absalom by David's commanding general, Joab (2 Sam 18). During those days, was he "followed by good"? It seems he was. Perhaps some of the time the good was behind him, protecting him, but he chose to turn aside from it. Yet as he looked back he could vividly remember the good that followed him.

The second word in David's list is *khesed* (mercy/grace/lovingkindness). This important theological word is like a coin with two sides. On one side it denotes *faithfulness* within a *covenant*.[58] On the other side *khesed* is *grace* that is *freely offered* to the undeserving. As Bultmann writes,

> In the OT *khesed* denotes an attitude of man or God which arises out of a mutual relationship. It is the attitude which the one expects of the other in this relationship, and to which he is pledged in relation to him. . . . On the other side *khesed* denotes help or kindness as the grace of a superior.[59]

Bultmann concludes, "the meaning of *khesed* fluctuates between (covenant) faithfulness, obligation and love or grace."[60] In our text David seems to be affirming that he lives his life, with all of its fears and dangers (see cameo 4), with the awareness that following behind him is a God who both supports him out of covenant faithfulness and at the same time extends grace (loving kindness) to him that he does not deserve.

David began with the first person (cameo 1, "the LORD is *my* shepherd"). As noted, the first person reappears in the center with his reflections on sin and death (cameo 4, "*I will fear no evil*") and now David concludes with the

---

[57]LVTL, *Lexicon*, p. 349.

[58]Nelson Glueck champions this view; Nelson Glueck, *Hesed in the Bible* (1927; repr., Eugene, OR: Wipf & Stock, 2011).

[59]Rudolf Bultmann, "ελεος," in *TDNT*, 2:479.

[60]Ibid. For a fine discussion of these two meanings and the long discussion regarding them see R. Laird Harris, "ḥsd," in *Theological Workbook of the Old Testament* (Chicago: Moody Press, 1980), 1:305-7.

assurance that he personally is followed by the covenant faithfulness/grace of God (cameo 7, "*I will dwell* in the house of the LORD").

Something of this same imagery appears in Hebrews 12:2, where the reader is urged to look to Jesus who is not only the "pioneer" *who goes before* but also the "perfecter of our faith" *who follows after* and encourages our faith in the direction of its goals.

The seventh cameo concludes the psalm (see fig. 1.11).

> and I will dwell in the house of the LORD
> for the length of the days.

Figure 1.11. House of all the days (Ps 23:6)

Following the centuries-old Syriac and Arabic versions, I have chosen to translate the Hebrew text literally. Does "the length of the days" mean "forever" (KJV, ESV)? Or does it refer to "my whole life long" (NRSV)? Is David discussing the days of *his life* or *God's days*? Both translations are possible. I prefer to leave the original Hebrew as it is and allow the text to stimulate the imagination of the reader. Why should it not mean both "my days" and "God's days"?

Furthermore, what does it mean that I am to "dwell in the house of the LORD" for the length of the day (be they my days, God's days or both)? This could mean that David is talking about his daily presence in the temple worship. But it could also mean that wherever he goes he senses that he is *in the house of God*. All things were made by him and all nature is his. Is God not present in all of it? If this is David's intent, would this not profoundly influence the way I look at, treat and preserve the natural world? Someone has said that the natural world is not an inheritance that I receive from my parents. Rather it is a trust that I am responsible to pass on to my children. That is a good start. But perhaps the psalm is affirming that the entire created universe is the house of God. Do I dump my garbage in the middle of the sanctuary of my church? Perhaps this psalm tells us that all of nature is sacred space and that we are to act accordingly.

In order to set a benchmark against which to measure the relationships between the various good shepherd accounts, it is important to observe the ten themes (already noted) that we intend to trace through the Bible. These themes (as they appear or fail to appear) in Psalm 23 are as follows:

1. The *good shepherd is God.* (The psalm opens with this declaration.)

2. A *lost sheep.* (There is no "lost flock.")

3. Opponents. (Death and "enemies.")

4. The *good shepherd* and the *good host(ess)?* (Male and female images are boldly presented.)

5. The *incarnation of the shepherd.* (Incarnation is declared with "You are with me.")

6. The *shepherd restores the lost.* (He "brings me back.")

7. *Repentance/return.* (The verb *shuv* appears.)

8. ———. (There are no *bad, unredeemed sheep.*)

9. A *celebratory* meal. (This meal is offered at great cost.)

10. The story concludes *in the house.* (My days and God's days are involved.)

With the original structure of the story of the good shepherd and the lost sheep in mind, we can attempt a summary of what we prefer to call a "theological cluster." Rather than a rational argument that comes to a conclusion at the end, the psalm is a story that like a diamond sheds light in a variety of directions. Such a cluster in this Psalm can include the following:

THE THEOLOGICAL CLUSTER OF PSALM 23

Cameo 1. *The Lord is my shepherd.*

      a. My deepest security is found in the Lord, who is my shepherd, not in the security forces or military might of my country.

      b. God cares for each sheep. That sheep is naturally a part of a flock, but at the same time he is *my* shepherd.

      c. The shepherd secures my legitimate needs.

Cameo 2. *The quiet water and the green pastures.*

      a. The shepherd leads with a gentle call. He does not drive with a stick.

      b. He provides good food and the needed quiet waters for his sheep.

    c. The shepherd daily leads the flock to where it can rest. It is not always on the move.

Cameo 3. *He brings me back—for his own name's sake.*

    a. A lost sheep and a good shepherd who brings it back are central to what the psalm is all about.

    b. The lost sheep cannot find its own way home. The shepherd alone can provide the rescue it needs.

    c. The shepherd leads me in paths of righteousness. It is not enough that he returns me to those paths; he must also lead me in them.

    d. The shepherd searches for the lost sheep out of loyalty to his own integrity. It is for "his own name's sake." Therefore my worth as a sheep, be it little or great, has nothing to do with his determination to (find and) restore me.

Cameo 4. *The valley of the shadow.*

    a. Evil and death are real and must be faced. But because of the assured presence of the shepherd we can be delivered from our fear of them.

    b. The flock does not remain in the valley of the shadow. The sheep follow the shepherd and pass through the darkness.

Cameo 5. *You are with me with your rod and staff.*

    a. The Lord suddenly appears "on stage," and David is able to address him directly.

    b. God is both able to protect me from predators (with his rod), and keep me on the right paths (with his staff).

Cameo 6. *You prepare a table.*

    a. The Lord, like a woman, prepares a meal for me.

    b. That meal is offered at great cost. My enemies observe what the Lord is doing for me and they are angry at him for doing it. This is part of the measure of his love.

    c. The special favors reserved for an honored guest are extended to me. Oil is poured on my head and my cup is filled to overflowing.

Cameo 7. *Goodness and mercy—all the days.*

    a. Each evening as I turn toward home (with the flock), I am fol-

lowed by goodness and covenant faithfulness/loving kindness—
not by wild animals and ruthless thieves.

b. This is true "all of the days," which includes my days (my life
long) and God's days (forever).

c. Wherever I go, I am in the house of God and I see the natural
world around me as sacred space in which God is present.

With this great psalm firmly implanted in our minds, we are ready to move
ahead four hundred years in order to reflect on Jeremiah's reuse and refor-
mulation of the same story.

2

THE GOOD SHEPHERD
AND JEREMIAH 23:1-8

It is well known that the various sections of the book of Jeremiah are not assembled in precise historical order. Jeremiah 21:1–24:10 is a series of oracles written and delivered under King Zedekiah leading up to the destruction of Jerusalem by the Babylonians and the Chaldeans (586 B.C.). During the last of those years, Jeremiah was under house arrest and at one point was lowered into a cistern. Convinced that the city would fall, sensing that his message had not been heard and denied his personal freedom, Jeremiah had every reason to despair. It is astounding that he did not do so.

Instead, he reflected critically on the past, sparing no one, particularly the kings of Jerusalem, and envisioned a future full of hope. One of the images that helped him formulate that hope was the good shepherd of Psalm 23. David's personal journey with God was reshaped by Jeremiah into a journey of the nation through defeat, destruction and dispersion to a vision of restoration and return. This retelling of the national story as a good shepherd saga required some dramatic changes and additions to the collection of images that make up the psalm. This chapter will examine Jeremiah's version of the good shepherd psalm and reflect on the points of continuity and contrast with David's original.

Jeremiah's reflections on the shepherds and the flock fall into five cameos. He opens with "Woe to the shepherds who destroy and scatter the sheep of my pasture [An oracle of Yahweh]" (Jer 23:1), and continues with reflections on what the Lord, the God of Israel, will do in response to his shepherd's failures.

1. [23:1] "*Woe* to the *shepherds* who destroy
And scatter the sheep of my pasture!"
    [An oracle of Yahweh][a]

BAD SHEPHERDS
Destroy & Scatter Sheep

2. [2]Therefore thus says the Lord, The God of Israel,
Concerning the shepherds who shepherd[b] my people:
"You have *scattered my flock*
and have *driven them away*,
and you have *not attended* to them.
Behold, I will attend to you
For *your evil deeds*.
    [An oracle of Yahweh]

BAD SHEPHERDS
Criticized
& Threatened

3. [3]Then *I will gather* the remnant of *my flock*
Out of all the countries where I have driven them,
And I will *bring them back (shuv)* to their fold,
And they shall be fruitful and multiply.
[4]*I will set shepherds over them*
Who will *shepherd them*,
And they shall *fear no more, nor be dismayed*,
Neither shall any be *missing*.
    [An oracle of Yahweh]

GOD: GOOD SHEPHERD
Bring Them Back *(shuv)*
& Give Good Shepherds
None Afraid or Lost

4. [5]Behold, the days are coming,
    [An oracle of Yahweh]
When I will *raise up for David* a righteous Branch,
And he shall *reign as king* and deal wisely,
And shall *execute justice*
and *righteousness in the land*.
[6]In his days Judah will be *saved*,
And Israel will *dwell securely*.
And this is the name by which he will be called:
'The Lord is our righteousness.'

DAVIDIC KING PROMISED
Judah Saved
Israel Made Secure
In the Land

5. [7]Therefore, behold, the days are coming,
    [An oracle of Yahweh]
  When they shall no longer say,
  'As the Lord lives
    who brought up the people of Israel
    out of the land of Egypt,' but,
[8]'As the Lord lives
    Who brought up and gathered[c] the offspring
    Of the house of Israel
      Out of the north country
      And out of all the countries
      where he had driven them.'

THE LORD
  Brought Israel Back
    From Egypt

THE LORD
  Brings Israel Back
    From the North

Then they shall *dwell in their own land*."

DWELL IN THEIR LAND

---

[a] My translation.

[b] The Hebrew has a play on words here. The same root (r'y) appears as a noun and means "shepherds" and then as a verb meaning "tend the sheep." I have tried to duplicate this in English. The translation "care for my people" suggests that these worthless shepherds are doing a good job. Such is not the case, as the text makes clear. Arabic versions preserve the play on words as does the Syriac Peshitta.

[c] My translation. See LVTL, *Lexicon*, pp. 112-13.

Figure 2.1. Jeremiah's reflections on the shepherds and the lost flock (Jer 23:1-8)

Yet at the time Jeremiah composed these five cameos, there had already been a significant dispersion of the people (Jer 23:3).[1] That text most certainly refers to the first deportation to Babylon, which took place in 597 B.C. After comparing Jeremiah 23:1-8 with Psalm 23, it appears that Jeremiah is giving his listeners/readers a new version of the psalm in the light of the collapsing world around him. David's phrase *he brings me back* (*nafshi yeshobeb* [Ps 23:3]) must have struck a particularly deep cord for Jeremiah. Jeremiah's text is seen in figure 2.1.

THE RHETORIC

The five cameos flow in a *straight line sequence* that concludes with the "flock" dwelling in "their own land." At the same time, special prominence is given to cameo 3, where God promises to round up the flock and "bring them back" to their fold (i.e., the land). The goal of that return is then specifically mentioned as noted. The center in cameo 3 is also carefully tied to the end of cameo 5 with the repetition of the phrase "out of all the countries where I have driven them." Cameo 1 also speaks of the sheep being "scattered." They are *scattered and driven out* in the beginning (cameo 1), and at the end (cameo 5) Israel is *gathered* from the places where *the Lord has driven* them. Figure 2.2 provides a brief summary of the flow of ideas through the five cameos.

1. Present: Bad shepherds exposed—*sheep scattered*
2. Present: Bad shepherds accused and threatened
3. God enters: To gather and *bring back (shuv)* and provide shepherds for his flock
4. Future: A new, good king is given (because of David)—Salvation & Security
5. Future: Remember not—deliverance from Egypt,
      But rather—deliverance from Babylon.
      Sheep gathered—They will dwell in their own land

Figure 2.2. A Summary of Jeremiah's account of the good/bad shepherd

The message of Jeremiah's good shepherd psalm is: The disasters of the present (1-2), because of God's saving actions in history (3), will be superseded in the future (4-5).

The final cameo (5) uses step parallelism.

---

[1]Jeremiah calls the cameos "oracles" (*ne'um-Yahweh*).

COMMENTARY

Each of the five connected cameos includes the phrase *ne'um-Yahweh,* which is often translated "declares the Lord" or "says the Lord." The phrase has no verb and literally translated reads "an oracle of Yahweh." Today in liturgical churches public readers of Scripture often conclude the reading by saying, "This is the Word of the Lord," which is roughly parallel to the Hebrew wording.[2] Cameos 1-3 deal with the *present* and repeat "oracle of Yahweh" at the *end* of each cameo. The final two cameos (4-5) look to the *future* and invoke this phrase near the *beginning* of each of the two cameos, after the expression "Behold, the days are coming." The phrase itself helps to mark off the cameos from one another. As we proceed I will repeat each cameo in turn for easy reference (see fig. 2.3).

1. 23:1 *"Woe* to the *shepherds* who destroy And scatter the sheep of my pasture!" [An oracle of Yahweh]	BAD SHEPHERDS Destroy & Scatter Sheep

Figure 2.3. Bad shepherds destroy and scatter the sheep (Jer 23:1)

God is the *good shepherd* in Psalm 23, and there is no *bad shepherd* in that psalm. Jeremiah opens with a blunt condemnation of bad shepherds "who destroy and scatter" the sheep (see fig. 2.3). He is attacking the kings of Israel who reversed Josiah's reforms and reintroduced the worship of idols while neglecting the poor, the widows and the orphans. Those evil shepherds tried to undermine the prophets, and Jeremiah may well be writing at a time when he was imprisoned or under house arrest.

The second cameo continues this attack on the kings of Israel (see fig. 2.4).

2. 2Therefore thus says the Lord, The God of Israel, Concerning the shepherds who shepherd my people; "You have *scattered my flock* and have *driven them away,* and you have *not attended* to them. Behold, I will attend to you For *your evil deeds.* [An oracle of Yahweh]	BAD SHEPHERDS Criticized & Threatened

Figure 2.4. Sins of the bad shepherds and God's response (Jer 23:2)

[2]The modern phrase may have evolved from the Hebrew.

The bad shepherds have not only scattered the sheep (cameo 1) but have also driven them away and "not attended to them." God will reverse the scene by "attending to the shepherds" for these failures. But all is not lost. The double use of the word *attend* is lost in formal English. When a character in a novel says, "You haven't *taken care of your assignment,* so I'm going to *take care of you,*" the reader quickly catches the double use of the phrase *take care of*, and expects the speaker to follow this strong language with some form of retaliation against the person so addressed. In like manner here in our text, God is still in control of history, and he is not powerless when the designated shepherds of his flock fail to care for his sheep. These worthless shepherds have "not attended" to God's sheep, so he responds with "I will attend to you for your evil deeds."

God's response follows (see fig. 2.5).

3. ³Then *I will gather* the remnant of *my flock*
Out of all the countries where I have driven them,
And I will *bring them back (shuv)* to their fold,   GOD: GOOD SHEPHERD
And they shall be fruitful and multiply.   Bring Them Back *(shuv)*
⁴*I will set shepherds over them*   & Give Good Shepherds
Who will *shepherd them,*   None Afraid or Lost
And they shall *fear no more, nor be dismayed,*
Neither shall any be *missing.*
          [An oracle of Yahweh]

Figure 2.5. God gathers and brings back his flock (Jer 23:3-4)

It was not only the Babylonians who drove the people out of their land. Rather, God himself drove them into Egypt and Babylon. Now God will again enter history and "gather the remnant" of his flock. He will "bring them back" (*shuv*) to "their fold" (read, "their land"). Then it will be possible for them to take up God's commandment to Adam and Eve in Genesis 1:28, where they are told to "Be fruitful and multiply."

Once God has personally carried out the critical task of "gathering" and "bringing back," he will appoint "shepherds . . . who will shepherd them." The same play on words using the word *shepherd* that appears in cameos 1-2 is repeated here. The *shepherds* scatter the flock rather than *shepherding* them (cameo 1). God will supply *other shepherds* who will truly *shepherd the flock* (cameo 3).

Furthermore the flock will be delivered from its fear. The theme of deliverance from fear that appeared in Psalm 23:4 is here repeated. An additional connection to the great psalm surfaces in the phrase "Neither shall any be missing." David himself was lost, and God had to bring him back (Ps 23:3). Finally, the important verb *shuv* (bring back) forms yet another thread tying the two texts together.

Cameo 4 moves ahead to reflect on a particular shepherd that God is planning for the scattered flock (see fig. 2.6).

4. ⁵Behold, the days are coming
    [An oracle of Yahweh]
When I will *raise up for David* a righteous Branch,
And he shall *reign as king* and deal wisely,   DAVIDIC KING PROMISED
And shall *execute justice*   Judah Saved
and *righteousness in the land*.   Israel Made Secure
⁶In his days Judah will be *saved*,   In the Land
And Israel will *dwell securely*.
And this is the name by which he will be called:
'The Lord is our righteousness.'

Figure 2.6. The flock is safe and secure (Jer 23:5-6)

The text now moves to the future. Jeremiah dreams of a righteous branch that God will raise up "for David" (that is, he will be a descendent of David).[3] This future ruler will reign as king and will deal wisely and execute justice and righteousness. Judah will be saved, and Israel will dwell securely. Clearly, Jeremiah is reflecting on a future king who will reign *in history*, not at its end. This kind of a projection is common in the prophets (see Is 9:5-6; 11:1-9; Mic 5:1-5; Amos 9:11; Hos 3:5). This future king will be called *Yahweh-tsidqenu* (the Lord is our righteousness). This is a play on words with the name of the king at the time of composition, which was Zedekiah (*Tsadqiyahu*: Yahweh is my righteousness). The standards that this future king will keep are far from the kingship Zedekiah was maintaining in the days of Jeremiah. The "righteousness" Jeremiah was invoking was an appropriate response to God's acts in history to save and "justice" involved ethical standards modeled after God's righteousness. Again, Zedekiah had

---

[3]Isaiah 11:1 also speaks of a "branch" that is in the lineage of David.

abandoned any effort to emulate such kingship. Guy Couturier comments on this text:

> Therefore, like his predecessors, Jeremiah predicts the restoration of David's dynasty, not so much on political grounds, but on the level of the religious and moral obligations of the covenant. Knowing the full course of history and being witnesses of the end of revelation we now see that Jesus alone has accomplished this hope and on a much higher level.[4]

Jeremiah 23:1-8 can thus be read along with the more familiar passage in Jeremiah 31:31-34 on the new covenant. The text continues (see fig. 2.7).

5. [7]Therefore, behold, the days are coming
       [An oracle of Yahweh]
    When they shall no longer say,
    'As the Lord lives   THE LORD
        who brought up the people of Israel   Brought Israel Back
        out of the land of Egypt,' but,   From Egypt
    [8]'As the Lord lives
        Who brought up and gathered the offspring
        Of the house of Israel   THE LORD
            Out of the north country   Brings Israel Back
            And out of all the countries   From the North
            where he had driven them.'

    Then they shall *dwell in their own land.'*   DWELL IN THEIR LAND

Figure 2.7. Return from Babylon surpasses return from Egypt (Jer 23:7-8)

This same cameo also appears in Jeremiah 16:14-15, which indicates that it had something of a life of its own. Yet it is a fitting conclusion to the shepherd text before us.

It is amazing to contemplate the strong faith and unshakable hope of a man who can compose such a text while living, probably under house arrest, in a doomed city about to fall. The sack of the city was inevitable, and anyone alive after it was over would most likely face a lifetime of slavery in a foreign land. How many of them would die on the trek to Babylon? Jeremiah ex-

---

[4]Guy Couturier, "Jeremiah," in Raymond E. Brown, Joseph A. Fitzmyer and Roland E. Murphy, *The Jerome Biblical Commentary* (Englewood Cliffs, NJ: Prentice-Hall, 1968), p. 321.

hibits raw courage and greatness of heart. Not only is he saying "all things will yet be well," but he is also affirming that the return from Babylon will *exceed in greatness* the exodus from Egypt! In short the text can be understood to mean,

> God got us out of Egypt with the parting of the Red Sea, the drowning of Pharaoh's army, the giving of the law and all of that. But the return from Babylon will overshadow those astounding events. In the future, when you make an oath, you will swear by the God who brought you back from *Babylon*, not *Egypt*.

And there is more. We *are* what we *remember*. Individuals and communities select what they choose to remember. That selection shapes their identity. A family has a serious automobile accident involving a drunk driver and some members of the family are killed. Then out of nowhere a total stranger at risk to herself stops, picks them up and takes them to the nearest hospital, saving the lives of other family members. Their losses will never be forgotten, but what will *dominate* their memories as a family? Will it be the horrors of the accident and its cause, or the extraordinary grace of their "good Samaritan"? Their choice of a dominant memory will influence the inner core of their being for the rest of their lives.

Jeremiah asks his readers to remember the Lord who returned them from "the north country." Was it dangerous to pen a negative reference about the Babylonians? Perhaps. But he does not say, "Never forget the horrors of the siege and fall of the city." How much they had *suffered* was not forgotten, but neither was it their primary focus. Rather Jeremiah tells the people that one day they will be able to look back and remember the Lord who brought the people back "out of the north country." What mattered was their *redemption* and their *Redeemer*, not their *suffering*. There is no nursing of community grievances—only gratitude for divine intervention. What then of the emphasis on the *return* from "the north country"?

Israel returned from Egypt as a powerful conquering army that was able to wipe out villages like the town of Ai (Josh 8:1-29) killing all twelve thousand people, burning the town, hanging their king and leaving the city a smoking ruin. Ezekiel, a contemporary of Jeremiah, was given a vision and heard a voice (Ezek 40:1-4) telling him, among many other things, what the people must do on their return from Babylon. The text reads:

So you shall divide this land among you according to the tribes of Israel. You
shall allot it as an inheritance for yourselves and for the sojourners who reside
among you and have had children among you. *They shall be to you as native-
born children of Israel.* With you they shall be allotted an inheritance among
the tribes of Israel. In whatever tribe the sojourner resides, there you shall
assign him his inheritance, declares the Lord GOD. (Ezek 47:21-23)

In effect Ezekiel is told, "You have been gone for fifty years. Other people
have moved in. They have now equal rights with you to the land, and you
must treat them accordingly."

Ezekiel was writing shortly after Jeremiah. To what extent did Ezekiel
reflect Jeremiah's views? We cannot tell. We can be sure of significant influence and of the fact that Jeremiah wanted the return from Babylon to
supersede the return from Egypt. Surely Jeremiah did not envision the
return from Babylon as more important, simply because it would be chron-
ologically later. It appears that he dreamed of it being superior in nature to
the return from Egypt. Perhaps Ezekiel reflected something of that quality
when he composed the lines noted previously.

If Israel envisions itself returning from Babylon following these writings
of Jeremiah and Ezekiel, it will see itself and its world through the lenses of
God's concern for justice to the non-Jew and not through the glasses of the
horrors of Babylonian slavery.

Miroslav Volf, professor of theology at Yale Divinity School, has written
a deeply moving book on suffering and our memory of it. He says,

> We will not "forget" so as to be able to rejoice; we will rejoice and therefore
> let those memories slip out of our minds! The reason for our non-remembrance
> of wrongs will be the same as its cause: Our minds will be rapt in the goodness
> of God and in the goodness of God's new world, and the memories of wrongs
> will wither away like plants without water.[5]

Jeremiah tells his listeners/readers to focus their memories on God's grace
demonstrated in history, not on human sin and its devastation. This selection of what needs to be remembered can dramatically shape a future full
of justice, peace and security.

The story ends in the land (Jer 23:8).

---

[5]Miroslav Volf, *The End of Memory* (Grand Rapids: Eerdmans, 2006), p. 214.

What then can be observed when Psalm 23 is compared to Jeremiah 23:1-8? The comparisons appear in figure 2.8.

Psalm 23:1-6	**Jeremiah 23:1-8**
(a personal story)	(community exile and return)
1. Good shepherd is God	Good shepherd is God
2. Lost sheep	———
	Lost flock
3. Opponents:	Opponents:
Death and evil	Bad shepherds
	destroy/scatter
4. Female presence:	
Good host(ess?)	———
5. Incarnation	Incarnation
implied in the present	promised for the future
6. Price paid:	Price paid:
bring back	gather
	bring back
7. Return is to God	Return is to the land
(*shuv*)	(*shuv*)
8. Good and bad sheep missing	———
9. A celebration	———
10. Story ends in	Story ends in
the *house*	the *land*

Figure 2.8. Comparison between David and Jeremiah on the good shepherd

Jeremiah has made a number of important changes to the original story line of the psalm. Following the ten components of the story listed earlier, these include the following:

1. Identity of *the Shepherd*. The good shepherd is still God who is the owner of the sheep. God will gather and bring back the sheep and will appoint new shepherds along with a Davidic king to lead them.

2. The *lost sheep*. The lost sheep has morphed into a lost flock. The entire community is now lost.

3. *Opponents*. David's opponents were "death and evil." Here bad shepherds are introduced for the first time.

4. *Female* presence. David's introduction of female participation is dropped by Jeremiah.

5. *Incarnation*. For David, God was already present and active as his shepherd, leading him and bringing him back (*shuv*). For Jeremiah, God would one day in the future gather the entire flock.

6. *Cost*. The psalm remembers that God brings David back. In Jeremiah, God gathers, raises up (for David), brings back (*shuv*), saves and provides security.

7. The *return* is: David's return is to God. Jeremiah's return is to the land. This is a critical shift of emphasis. A psalm describing David's personal restoration to God is reshaped into a national story of return to a particular piece of geography.

8. *Bad sheep*. Later in the tradition, Ezekiel will reflect on the nature of the sheep. Jeremiah, like David, has no such discussion.

9. The *celebration*. The celebratory meal that David describes is omitted by Jeremiah.

10. The *ending*. The story for Jeremiah ends in "the land" not in the "house of the Lord."

By way of summary, what can be said regarding Jeremiah's vision of the shepherd and the flock?

THE THEOLOGICAL CLUSTER OF THE GOOD SHEPHERD IN JEREMIAH 23:1-8

1. *Leadership failure is a serious matter.*
   Jeremiah emphasizes that failures on the part of the leadership of the commu-

nity of faith are very serious and that those failures will not be overlooked.

2. *Communities can be lost, not just individuals.*
   Communities can go astray or be lost, scattered and destroyed.

3. *The flock belongs to God (not to the shepherds).*
   The flock is God's flock and he still cares for it when the shepherds fail.

4. *In the midst of devastation, hope dies not.*
   Jeremiah affirmed unshakable hope for the future at the very time the world around him was descending into the abyss of destruction, death, slavery and exile.

5. *Incarnation is the only solution.*
   Jeremiah was sure that one day *God himself would appear* to gather and bring back the flock that still belonged to him, even though the sheep were scattered and lost.

6. *The promise of new shepherds and a Davidic king make the future bright.*
   For the flock, God will provide other shepherds and raise up a Davidic king who will rule with *wisdom, justice* and *righteousness*, while offering *salvation* and *security*. This language participates with Jeremiah 31:31-35 in the projection of a new and hopeful future.

7. *Freedom from fear is central to all meaningful life.*
   Fear is again specifically mentioned (cameo 3). They will "fear no more, nor be dismayed."

8. *The anticipated return of the scattered flock is "to the land" and not "to God."*
   Jeremiah has given the story a new political frame of reference that the psalm does not have. But Psalm 23 is not a song about a disembodied soul. David writes about food, drink, security, shelter and a permanent abode. The traditional translation of Psalm 23:3 of "He restoreth my soul" has often been given a Platonic interpretation where the "soul" has nothing to do with the "body." But the Psalm in Hebrew is talking about *nafshi* (my whole person), and the Psalmist is indeed concerned about food, drink and shelter. Furthermore Jeremiah does indeed discuss refugees going home, but there is no space for the displacement of those who live there, as Ezekiel makes clear. Goodness, absence of want, mercy/grace, along with justice and righteousness are essential compo-

nents of the Prophets' dreams.

9. *Jeremiah has set aside some of David's vision.*

In Jeremiah 23 there is no *celebration*, no *house* and no recognition of *female activity* in the work of God.

10. *The return from exile trumps the exodus.*

The projected salvation from Babylon will overshadow the salvation experienced at the sea of reeds. Recollection of the new salvation will focus on the goodness of God, not on the brutalities of humans and the return envisioned has no military component attached to it, which is central to the story of the Exodus.

Jerusalem falls and Jeremiah is exiled to Egypt, where he dies. A few years later, writing from Babylon, Ezekiel's voice is raised and that voice includes an expansion of David's (and Jeremiah's) great hymn about the good shepherd. To that new voice we now turn.

3

THE GOOD SHEPHERD
AND EZEKIEL 34

As a younger contemporary of Jeremiah, it is clear that Ezekiel knew what Jeremiah had said about the good shepherd. This is evident from a comparison between the two texts, as will be noted. Ezekiel was taken captive by the Babylonians and removed to Babylon in 598 B.C. as part of the first wave of deportations from Jerusalem.

A few years later there was a second revolt and Judah was invaded yet again. In 586 B.C. the city of Jerusalem fell and was destroyed. During the final conflict, Ezekiel, in far off Babylon, remained quiet. When word of the fall of the city reached him, he wrote, "my mouth was opened, and I was no longer dumb" (Ezek 33:22). After months of silence, what could he say to the Hebrew refugees by way of reaction to the devastating news of the fall of their capital?[1] As Lawrence Boadt has written succinctly,

> Ezekiel lived through the greatest crisis in ancient Israel's history: the final destruction of Judah and its capital, Jerusalem; the loss of independence in the promised land, exile of all the leading citizens to Babylonia; and the tearing down of the temple and removal of the House of David from kingship.[2]

---

[1] The book of Ezekiel is well organized. The order of the material in chapters 33-34 may be historical or theological. In either case, the reader is presented with the order before us. The question is, what does this order say to the reader?

[2] Lawrence Boadt, "Ezekiel, Book of," in *Anchor Bible Dictionary*, ed. David Noel Freedman (New York: Doubleday, 1992), 2:713.

The prophet's first response was to dash their hopes that the nation might easily and quickly be restored (Ezek 33:23-27). He announced that depopulation and devastation was what awaited those who remained in Judea. He then reflected on the fact that the people really didn't want to hear a word from the Lord, at least not through him! Speaking for God, Ezekiel prophesied (see fig. 3.1):

They hear what you say
but they will not do it;
for with their lips they show much love,
but their heart is set on their gain.
    And lo, you are to them like a love song,
    sung with a beautiful voice
    and played well on an instrument,
for they hear what you say,
but they will not do it. (Ezek 33:31-33)[a]

---

[a]The RSV along with my restoration of the original Hebrew in the fifth line.

Figure 3.1. Ezekiel and the parable of the singer of love songs (Ezek 33:31-32)

Ezekiel's prophecy of destruction (vv. 27-28) was thus spoken in a kindly fashion (it sounded like a love song), but Ezekiel knew only too well that they would hear his words but not do them. Yet judgment was not all he had to offer.

The more distant future was full of hope, and to express that hope Ezekiel retold the classical story of Psalm 23 (already reshaped by Jeremiah). In the shadow of the devastating news of the fall of Jerusalem and the destruction of the Jewish state, Ezekiel created a new version of the story of the good shepherd. He did not whitewash the present, nor did he dim the bright hope that burned within him that God was not finished with his people. In four sections (see figs. 3.2-3.5) he says,

A. Bad shepherds are accused, found guilty and condemned.

1. ^{34:1}The word of the LORD came to me:
   ²"Son of man, prophesy against the shepherds of Israel;   PROPHET CALLED
   Prophesy, and say to them, even to the shepherds,   Prophesy Against Shepherds
   Thus says the Lord GOD:

2. Ah, shepherds of Israel
   Who have been shepherding/tending^a yourselves!
   Should not shepherds shepherd/tend the sheep?
 ³ You eat the fat,   BAD SHEPHERDS
   You clothe yourselves with the wool,   Tend Themselves
 You slaughter the fat ones,   Not the Flock
   But you do not shepherd/tend the sheep.

3. ⁴The *weak* you have *not strengthened,*
   The *sick* you have *not healed,*   SHEPHERDS FAIL
 The *injured* you have not *bound up,*   To Bring Back
 The *strayed* you *have not brought back [shuv],* & in Many Things
 The *lost* you have *not sought,*
   And with *force* and *harshness* you have ruled them.

4. ⁵So they were scattered,
   Because there was no shepherd,
 And they became food for all the wild beasts.
     ⁶My sheep were scattered;   RESULTS OF THEIR FAILURES
 They wandered over all the mountains   Sheep Scattered
   And on every high hill.   Eaten, Wandering
 My sheep were scattered over all the face of the earth,
   With none to search or seek for them.

5. ⁷"Therefore, you shepherds,
   Hear the word of the Lord:
 ⁸As I live, [An oracle of the Lord GOD]   BECAUSE OF THESE FAILINGS
   surely because my sheep have become a prey, Sheep Eaten by Beasts
 And my sheep have become food for all the wild beasts, And Shepherds Serve Themselves
   Since there was no shepherd,
 And because my shepherds have not searched for my sheep,
   But the shepherds have shepherded/tended themselves,
   And not fed my sheep.

6. ⁹Therefore, you shepherds,
   Hear the word of the LORD:
 ¹⁰Thus says the Lord GOD,   I DISMISS SHEPHERDS
   Behold, I am against the shepherds,   I Will Rescue Sheep
 And I will require my sheep at their hand
   And put a stop to their tending of the sheep.
 No longer shall the shepherds shepherd/tend themselves.
   I will rescue my sheep from their mouths,
   That they may not be food for them.

---

^aIn Hebrew the root *r'h* produces the words *flock, shepherds* and *tending/shepherding.* I have tried to preserve as much as possible of this play on words between "the shepherds" and what they do, which is shepherding/tending. It means far more than "feeding" as the texts themselves demonstrate.

Figure 3.2. The bad shepherds (Ezek 34:1-10)

B. *God, the good shepherd,* comes, searches, finds, gathers, rescues, feeds, brings back (*shuv*), binds up, strengthens and gives justice.

7. [34:11]"For thus says the Lord GOD:
> Behold, *I, I myself will search for my sheep*
> And will *seek them out.*
>> [12]As a shepherd seeks out his flock
>> When he is among his sheep that have been scattered,
>> So will *I seek out my sheep,*
>> And *I will rescue them*
>>> From all the places where they have been scattered
>>> On a day of clouds and thick darkness.
>> [13]And I will *bring them out* from the peoples
>> And *gather them* from the countries,

GOD HIMSELF WILL RESCUE
& Bring Them Back/Out
From the Peoples

8. And will *bring them* into their own land.
> And *I will shepherd them* on the mountains of Israel,
> By the ravines,
>> And in all the inhabited places of the country.
>> [14]*I will shepherd them in good pasture,*
>>> And upon the mountain heights of Israel
>> shall be their grazing land.
>>> There *they shall lie down* in *good grazing land,*
>> And on *rich pasture* they shall *feed*
>>> On the mountains of Israel.

GOD WILL FEED THEM
They will Lie Down
In Good Grazing Land

9. [15]*I myself will be the shepherd of my sheep,*
>> [16]And *I myself will settle them down,*[a]
>> [An oracle of the Lord God]
> *I will seek* the lost,
>> And I will *bring back* (*shuv*) the strayed,
> And I will *bind up* the injured,
>> And I will *strengthen* the weak,
> And the fat and the strong I will destroy.
> I will *feed them* in *justice.*

GOD WILL BE SHEPHERD
He will Seek the Lost
Bring Them Back
Destroy Fat/Strong

---

[a]The same verb רבץ (*rbts*) is used in Ps 23:2, which I have chosen to translate "he settles me down." The noun form of this verb means "a resting place." See LVTL, *Lexicon*, p. 871.

Figure 3.3. The good shepherd (Ezek 34:11-16)

C. *Bad sheep* are accused and judged.

10. [34:17] "As for you, my flock,
> says the Lord GOD:
> Behold, I judge between sheep and sheep,
>> Rams and male goats.
>> [18]Is it not enough for you to feed on good pasture,
>>> that you must tread down with your feet
>>> the rest of your pasture;
>> and to drink of clear water,
>>> that you must muddy the rest of the water with your feet?
>> [19]And must my sheep eat what you have trodden with your feet,
>>> and drink what you have muddied with your feet?

I, GOD, WILL JUDGE
Bad Sheep

11. [20]"Therefore, thus says the Lord GOD to them:
> Behold, *I, myself will judge* between the fat sheep
>> And the lean sheep.
> Because you push with side and shoulder,
>> And thrust at all the weak with your horns,
>> Till you have scattered them abroad,
>> [22]*I will rescue* my flock;
>>> they shall no longer be a prey.
>> And *I will judge* between sheep and sheep.

I, GOD WILL JUDGE
Bad Sheep &
Save Flock

Figure 3.4. The bad sheep (Ezek 34:17-22)

D. *God, the good shepherd,* will appoint leaders, tend, provide food, security, peace, blessing and freedom.

12. ^{34:22}And *I will set up* over them *one shepherd,*
    My servant David,
And he shall shepherd them:
    He shall tend them and be their shepherd.
  ²⁴And I, the Lord, will be their God,
    And my servant David shall be prince among them.
I am the Lord; I have spoken.

          I, GOD, WILL APPOINT
          David - Shepherd & Prince

13. ²⁵"I will make with them a covenant of peace
    and banish wild beasts from the land,
so that they may dwell securely in the wilderness
    and sleep in the woods.

          I, GOD, WILL MAKE
          Covenant of Peace/Security

14. ²⁶And I will make them
    and the places round about my hill a blessing,
And I will send down the showers in their season;
    They shall be showers of blessing.
  ²⁷And the trees of the field shall yield their fruit,
    And the earth shall yield its increase,
    And *they shall be secure in their land.*

          I, GOD, WILL GIVE
          Blessing, Prosperity &
          Security

15. And they shall know that I am the Lord,
    When I break the bars of their yoke,
    And deliver them from the hand of those who enslaved them.
  ²⁸They shall no more be a prey to the nations,
    Nor shall the beasts of the land devour them.
They shall dwell securely,
    And none shall make them afraid.
  ²⁹And I will provide for them renowned plantations
    so that they shall no more be consumed
    With hunger in the land,
    And no longer suffer the reproach of the nations.

          I, GOD, WILL BREAK YOKE
          No Foreign Threat (without)
          No Wild Beasts (within)
          Security & Prosperity

16. ³⁰And they shall know
    that I am the Lord their God with them,
  and that they, the house of Israel, are my people,
    Says the Lord God.

          THEY WILL KNOW
          I/Their God Am With Them
          They – My People

E. *Conclusion:* You are my sheep.

17. ³¹And *you are my sheep,*
    Human sheep of my pasture,
  And I am your God
    declares the Lord God."

          YOU ARE MY SHEEP &
          I Am ***Your God***

Figure 3.5. God the good shepherd (Ezek 34:23-31)

THE RHETORIC

This chapter is the longest of any of the biblical good shepherd accounts. Composed of seventeen cameos its outline is seen in figure 3.6.

A. *The bad shepherds are* accused, found guilty and condemned.

(Cameos 1-6; Ezek 34:1-10)

    B. *God, the good shepherd, promises,* I, I myself will come, search, find, gather, rescue, feed, bring back, bind up, strengthen, and give justice.   (Cameos 7-9; Ezek 34:11-15)

C. *The bad sheep are* accused and judged.   (Cameos 10-11; Ezek 34:17-22)

    D. *God, the good shepherd, affirms that* I myself will appoint, shepherd, provide food, security, peace, blessing, and freedom.   (Cameos 12-17; Ezek 34:23-30)

E. You are *my sheep*
  I am *your God.*   (Cameo 17; Ezek 34:31)

Figure 3.6. The overall outline of Ezekiel 34

A brief summary/outline of the chapter can be seen as

- The bad shepherds (A) and God's response to them (B).
- The bad sheep (C) and God's response to them (D).
- The conclusion to the matter (E).

COMMENTARY

Ezekiel retained (and expanded) all of the changes that Jeremiah introduced into the story line of the good shepherd. Ezekiel's only major innovation was the introduction of "bad sheep."

In the following reflections we will follow Ezekiel's five divisions (A-E).

A. *The bad shepherds are* accused, found guilty and condemned (cameos 1-6; Ezek 34:1-10).

Jeremiah began his telling of the story of "the good shepherd" with an attack on the "bad shepherds." Ezekiel's description of them is extensive, blunt and reflects considerable anger. Progression through the six cameos is as follows:

Cameo 1. *The prophet's mandate.* The prophet is ordered to "prophesy against the shepherds of Israel."

Cameo 2. *The self-centeredness of the shepherds.* The shepherds shepherd/tend themselves rather than the sheep. They kill the sheep, eat the fat and clothe themselves with the wool but do not tend the sheep.

After the fall of Jerusalem, King Zedekiah was captured, blinded and taken as a prisoner to Babylon (2 Kings 25:6-7). Ezekiel (presumably) was not aware of these details. But after everything had been lost, popular anger at Zedekiah (dead or alive) for having led the nation into such a disaster was no doubt high. Thus Ezekiel's criticism of "the shepherds" of Israel (cameo 2) was probably received sympathetically by the exiles around him in Babylon.

Cameo 3. *The suffering the shepherds have inflicted on the sheep.* Ezekiel lists seven failings of the shepherds:

The weak—not strengthened
The sick—not healed
The injured—not bound up
The strayed—not brought back (*shuv*)
The lost—not sought out
The people—ruled with force
  —and with harshness

Both "search for" (cameo 2) and "bring back" (cameo 3) are mentioned. Shepherds are not known to be rich. An *owner* of large flocks (like Job) can be wealthy, but not so the shepherd who must daily lead the sheep through winter cold and summer heat, facing dangers from wild animals and thieves. The one thing the shepherd possesses that is of supreme value to him is his reputation as a shepherd. This theme was already introduced in Psalm 23, where the good shepherd "brings me back . . . *for his own name's sake*" (Ps 23:3).

Ezekiel does not name names; he simply tells a story about worthless shepherds who failed and what God is going to do about it. The deportees around Ezekiel were already in exile and thus knew all about the "scattered flock" and, as noted, would have been pleased to hear this kind of harsh public criticism of their failed leaders. The key word *shuv* again appears. The shepherds had failed to "*bring back* [*shuv*] the strayed."

Cameo 4. *The result of these gross failures:*

The sheep are scattered over "all the face of the earth."
The sheep become food for the wild beasts,
  with "none to search or seek for them."

Both "*search/seek*" and "*bring back*" are mentioned. When a sheep is lost, the shepherd is expected to engage in both saving acts. A good shepherd must first *find*, and only then can he *restore* the lost. At whatever cost, the shepherd must tramp over the rugged hills until he finds the lost sheep. Having found it, the second task is still before him. He must hoist the 50 to 70-pound animal on his shoulders and stagger back to the village (probably uphill) regardless of the distance.[3] Psalm 23 only mentions the second, which is, "he brings me back." In Jeremiah, God "gathers" the flock and then "brings them back." Gathering assumes finding. But here in Ezekiel, for the first time both aspects of the task of saving the lost are clearly mentioned.[4] They are both important because theologically speaking the first is *incarnation* and the second is *atonement*. More of this later.

The bad shepherds become *like the wild beasts*. Both the shepherds and the beasts kill and eat the sheep.

Cameos 5-6. *What will happen to these self-centered, irresponsible shepherds?* Summarizing the results of the bad shepherds, Ezekiel says: (5) because the shepherds tended themselves rather than the flock and because the flock had become food for the wild beasts (read, Babylonians), (6) I therefore say to the shepherds, "you *are fired!*" I must now rescue my sheep *from you.*

Because the shepherds are as damaging to the flock as the wild beasts, God (the owner of the flock) is obliged to fire the current shepherds in order to save the flock.

Thus far Ezekiel's version of "the good shepherd" was no doubt well-received. The message was, blame the king and his administrators and blame the "wild beasts" (the Babylonians). Sitting in a slave labor camp at the edge of Babylon, Ezekiel chose to *blame the leadership of his own community* rather than merely point the finger at the Babylonians! The "wild animals" are out there, but Ezekiel knows that God must first deal with the crooked shepherds who continue to gradually destroy the flock. Amazing! Generally speaking, in times of great loss, loyalty to "king and country" produces the cry, "Blame

---

[3]In Judea the villages were on the top of the ridge, while the wilderness pastures sloped down from that ridge to the Dead Sea. They still do.

[4]Modern emergency crews are called "search and rescue" teams. The two tasks are related but distinguishable as separate activities. Talking to Zacchaeus Jesus uses the language of a shepherd when he says, "The son of man came to *seek* and to *save* the lost" (Lk 19:10). Both actions are specifically mentioned.

the oppressors!" Ezekiel also blames the leadership of his own community.

God "fires" *the shepherds*! Now what? This brings us to God's stunning response that appears in section B with its three cameos (Ezek 34:11-16). It was not enough to rail against the "bad shepherds." God now offers hope for the future. (Because of its importance we will reprint the text for easy reference.)

B. *The good shepherd (God)* searches for, finds, gathers, rescues, feeds, brings back (shuv), binds up, strengthens and gives justice (see fig. 3.7).

7. ³⁴:¹¹"For thus says the Lord GoD:
    Behold, I, I myself will search for my sheep
    And will seek them out.
        ¹²As a shepherd seeks out his flock   GOD HIMSELF WILL RESCUE
    When he is among his sheep that have been scattered,   & Bring Them Back/Out
        So will I seek out my sheep,   From the Peoples
    And I will rescue them
        From all the places where they have been scattered
        On a day of clouds and thick darkness.
    ¹³And I will bring them out from the peoples
        And gather them from the countries,

Figure 3.7. God comes in person to his flock (Ezek 34:11-13)

The language is very forceful. The leaders of the community were part of the problem, not part of the solution. The only hope for salvation was *divine incarnation*. "I, I myself will search for my sheep," reads the text. The verbs tell their own story. God will *search* for, *seek* out, *rescue*, *bring out* and *gather* his people from the lands where they are scattered. Then what? (See fig. 3.8.)

8. And will bring them into their own land.
        And I will shepherd them on the mountains of Israel,
    By the ravines,
        And in all the inhabited places of the country.
    ¹⁴I will shepherd them in good pasture,   GOD WILL FEED THEM
        And upon the mountain heights of Israel   They will Lie Down
    shall be their grazing land.   In Good Grazing Land
        There they shall lie down in good grazing land,
    And on rich pasture they shall feed
        On the mountains of Israel.

Figure 3.8. God himself shepherds the flock (Ezek 34:13b-14)

God is not just the first-responder rescue team. Rather, he *himself* will be their shepherd. He will bring them to their own land and will lead them to good pasture. In the psalm David affirmed that God led him to "green pasture." After eating his fill he was allowed to settle down in that place of repose and abundance. Once again, an idea first found in the psalm is repeated by Ezekiel as he writes, "they shall lie down in good grazing land."

The cameo opens and closes with the phrase *the mountains of Israel*. Ezekiel had just told the people that God would make the "land of Israel" an utter waste, to the extent that "the mountains of Israel shall be so desolate that none will pass through" (Ezek 33:28). Those same mountains of Israel had become "high places" for the worship of idols, and were therefore ripe for special condemnation. The dead bodies of the people of Israel would be dumped in front of their idols on those same "high places" in the mountains of Israel (Ezek 6:1-7). Now those mountains will become "rich pasture" for a restored flock.

A bright hope for the future can easily dance before the eyes of any dreamer on a sunny day, but in the wake of a devastating storm with destruction on all sides overwhelming the mind and heart, how can such a vision survive?

Many of the themes of cameo 8 are repeated in cameo 9 (see fig. 3.9).

9. ¹⁵*I myself will be the shepherd of my sheep,*
    ¹⁶And *I myself will settle them down,*
      [An oracle of the Lord God]   GOD WILL BE SHEPHERD
    I *will seek* the lost,   He will Seek the Lost
      And I will *bring back (shuv)* the strayed,   Bring Them Back
    And I will *bind up* the injured,   Destroy Fat/Strong
      And I will *strengthen* the weak,
    And the fat and the strong I will destroy.
      I will *feed them* in *justice.*

Figure 3.9. God himself will bring back, bind up and feed his sheep (Ezek 34:15-16)

Now for the third time Ezekiel reaffirms that, humanly speaking, Israel's problems are unsolvable. The answer already given in cameos 7-8 is repeated here in cameo 9 with some expansion. God understands and declares through the prophet that *one day* he, *himself*, will *enter history* and put things right. The redemptive acts promised by the incarnate God are now presented in a list (see fig. 3:10).

9. I myself will be the shepherd and I will:
    Let them lie down
    Seek the lost
    Bring back *(shuv)* the strayed,
    Bind up the injured
    Strengthen the weak
    Feed them in justice (having overpowered the bullies)

Figure 3.10. Six great saving acts of Ezek 34:15-16

"Lie down" and "bring back" are both prominent in Psalm 23. Earlier in this chapter (cameo 3) Ezekiel discussed shepherds who will "Not bring back [*shuv*]" the lost. But in cameo 9 the same verb appears in the center of the list of positives.[5] Ezekiel is confident that a human shepherd cannot accomplish these tasks; only a divine shepherd can manage.

Having discussed the "bad *shepherds*" (A) and noted God's response (B), Ezekiel now turns to reflect on "the bad *sheep*" (C). His views on the "bad sheep" fall into two cameos (10-11) (see fig. 3.11).

C. Bad sheep are accused and judged.

10. [17] "As for you, my flock,
        says the Lord GOD:
     Behold, I judge between sheep and sheep,
        Rams and male goats.   I, GOD, WILL JUDGE:
     [18]Is it not enough for you to feed on good pasture,   Bad Sheep
        that you must tread down with your feet
        the rest of your pasture;
     and to drink of clear water,
        that you must muddy the rest of the water with your feet?
     [19]And must my sheep eat what you have trodden with your feet,
        and drink what you have muddied with your feet?

11. [20]"Therefore, thus says the Lord GOD to them:
     Behold, *I, myself will judge* between the fat sheep
        And the lean sheep.   I, GOD WILL JUDGE:
     Because you push with side and shoulder,   Bad Sheep &
        And thrust at all the weak with your horns,   Save Flock
        Till you have scattered them abroad,
     [22]*I will rescue* my flock;
        they shall no longer be a prey.
        And *I will judge* between sheep and sheep.

Figure 3.11. Flock saved from bad sheep (Ezek 34:17-22)

---

[5]If "becoming a shepherd" is understood as the first item on this list, the number of promised positives totals seven.

Prophets of Israel were known to criticize wayward people, but that was within the safety of their own land. However, Ezekiel and the people were now in exile. Yes, he could be expected to criticize the failed leadership. The public mood could well be: "Those leaders got us into this mess. The prophet has every right to criticize them." But having done so (Ezek 34:1-10), Ezekiel goes on to offer some harsh words about the *sheep themselves*. They are not innocent. The *battered flock* has *bullies in its midst*. Yes, they are oppressed by the Babylonians (the wild animals) and also by their own leadership (the bad shepherds). But the flock also suffers from bad sheep who *start oppressing the rest of the flock!*

"How dare you criticize us—look at how much we have suffered" is a shallow cry that echoes across the millennia. It is often the case that the more people suffer the more they are convinced that their oppressors are guilty, while they are innocent. Their very suffering, they suppose, grants them the right to assume innocence. Woe to the preacher or prophet who dares to tell them, "Yes, you have suffered, but don't forget—there are serious faults to be found within the flock!" In cameos 7-8 (figs. 3.7-3.8) the reader can see that the flock needs to be rescued from bad shepherds, wild animals *and from bad sheep!*

This theme is bold and unmistakable in Ezekiel, but there is one faint hint of it in Psalm 23. David writes, "He brings me back." The text allows the reader to imagine that David is responsible for getting himself lost. David's personal life encourages such imaginings. In the psalm this idea is reinforced by the second phrase that reads, "He leads me in the paths of righteousness." Clearly the psalmist was in the paths of "unrighteousness" and needed help to return to the paths of righteousness. David knew he needed to be "brought back" and led in the right paths.

Returning for a moment to Jeremiah we note that the prophet introduces flawed, human shepherds who "scatter the sheep . . . and drive them away" (Jer 23:1-2). At the same time, in Jeremiah 23:3 God will gather the remnant "of my flock out of all the countries where *I have driven them*." God is active and sovereign in history, and *he scatters the sheep*, and at the same time the bad shepherds are blamed for *their acts* of *scattering* those *same sheep*. God acted, and so did the bad shepherds. One can make peace with such a paradox, but can never resolve it.[6]

Ezekiel adds a creative flourish to this paradox. He presents three actors in this "divine drama." In some deep, indefinable sense, *God is in control* of history. Yet both the *bad shepherds* and the *bad sheep* were fully responsible for their actions in scattering the flock.

God has no illusions. He acts in history out of loyalty to his own integrity. He is a witness to the brutalities of the strong (who in Ezekiel's day were themselves downtrodden refugees) who treat the weak among them with merciless cruelty. Once again, the flock cannot sort itself out. The only solution is the *intervention* of the *divine into human history*.

In cameos 12-16 (Ezek 34:23-30) the prophecy focuses on what God will do once he gathers the flock and returns it to the land. Summarized, these cameos project the following:

- Cameo 12. Yahweh is their God and he will appoint his "servant David" as prince among them.

- Cameo 13. God will make with them a covenant of peace and offer security from wild beasts, even in the wilderness. The *covenant of peace* here promised is a longed for gift, desperately desired by refugees, especially when they had just lost a devastating three-year war.

- Cameo 14. The places "around my hill" (recently destroyed) will be a blessing. Bountiful rain, abundant harvests and security in the land will be theirs. The readers are assured that the war-ravaged areas around the recently destroyed city of Jerusalem will become places of blessing. Fruitful fields and orchards will banish hunger.

- Cameo 15. The yoke of slavery and its public humiliation before the nations will disappear. The resulting security will assure freedom from slavery, fear, hunger and reproach. They shall know that "I am the LORD their God with them."

Seen together, this fourth section of Ezekiel's retelling of the good shepherd story (D) focuses on the life of the community after their return. The setting is no longer Babylon but Israel. There will be rain

---

[6]Ezekiel is not embarrassed to present such a paradox. He had not read Aristotle.

and good crops along with an absence of hunger and wild beasts. Yet the
text has hints of something more. As they settle in the land they will
experience

- a covenant of peace
- security (even) in the wilderness (They will "sleep in the woods")
- freedom from fear (none shall make them afraid)

Ezekiel has a great deal to say about the covenant Israel has with God,
which they have broken (see chaps. 16-17). But only in connection with "God
the good shepherd" do we have reference to "a covenant of peace."[7] Because
of its rarity and its content, it becomes "a showstopper" for the reader. If on
return the people are to be so secure that they can "sleep in the woods"
without fear, then that "covenant of peace" must necessarily include peace
with the non-Jews who already live there. Does Ezekiel have anything to say
on this topic? He does.

As noted earlier in our discussion of Jeremiah 23, Ezekiel firmly tells
the returnees that the non-Jews who had moved in during their relatively
short absence had rights to the land equal to their rights (Ezek 47:13–
48:35). Thus Ezekiel takes the argument one giant step beyond Jeremiah.
Jeremiah affirmed that the new king would "execute justice and righteousness in the land" (Jer 23:5), and that the return from Babylon would
be greater than the return from Egypt (Jer 23:7-8). Now Ezekiel spells
out an important part of that justice. Namely, the Jew and non-Jew have
equal rights that include rights to the land. This is a new day! When
Israel returned from Egypt, the pattern of interaction with the people
who lived in the Holy Land was to kill them or drive them out (cf.
Joshua). For Ezekiel that pattern was no longer good enough. Now the
returnees are to have a "covenant of peace" in the land, and they will be
so secure that they can "sleep in the woods" because the non-Jewish
village next to them, having been treated justly will inevitably be a part
of that *covenant of peace*.[8]

---

[7]Bits and pieces of the good shepherd parable (chap. 34) reappear in Ezekiel 37:24-28. One of the
items that is repeated is the "covenant of peace." This phrase, *covenant of peace*, appears in Ezekiel
only in these two texts.

[8]The European Americans who settled America across the last 350 years did not allow themselves
to be informed by these texts.

Three themes are particularly close to Psalm 23. The *first* is the phrase "I will fear no evil," which we noted in Psalm 23:4b. This theme is repeated Ezekiel 34:28, which reads, "None shall make them afraid." The *second* has to do with Psalm 23:4: "for you are with me." This affirmation is in harmony with Ezekiel 34:16, which says, "I the Lord their God will be with them." *Third* is a repetition of a dramatic element already noted in Psalm 23:4-5, where God "walks on stage." The pronoun "he" gives way to "you" as God is addressed directly. These are

- *You* are with *me* . . .

- *Your* rod and staff . . . comfort *me*

- *You* prepare a table for *me* . . . [before] *my* enemies

- *You* anoint *my* head.

In like manner, here at the end of Ezekiel's account of the good shepherd (cameo E), God is no longer addressed as "he" but rather for the first time God addresses his flock directly saying,

> And *you* are *my* sheep
>> Human sheep of *my* pasture,
> And *I am your God*
>> Declares the Lord GOD. (v. 31)

God is now among the people.

It is now time to trace the major elements that tie the good shepherd stories together. As regards the first three accounts those elements are displayed in figure 3.12 (p. 94).

From what we have seen, it is evident that Ezekiel is following Jeremiah's lead. As noted, all of the revisions that Jeremiah introduces into David's story line, Ezekiel maintains. The hint of "bad sheep" in Psalm 23:3 is picked up by Ezekiel and expanded into a full section. We conclude with a summary of what Ezekiel is saying as he expands Jeremiah's revision of Psalm 23 (see p. 95).

Ps 23:1-6	*Jer 23:1-8*	*Ezek 34:1-31*
David is: Lost & Found	(exile and return)	(exile and return)
1. Good shep. is God	Good shep. is God	Good shep. is God
2. Lost sheep (no flock)	----- Lost flock	----- Lost flock
3. Opponents: Death & "enemies"	Opponents: Bad shepherds destroy/scatter the flock	Opponents: Bad Shepherds scatter/eat the flock
4. Good Host(ess?)	-----	-----
5. Incarnation implied	Incarnation promised	Incarnation promised
6. Price paid: Deliver from fear, bring back	Price paid: Deliver from fear, gather, bring back	Price paid: deliver from fear, search for
7. Repentance is return to God *(shuv)*	Repentance is return to land *(shuv)*	Repentance is return to land *(shuv)*
8. (bad sheep?)	-----	good/bad sheep
9. A celebration	-----	-----
10. Story ends in house	Story ends in the land	Story ends in the land

Figure 3.12. David, Jeremiah and Ezekiel on the story of the shepherd and the sheep

THE THEOLOGICAL CLUSTER OF EZEKIEL 34:1-31

Section A: *Bad shepherds* (cameos 1-6)

>
> 1. Bad shepherds are criticized bluntly and dismissed from being shepherds.
> 2. The entire flock is scattered and lost as a result of their poor leadership.

Section B: *God, the good shepherd* (cameos 7-9)

>
> 3. The situation is so desperate that the *only solution is incarnation*. God must and will come *himself* to gather, bring back (*shuv*) and care for the lost flock.
> 4. God will bring them to their land and the devastated "heights of Israel" will become "grazing land." (The focus of the verb "to return" [*shuv*] is changed.) In Psalm 23 God "brings me back" to himself, that is, to his house. Now the return is to the land.
> 5. There is a special promise that God incarnate will strengthen the weak and "feed them in justice."

Section C: *Bad sheep* (cameos 10-11)

>
> 6. The abused sheep are not necessarily righteous. Some of them are judged as evil because of their brutality toward other sheep.
> 7. Like the enemies of the flock, these aggressive sheep *scatter* the weak sheep.

Section D: *God, the good shepherd* (cameos 12-16)

>
> 8. God will provide "My servant David" as their shepherd and prince.
> 9. God will secure for them a "covenant of peace."
> 10. God will provide security (even when exposed) in the midst of all.

Section E. *God speaks to them directly* (cameo 17)

>
> 11. "You are my sheep," and I am "your God."

We turn now to Zechariah and the fourth telling of the story of the good shepherd and the lost sheep/flock.

4

THE GOOD SHEPHERD
AND ZECHARIAH 10:2-12

It is with some hesitation that I include in this study a brief discussion of Zechariah 10:2-12. The first eight chapters of this book have long been attributed to Zechariah the prophet, and they are internally dated from 518 B.C. (Zech 1:1) to 520 B.C. (Zech 7:1). Chapters 9–14 are almost universally accredited to "Deutero-Zechariah"[1] and are assumed to be composed after the conquest of the Holy Land by the Greeks under Alexander the Great (332 B.C.). The presence of the Greek military is mentioned in Zechariah 9:13. This study focuses on Zechariah 10:2-12, which is full of references to sheep and shepherds.

However, I am omitting chapter 11, where the prophet is told to "become shepherd of the flock doomed to slaughter" (Zech 11:4). He destroys three shepherds. Two staffs are broken and severe "woes" are pronounced against the "worthless shepherds" (Zech 11:15-17). There appears to be almost no trace of the story line of Psalm 23 in these most puzzling verses. In chapter 10, however, such influence from the shepherd psalm can be found even if it is not as bold as in Jeremiah and Ezekiel. Our focus will be limited to Zechariah 10:2-12 (see fig. 4.1).

---

[1]For a summary of recent scholarship on Zechariah see David L. Petersen, "Zechariah, Book of," in *The Anchor Bible Dictionary*, ed. David Noel Freedman (New York: Doubleday, 1992), 6:1065-66.

1. [10:2]Indeed, the household gods utter nonsense,	
and the diviners see lies;	FALSE LEADERS
they tell false dreams	Fail
and give empty consolation.	
Therefore *the people wander like sheep;*	LOST FLOCK
they are afflicted with no shepherd over the sheep.[a]	No Shepherds
[3]My *anger is hot against the shepherds,*	Lord Angry
and I will *punish the leaders;*	Bad Shepherds Punished
2. For the *Lord of hosts cares for his flock,* the house of Judah,	GOD: SHEPHERD
and will make them like the steed *of his majesty in battle.*[b]	War Horse for God
[4]From him shall come the *cornerstone,*	Cornerstone
from him the *tent peg,*	Tent Peg
from him the *battle bow,*	Battle Bow
from him every *ruler* – all of them together.	Ruler
[5]They shall be like *mighty men in battle,*	Mighty in Battle
trampling the foe in the mud of the streets;	Trampling Foe in Mud
they shall fight because *the Lord is with them,*	GOD WITH THEM
and they shall put to shame the *riders on horses.*	Cavalry Shamed
3. [6]"I will make strong (*gabar*) the house of Judah,	GOD: GOOD SHEPHERD
and I will *save* the house of Joseph.	Joseph Saved
I will bring them back (shuv)	Brought back *(shuv)*
because I have *compassion* on them,	Shown Compassion
and they shall be as though I had *not rejected them,*	Not rejected
for *I am the Lord their God* and I will *answer* them.	Answered
4. [7]Then Ephraim shall become like a mighty warrior	EPHRAIM
and their hearts shall be glad as with wine.	A Mighty Warrior
Their children shall see it and be glad;	Children Glad
their hearts shall rejoice in the Lord.	
5. [8]I will whistle for them and gather them in,	
for I have redeemed them,	I WHISTLE
and they shall be as many as they were before.	I Gather/Redeem Them
[9]Though I scattered them among the nations,	They Remember
yet in far countries they shall remember me,	They Return *(shuv)*
and with their children they shall live and *return (shuv).*	
6. [10]I will *bring them back (shuv)* from the land of Egypt	
and gather them from Assyria	I BRING BACK *(shuv)*
and I will bring them to the land of Gilead and to Lebanon,	Egypt
till there is no room for them.	Assyria
7. [11]He shall pass through the sea of troubles	
and strike down the waves of the sea,	
and all the depths of the Nile shall be dried up.	EGYPT &
The pride of Assyria shall be laid low,	Assyria Overcome
And the scepter of Egypt shall depart.	
8. [12]I will make them strong in the Lord,	STRONG IN LORD
and they shall walk in his name [an oracle of Yahweh].	Walk in His Name

[a]My translation.

[b]My translation. The text is describing the majesty of the Lord, not the greatness of the horse. Granted, the horse must be a powerful and magnificent animal to showcase the majesty of the Lord, but it is the Lord who is on display, not the horse. Queen Elizabeth's formal attire displays the majesty of her person and presence, not the other way around. Here we follow the Syriac Peshitta and the Arabic versions.

Figure 4.1. Zechariah's good shepherd (Zech 10:2-12)

THE RHETORIC

There appear to be eight cameos in this account of the shepherds and the flock. The eight present a straight line sequence. The first cameo attacks the bad shepherds and expresses God's "hot anger" against them. The second and third cameos focus on how God himself will enter history, transform the sheep, save them and bring them back (*shuv*). As in Psalm 23, Jeremiah 23 and Ezekiel 34, here in Zechariah, God is referred to in personal terms. That is, "*He will* do [thus and so]" (cameo 2) turns into "*I will* strengthen, save, bring . . ." (cameo 3). The peoples' response appears at the very end and reads, "And they shall walk in his name." As is expected in a straight line sequence, the climax appears at the end.

COMMENTARY

Cameo 1 begins with an attack on false leaders (see fig. 4.2).

1. [10:2]Indeed, the household gods utter nonsense,	
and the diviners see lies;	FALSE LEADERS
they tell false dreams	Fail
and give empty consolation.	
Therefore *the people wander like sheep;*	LOST FLOCK
they are afflicted with no shepherd over the sheep.	No Shepherds
[3]My *anger is hot against the shepherds,*	Lord Angry
and I will *punish the leaders;*	Bad Shepherds Punished

Figure 4.2. God is angry with the bad shepherds (Zech 10:2-3a)

The opening word (*ki*) in this cameo can best be read as a *demonstrative particle* and translated "indeed" rather than a causative "for" or "because."[2] This option strengthens the reading of Zechariah 10:2 as a new beginning.[3]

The focus of cameo 1 is on the failure of the "household gods" and the "diviners," who deceive the people and leave them (the flock) without a shepherd. Thus this text, like Jeremiah and Ezekiel, opens with an attack on the "bad shepherds," who will be punished for their neglect of the flock. The language used here reflects the influence of Jeremiah and Ezekiel.

The second cameo describes some amazing transformations of the flock that God will accomplish (see fig. 4.3).

---

[2]William L. Holladay, *A Concise Hebrew and Aramaic Lexicon of the Old Testament Based upon the Lexical Work of Ludwig Koehler and Walter Baumgartner* (Grand Rapids: Eerdmans, 1971), p. 155.
[3]The promise of "showers of rain" (Zech 10:1) attaches naturally to the end of chapter 9.

2. For the *Lord of hosts cares for his flock,* the house of Judah,	GOD: SHEPHERD
and will make them like the steed *of his majesty in battle.*	War Horse for God
[4]From him shall come the *cornerstone,*	Cornerstone
from him the *tent peg,*	Tent Peg
from him the *battle bow,*	Battle Bow
from him every *ruler* – all of them together.	Ruler
[5]They shall be like *mighty men in battle,*	Mighty in Battle
trampling the foe in the mud of the streets;	Trampling Foe in Mud
they shall fight because *the Lord is with them,*	GOD WITH THEM
and they shall put to shame the *riders on horses.*	Cavalry Shamed

Figure 4.3. The sheep become God's horse, God's soldiers, and their weapons (Zech 10:3b-5)

God *cares* for "his flock," which is identified as "the house of Judah." The motive for God's actions is thus made clear. The word *care for (fqd)* includes the idea of "worry about." God will not only act to save the flock because he *owns it.* Nor is he acting simply for "his own name's sake" (Ps 23:3), but also because he *cares for them.*[4]

The image of *horse(s) (sus)* opens and closes the cameo. At the beginning (v. 3) the sheep are told that God will make them like "the horse of his majesty in battle." As observed (note 3), the majesty described is the majesty of God (not the majesty of the horse), but at the same time the flock is to become like the horse on which the king rides into battle. Naturally, the king must be "well mounted" when he appears at the front of his troops. He cannot be seen leading his people into combat riding on an old toothless nag. Only a powerful, stomping war horse, with an appropriate saddle, bridle and frontlets, is adequate for the king. His very presence is intended to inspire confidence in his troops and strike fear in the hearts of his enemies. The metaphor is both vivid and powerful. But the amazing thing is that the king's *flock of sheep* will become "like the horse of his majesty in battle." They will be transformed and will resemble the powerful, terrifying mount on which the king himself rides.

The "house of Judah" is "his flock," and out of them will come a *cornerstone* if you happen to live in a stone house in a village. If however you dwell in a tent, God will create *tent pegs* from the flock. We note in passing that all across the Middle East, tents inhabited by nomadic or seminomadic people are always erected and stabilized with four tent pegs, each of which mea-

---

[4]This theme will reappear in John 10:13, where the hireling fails to *care* for the sheep.

sures about five feet in length.[5] These pegs are driven firmly into the ground about fifteen feet outside the tent (front and back) and extend into the air about four feet. The tops of these pegs are attached to the edges of the roof of the tent with long ropes. This elevates the front and back edges of the top of the tent to allow for maximum ventilation. They are functionally more important for a tent home than a cornerstone is for a stone house.

From the flock will also appear "the battle bow," and the sheep will be transformed into "mighty men in battle." Furthermore, their victories will be so complete that they will not only be able to defeat their enemies but also to humiliate them by trampling them "in the mud of the streets." Horses (and chariots) were the "tanks" of ancient warfare. This transformed flock will even be able to shame (humiliate) mounted troops.

These sheep (transformed into soldiers) will fight because "The LORD is with them." David sensed that the Lord was with him (Ps 23:4) to *deliver him* from *death* and *evil*. Here "the LORD is with them" to give them *victory over opposing armies*. These remarkable transformations of a flock of docile sheep into soldiers, war horses and all the rest are unique to Zechariah. They illustrate the extent to which the prophets were free to recast this ancient story to fit a new set of circumstances. But this leaves us with a dilemma.

In the previous chapter (Zech 9:9-10) the reader is told:

Behold, your king is coming to you;
     righteous and having salvation is he,
humble and *mounted on a donkey*,
     on a colt, the foal of a donkey.
I will cut off the chariot from Ephraim
     and the *war horse from Jerusalem*;
and the *battle bow* shall be cut off,
     and he shall speak *peace to the nations*.

Here in chapter 9 the war horse and the battle bow are "cut off" from Jerusalem. But in chapter ten the *war horse* and the *battle bow* are boldly reintroduced. Peace with the nations is dropped from the text and instead enemy soldiers are trampled in the mud of the streets, and cavalry are hu-

---

[5]They could be described in English as "exterior tent poles."

miliated. It is even more surprising to discover that the aggressive military language in chapter ten is attached to a discussion of the flock of God. The *sheep of the flock* will be turned into a war horse, a battle bow and mighty men in battle. The tension between these two texts is not easily resolved. Perhaps together they illustrate Ecclesiastes 3:8, which reads, "[there is] a time for war, and a time for peace." Thoughtful people in every age struggle with this tension. Perhaps we can somehow make peace with this struggle instead of resolving it.

Looking ahead to the New Testament, clearly Jesus had both texts available to him and he chose the donkey of chapter 9 over the horse of chapter 10.[6] Matthew appropriately quoted the first as a scriptural foundation for Jesus' famous ride into Jerusalem on a donkey (Mt 21:2). Earlier in his ministry Jesus was faced with a choice between "war and peace" as he fashioned a nonviolent option for his response to the murder of John the Baptist (cf. Mk 6, discussed later).

The transformation of sheep into "mighty men in battle" occurs only here in all of the good shepherd accounts in both the Old and New Testaments.

Cameo 3 promises the incarnation (see fig. 4.4).

3. [6]"I will make strong (*gabar*) the house of Judah, and I will *save* the house of Joseph. *I will bring them back (shuv)* because I have *compassion* on them, and they shall be as though I had *not rejected them,* for *I am the Lord their God* and I will *answer* them.	GOD: GOOD SHEPHERD Joseph Saved Brought back *(shuv)* Shown Compassion Not rejected Answered

Figure 4.4. Incarnation promised (Zech 10:6)

Not only is the southern kingdom (the house of Judah) to be "brought back" (*shuv*) but also the northern kingdom (the house of Joseph). The prophet's vision of salvation for the flock reaches back to before the fall of the northern kingdom to the Assyrians in 722 B.C. This salvation will take place because of God's compassion, not because of their inherent worth. Indeed, his grace will be extended to them "as though I had not rejected them."

An impressive list of positives now appears. God's compassion motivates

---

[6]If no horse was available to him, he could have walked into the city.

him to *strengthen, save, claim* and *bring back* (*shuv*) the lost sheep. Since their exile, the people had been earnestly praying (to no avail) for salvation. At last God will "answer them."

As noted, third person pronouns here give way to first person. The text addresses God in more personal terms as it unfolds. This is in harmony with how the good shepherd story had been told in the past. In the second half of Psalm 23 God appears "on stage" and the psalmist addresses him directly with "*you* prepare a table" and so on. In Jeremiah's account of the same story, God promises "*I will gather* my flock" and "*I will bring them back.*" For Ezekiel, God appears in person and emphatically affirms, "Behold, I, I myself will search for my sheep." There God promises repeatedly to enter history himself and bring back, bind up, strengthen and feed the flock. In like manner here in the third cameo, the prophet shifts to, "*I* will *strengthen . . . save . . . bring back . . .* have *compassion . . . not reject . . .* and *answer.*" The promise that God will enter personally into history to save gains momentum through repetition.

Cameo 4 reinforces the military images in cameo 2 (see fig. 4.5).

4. ⁷Then Ephraim shall become like a mighty warrior	EPHRAIM
and their hearts shall be glad as with wine.	Mighty Warrior
Their children shall see it and be glad;	
their hearts shall rejoice in the LORD.	

Figure 4.5. The mighty warriors and their children are glad (Zech 10:7)

Having survived in Beirut, Lebanon, through the first ten years of the long Lebanese civil war (1975–1991), I know that war is *horrible* and tragically *very exciting.* War can produce people who are caught up in the "pornography of suffering." Woe to the lost souls who are hooked on their own adrenaline. The prophet describes this condition as a form of drunkenness which children observe and in which they participate.

The account continues with cameo 5 (see fig. 4.6).

5. ⁸I will whistle for them and gather them in,	
for I have redeemed them,	I WHISTLE
and they shall be as many as they were before.	I Gather/Redeem Them
⁹Though I scattered them among the nations,	They Remember
yet in far countries they shall remember me,	They Return (*shuv*)
and with their children they shall live and *return* (*shuv*).	

Figure 4.6. God will gather and redeem (Zech 10:8-9)

The verb "whistle" in its noun form (*sheriqah*) refers to flute playing. Isaiah 5:26 reads,

> He will raise a signal for a nation afar off,
> And whistle for it from the ends of the earth.

Isaiah is talking about God calling Assyria "from the ends of the earth" to punish wayward Israel.

From the parallel line it is clear that "to whistle" can mean "to raise a signal." Returning to Zechariah, God is now "whistling" or "raising a signal" for Israel to return home. This can be seen as the language of a shepherd calling his sheep. The shepherd either gives a special call or plays a special tune on his pipe to lead the sheep in the direction he wants them to go. This possibility is reinforced by the rest of the sentence that reads "and gather them in." He scattered them and now they will return (*shuv*), following the tune he plays (or sings/whistles) for them. The cameo is full of the language of a shepherd calling and gathering his flock.

Cameo 6 describes the return (see fig. 4.7).

6. ¹⁰I will *bring them back (shuv)* from the land of Egypt
   and gather them from Assyria   I BRING BACK *(shuv)*
   and I will bring them to the land of Gilead and to Lebanon,   Egypt
   till there is no room for them.   Assyria

Figure 4.7. Return from Egypt and Assyria (Zech 10:10)

At the end of the previous cameo the people themselves "return." The same verb (*shuv*) appears here, but now God is the actor. He will "bring them back" (*shuv*). The mystery of God's sovereignty on the one hand, and human freedom and responsibility on the other, are embossed on to the two sides of this theological coin. The people (the flock) must themselves *come back* and at the same time God incarnate as the shepherd must *bring them back*.

The prophet now expands the idea that he presented in cameo 3. It is not just Babylon (and the people's recent history) who are involved. Rather, God's actions to "bring back" the scattered flock involve *Egypt and Assyria*.

The scope of this restoration is continued in cameo 7 (see fig. 4.8).

7. ¹¹He shall pass through the sea of troubles
        and strike down the waves of the sea,
        and all the depths of the Nile shall be dried up.   EGYPT &
The pride of Assyria shall be laid low,   Assyria Overcome
        And the scepter of Egypt shall depart.

Figure 4.8. Assyria and Egypt overcome (Zech 10:11)

Reusing imagery from the exodus, God is pictured as the one who moves ahead of the people in their fearsome passage through the "sea of troubles." He will "strike down" the waves ahead of them in their passage through the waters, and the Nile behind them (the power of Egypt) will dry up. Without the Nile, Egypt is dead. The scepter/rod (*shebet*) of Egypt will depart. This same word is used to describe the *rod* of the shepherd in Psalm 23:4. Indeed it is the shepherd's only offensive weapon. Pharaoh's rod/scepter, with which he held sway over the Hebrews, disappears.

Both Assyria and Egypt are again mentioned. Jeremiah's account of the bad/good shepherds also concludes with references to the ingathering from both Egypt and "the north country" (which included Assyria and Babylon).

The passage ends with cameo 8 (see fig. 4.9).

8. ¹²I will make them strong in the LORD,   STRONG IN LORD
        and they shall walk in his name. [an oracle of Yahweh]   Walk in His Name

---

Figure 4.9. Strong in the Lord (Zech 10:12)

This conclusion is a brief summary of the passage. The first line tells of what God will do for them. The second affirms their expected response.

As with previous discussions, it is now appropriate to look at how Zechariah has dealt with our list of key components that make up the biblical good shepherd tradition. To do this, it is necessary to compare Zechariah's account with the three previous recitations of the good shepherd(s) and the lost sheep/flock (see fig. 4.10).

Ps 23:1-6	Jer & Ezek (exile & return)	Zech 10:2-12
1. Good shep. is God	Good shep. is God	Good shep. is God
2. **Lost sheep**[a] (no flock)	----- Lost flock	----- Lost flock
3. Opponents: Death "Enemies"	Opponents: Destroy, scatter Eat the flock	Opponents: Abandon the flock
4. *Good Host(ess?)*	-----	-----
5. Incarnation assumed	Incarnation promised	Incarnation promised
6. Good shep. will deliver from fear, bring back *(shuv)*	Good shep. will search for, save, deliver, rescue, bring back *(shuv)*	Good shep. will strengthen, save, have compassion, bring back *(shuv)*
7. Return is **to God** *(shuv)*	Return is to the land *(shuv)*	Return is to the land[b] *(shuv)*
8. -----	Good and bad sheep	Flock was rejected by God
9. *A celebration*	-----	(they will rejoice)
10. Story ends in **the house**	Story ends in the land	Story ends in the land
		Flock is transformed into: God's war horse, a battle bow, victorious and arrogant military, tent peg/cornerstone, rulers

[a]The bold type in the first column indicates aspects of the story that are changed or omitted in the later accounts.
[b]Zechariah 10:2-12 does not mention the place of return. However "the land" appears just before (Zech 9:16) and just after (Zech 10:10) the good shepherd account in Zech 10:2-6. Thus it is assumed in the present text.

Figure 4.10. The good/bad shepherd in Psalm 23, Jeremiah/Ezekiel and Zechariah (Zech 10:2-12)

The foundation laid in Psalm 23 is still present, and the major changes and additions made by Jeremiah and Ezekiel are retained in Zechariah. Observing the above comparisons, the following can be briefly noted:

1. *The good shepherd.* The entire text is full of "good shepherd" language. But God, the "Lord of hosts," who "cares for his flock," appears in this text as a military leader seated on "the horse of his majesty in battle."

2. *The bad shepherd.* Bad shepherds seem to have abandoned the flock to wander on their own. God is angry with them and will punish them.

3. *The lost flock.* As in Jeremiah and Ezekiel, it is the entire flock that is lost.

4. *Female qualities.* There is no hint of female qualities in the text. Quite the opposite, this text is more boldly male in its references and resonances than Jeremiah or Ezekiel.

5. *The incarnation.* Incarnation is again promised. The Lord will be with them and bring victory to the people along with humiliation for the enemy.

6. *The cost of the shepherd's efforts.* The shepherd/military commander will strengthen, save and bring back "his flock."

7. *Repentance/return.* They "return," and at the same time God will "bring them back" (*shuv*).

8. *Bad sheep.* Here in Zechariah the "bad sheep" theme is limited to the fact that God will treat them as though he had "not rejected them." Obviously if at some previous time God had "rejected them," then he must have found some flaw in them, but nothing specific is mentioned in this text. (Everyone knows that they worshiped idols!)

9. *A celebration.* There is no mention of any specific celebration. The only hint of anything of the kind is the fact that the sheep (now transformed into "mighty men in battle") will trample the foe "in the mud of the streets." By the time the army is so engaged it has clearly won the battle and is in the "full flush" of exuberant total victory. It is natural to assume that the "celebration" will take place later that night.

10. *The location for the ending.* Again there is only a brief hint of this topic. The text affirms, "I will bring them back" but no particular lo-

cation is affirmed in this text. However, as observed (see note 12) "the land" appears in Zechariah 9:16 and 10:10, and can be assumed in this text.

The striking addition to the story is the dramatic transformation of sheep into a war horse, a battle bow and soldiers who defeat and then humiliate the enemy. As noted, these themes do not appear elsewhere in the good shepherd accounts. Zechariah 10:2-12 is clearly following the good shepherd tradition while making dramatic changes to it.

Finally, what ethical and theological content is embedded in Zechariah's retelling of this ancient story? I suggest the following:

THE ETHICAL/THEOLOGICAL CLUSTER OF ZECHARIAH 10:2-12

1. The *leaders of the community of faith* are seen as having abandoned their calling and failed the very people they were expected to lead. This failure angers God, and the consequences are serious.

2. God cares for his *abandoned flock*, and he is able to create new leadership out of the sheep in the scattered flock. That is, some of the sheep will become rulers (Zech 10:4).

3. An aggressive *military option* is offered to the people where the "war horse" is prominent. At the same time, the larger setting of the text includes a gentle savior who comes "humble and riding on an ass" (Zech 9:9-10) and the "war horse" is named and rejected. Readers of the text are presented with the tensions that "war and peace" offer. (This contrast occurs only here in the nine good shepherd songs under examination.)

4. *God promises to come himself* and make strong, save, bring back and answer the people in their desperate need.

5. The military option brings with it a special kind of *intoxication* (that is not criticized!). Even the children are caught up in it.

6. *God, the good shepherd, will bring them back* in spite of their faults. In previous years God scattered them because of their failures. He now promises to come and restore them because he is the good shepherd, not because they are good sheep.

7. The *vision* for "gathering and redeeming" *reaches back* for more than *four hundred years*. History is important, and the prophet writing in the fourth century B.C. looks back to the eighth century and the losses sustained in it. There is no trashing of the past and no ignoring of its present significance.

8. The passage concludes with a balancing of *identity* and *lifestyle*. As to identity, they will be "strong in the LORD." Regarding lifestyle "they shall walk in his name."

With this passage the Old Testament telling of the story of the good shepherd ends. We turn now to see what happens to this classical account in the Gospels.

5

JESUS THE GOOD SHEPHERD
AND THE GOOD WOMAN
IN LUKE 15:1-10

As noted in our introduction, it seems appropriate to look first at the nature and then at the practice of the good shepherd in the Gospels. In Luke 15 Jesus presents his understanding of the good shepherd in two linked parables. Then in Mark 6 we see him *applying* that understanding to a specific crises in his ministry. Thus we open with an examination of the twin parables in Luke 15:1-10.

It has been my privilege to publish a number of studies on Luke 15:1-10.[1] Along with an occasional reference to what I have already written, the focus of this chapter will be to examine the good shepherd account in Luke 15:4-7 (followed by the good woman of Lk 15:8-10) in the light of the four Old Testament biblical texts on the same topic (chaps. 1-4). I will also note a few treasures from the extant Arabic language New Testament commentaries from the last thousand years, along with the relevant early Jewish sources that help us understand the conflict between Jesus and his opponents.

The setting for the twin parables is crucial (see fig. 5.1).

---

[1]Kenneth E. Bailey, *Poet and Peasant and Through Peasant Eyes* (1976; repr., Grand Rapids: Eerdmans, 1983), pp. 142-58; Kenneth E. Bailey, *Finding the Lost* (St. Louis: Concordia, 1992), pp. 54-92; Kenneth E. Bailey, *Jacob and the Prodigal* (Downers Grove, IL: IVP Academic, 2003), pp. 65-94; Kenneth E. Bailey, *The Cross and the Prodigal*, 2nd ed. (Downers Grove, IL: IVP Academic, 2005), pp. 23-37.

¹Now the tax collectors and sinners were all drawing near to hear him.
²And the Pharisees and the scribes mumbled, saying,
"This . . . receives sinners and eats with them."ᵃ
³So he told them this parable:

ᵃMy translation. The word "man" is usually added to the verse by translators but is missing in the Greek text.

Figure 5.1. The setting (Lk 15:1-3)

Jesus welcomed outcasts. Ibn al-Tayyib notes in passing that "all sinners" means "many of them."² The phrase "all sinners were drawing near to him" also catches the nuance of "on all occasions" they were attracted to him.³ Ibn al-Tayyib writes,

> Sinners regularly drew near to the Christ, not just in order to watch wondrous works or miracles but rather to listen to his teaching because he, like a physician who labors to heal the sick, accepts invitations to enter homes and takes the opportunity to win them with his kindness.⁴

In his reference to a "physician" who calls on his patients, Ibn al-Tayyib reflects his own background as a medical doctor. He was also fully aware of the fact that in other texts Jesus compared himself to a physician (Mk 2:17; Lk 4:23).

Furthermore, Jesus had his own house, probably in Capernaum, into which he invited "tax collectors and sinners" for meals with his disciples (Mk 2:15-17). The Pharisees were complaining that Jesus "receives" sinners (Lk 15:2). The Greek word *receives* includes the idea of receiving someone as a guest.⁵ Jeremias has observed, "Sometimes he [Jesus] entertained his own guests (Lk 15.1f.)"⁶ Does this mean that he hosted meals? It does, and this was a problem.

---

²Ibn al-Tayyib, *Tafsir*, 2:261.
³Ibid.
⁴Ibid. Later on the same page, Ibn al-Tayyib talks about Jesus doing the inviting. In addition to being a monk and a biblical scholar, Ibn al-Tayyib was a famous medical doctor who lived in Baghdad in the eleventh century. See Samir Khalil, "The Role of Christians in the Abbasid Renaissance in Iraq and in Syria (750-1015)," in *Christianity: A History in the Middle East*, ed. Habib Badr (Beirut: Middle East Council of Churches Studies & Research Program, 2005), pp. 518-19.
⁵Naturally the reader of the entire chapter soon discovers that at the end of the third story the father "receives" the prodigal by running down the road and showering his wayward son with kisses. The father, as it were, "drags him in" that he might *eat* with him. Lk 15:2 foreshadows that dramatic climax.
⁶Joachim Jeremias, *The Eucharistic Words of Jesus* (New York: Scribner's, 1966), p. 47.

The rabbinic tradition is very clear on the question of table fellowship. In our text the Pharisees complain about Jesus in this regard. Who then were the Pharisees? From the writings of Josephus and from the pages of the New Testament, it is evident that they were a fairly broad group with no particular membership requirements except a serious commitment to the law and a concern to apply it in their day. They had an imprecise set of theological and ethical concerns that included tithing, sabbath observance, food laws and ritual purity. But within that larger group of serious-minded Jews there was a society called the *haberim* that did have a specific membership along with strict requirements for joining the "club."[7] The word *haberim* is usually translated into English as "associates." The Hebrew word *haber* literally means "friend." The *haberim* were a kind of guild pledged to kept the law in a very precise fashion. Gillihan notes that the *haberim* are "commonly regarded as a Pharisaic movement."[8] The Babylonian Talmud has a detailed discussion of the requirements for membership in the *haberim.*[9] As regards the eating of meals, George F. Moore notes that a member of the "associates/ friends" (*haberim*) was not allowed to deal with the common people, who were called the *'am ha–arets,* literally "the people of the land." The associates/ friends (*haberim*) could not "be the guest of the people of the land, or entertain [them] in his house. . . . He should not travel in company with one of the class, visit him, study the Law in his presence, and much more to the like effect."[10] Some of these strict rulings may not have been in force in the first century, but they indicate a climate that most certainly pervaded the period. Some of the material from the Tosefta, noted earlier, may be older than the Mishnah, which includes pre-Christian material. Aharon Oppenheimer refers to this "guild of Friends" (*habera*) as being "elite Pharisees."[11] Today, every country has security forces. From among such forces there is

[7]Tosefta, *Demai* 2:2–3:9, in *The Tosefta, First Division Zeraim,* ed. Jacob Neusner (Hoboken, NJ: KTAV, 1986), 1:82-90.

[8]Yonder M. Gillihan, "Associations," in *Eerdmans Dictionary of Early Judaism,* ed. John J. Collins and D. C. Harlow (Grand Rapids: Eerdmans, 2010), p. 398.

[9]Babylonian Talmud *Bekorot* 30b.

[10]George F. Moore, *Judaism in the First Centuries of the Christian Era* (1927; repr., New York: Schocken, 1971), 2:159.

[11]Aharon Oppenheimer, "People of the Land," in *Eerdmans Dictionary of Early Judaism,* ed. John J. Collins and Daniel C. Harlow (Grand Rapids: Eerdmans, 2010), pp. 1042-43. For a detailed discussion of the same topic see Aharon Oppenheimer, *The 'Am ha-Aretz: A Study in the Social History of the Jewish People in the Hellenistic-Roman Period* (Leiden: Brill, 1977).

usually a specially trained group known as "special forces." The *haberim*, it appears, were the "special forces" of the Pharisaic movement. They were indeed Pharisees, but known to be *very strict* Pharisees. What then does this have to do with Luke 15?

The parable of the good shepherd in Luke mentions the shepherd's "friends" (Lk 15:6). No Pharisee could hear that word without thinking about the special guild among the Pharisees called "the friends." Some of those who were complaining about Jesus' guests may have been members of the guild of the *haberim*. Thus, the "sinners and tax collectors" (otherwise known as "the people of the land") were what Oppenheimer appropriately calls "the lowest stratum of society," while the "friends" among the Pharisees were the *highest* stratum (the elite) of that same society. Jesus was called "rabbi" by the people and by his disciples. Thus it was unthinkable to the society around Jesus that he would violate the Pharisaic standards governing things like tithing, the sabbath and ritual purity. Yet he was inviting the "dregs" into his house and hosting them at meals! Jesus was obliged to reply to these complaints, and he did so by telling the parables of Luke 15. But the very substance and direction of his reply is astounding.

Jesus could have responded to the Pharisees in a variety of ways. (1) He could have started by referring to the Wisdom of Ben Sirach, where the text discusses "trades and crafts" (Sir 38:24-29) and pointed out that farmers, potters, blacksmiths and other skilled workers hold no rank and have no "grasp of the law" (Sir 38:33) but are important in their own way. "A town could not be built without them," continues Ben Sirach (Sir 38:32). So if we need such people for the smooth operation of any town, the argument might go, why not be friendly to them? (2) A second option would be to discuss what God really wants from us and quote the famous verse from Micah 6:8 that states, "what does the LORD require of you but to do justice, and to love kindness, and to walk humble with your God?" If we take that directive seriously, Jesus could argue, the barriers between "the friends" (*haberim*) and the "people of the land" (*'am ha-arets*), that is, "sinners," would begin to come down. (3) Jesus could discuss the possibility of relaxing the requirements for membership in the guild of "friends" because such an act would give a voice to ordinary people in the councils of the religious elite, and help build understanding. (4) Another option would be to argue the classifications of what causes ritual impurity. Perhaps the rules were too strict? (5) Barring all of the above, perhaps the "righteous" could keep a special bench near the door for the "sinners" (people of the land) to sit on when they visited the "righteous." (6) Or Jesus could discuss ritual purity and repeat his own views that real impurity results from what comes out of the mouth, not by what goes into it (Mt 15:11). But Jesus set aside all such approaches; he refused to allow his critics to frame the discussion but rather did so himself.

Jesus turned to the classical parable of the good shepherd, first set out in Psalm 23, and offered his own version of that great story. This is astounding! In the process he reshaped the "doctrine of salvation" as we will see. This choice in itself speaks volumes. In effect Jesus said to his critics:

> Fellow Israelites, I perceive that you want to discuss with me "*Who* must *keep what laws* and *how* must they *keep them*." I grant that your concern is important, but first I feel the need to frame for you the big picture of how we are to relate to God so that you can understand who I am and what I am here to do. I want to talk to you about *salvation* (repentance) because it is only within that larger picture can you correctly perceive why I eat with sinners.

Jesus refuses to discuss the laws of ritual purity that he is accused of breaking. Instead he opts to set out his views on repentance, and repentance for the Pharisees was one of the *most important* aspects of the faith. In his classical work *Judaism in the First Centuries of the Christian Era*, George F. Moore describes repentance as "the indispensable condition of the remission of every kind of sin," and as "a cardinal doctrine of Judaism." He calls it "the Jewish doctrine of salvation."[12]

Consequently, if Jesus opts to present his understanding of repentance/ salvation, what "big picture" will he choose? Will it be that of an athlete who trains tirelessly to win a big race or a climber who struggles to reach the top of a high mountain? What will it be? To the inevitable shock of all listeners, Jesus opens his reply with his version of the classical story of the good shepherd that was launched by David in Psalm 23.[13] The implications of that choice are enormous.

Both the good *shepherd* and the good *host* appear in Psalm 23 and in

---

[12]George F. Moore, *Judaism in the First Centuries of the Christian Era* (1927; repr., New York: Schocken, 1971), 1:500.

[13]Bailey, *Finding the Lost*, pp. 63-92.

Luke 15. Psalm 23 opens by affirming "The LORD is my shepherd." But, as noted earlier, God is not only a *shepherd*, he is also a *host*. The text of the psalm reads, "You prepare a table before me / in the presence of my enemies" (Ps 23:5). Enemies of the psalmist were angry at God for having chosen him as a dinner guest. Jesus followed the same pattern, only Jesus invited the "unclean" to be his guests at table. A few years ago an African head of state was questioned as to how his country managed to keep good relations with both Israel and the Arab states. He is said to have replied, "We choose our friends. We do not encourage our friends to choose our enemies."[14] Jesus would have understood. He was happy to eat with Pharisees (Lk 14:1), but at the same time he never granted them control over his guest lists.

But the Pharisees had an additional problem related to eating with "sinners." A part of why the Pharisees dared not eat with "sinners" was due to the Qumran community. The Qumran sect that produced the famous Dead Sea Scrolls lived totally apart from the common people in order to preserve ritual purity. The Pharisees, by contrast, chose to live among ordinary folk, which exposed those Pharisees to defilement. The Pharisees insisted that as long at they *ate their meals in isolation* they could maintain their ritual purity. Thus the choice of table companions was, for those Pharisees, extremely important. Rabbi Akiba is quoted as saying, "Whoever joins himself to those that commit a transgression, even though he does not act like them, is punished as they are."[15] The distinguished American Jewish scholar Jacob Neusner writes,

> Common folk ate everyday meals in an everyday way, among ordinary neighbors who were not members of the sect, and who engaged in workaday pursuits like everyone else. This fact made the actual purity rules and food restrictions all the more important, for they alone set the Pharisee apart from the people among whom he constantly lived.[16]

The Pharisees' irritation with Jesus on this question is reflected in the way they worded their complaint against Jesus regarding table fellowship. Lit-

---

[14]This unforgettable reply was told to me in Jerusalem the summer of 1957 by an American Quaker serving in Kenya.

[15]Babylonian Talmud, *'Abot de Rabbi Nathan* 30.

[16]Jacob Neusner, "Pharisaic Law in New Testament Times," *Union Seminary Quarterly Review* 26 (1971): 340.

erally translated, the Greek text reads, "This . . . receives sinners and eats with them." The word *man* is usually added by modern translators, and thus English readers miss the fact of its absence in the original text. The word *this* (*houtos*), when standing without a following noun, gives "a connotation of contempt."[17] The listener/reader can add the missing word, be it "this *fool*" or "this *ignorant peasant*" or "this *little boy*" or something stronger.[18]

The Babylonian Talmud summarizes the matter by saying, "do not eat food with the *'am ha-'arez* lest you come to profane the sacred food of Heaven."[19] The issue was critical for Jesus and for his critics. This has been noted by Eastern Scripture scholars. The great Coptic Orthodox monk and New Testament scholar Matta al-Miskin writes regarding this text,

> It is clear that Christ himself was responsible for the drawing near of sinners who came to him and sat to eat with him. They came because in him they discovered themselves to be lost, and their tormented consciences found rest and peace. They loved him because they felt his love for them.[20]

This same kind of attraction and response is on display in Isaiah 6, where the prophet went up to the temple and saw a vision of the holiness of God. *As a result of that vision* he cried out, "I am a man of unclean lips, and I dwell in the midst of a people of unclean lips; for my eyes have seen the King, the LORD of hosts!" (Is 6:5). Matta al-Miskin observed the same dynamic in this text. The sinners came because, he surmises, they knew Jesus loved them, and *as they drew near* they sensed (like Isaiah) that they were sinners. Father Matta also notes that the very sin of these sinners was the reason for Jesus' presence as their redeemer. He writes thoughtfully, "They [the sinners] adorned the cross with the fact of their approach to him."[21]

Ibn al-Tayyib also reflects on this introduction and writes,

> The Pharisees blamed Christ because of his invitation to sinners and his ac-

---

[17]BAGD, p. 596. Joseph A. Fitzmyer refers to "The pejorative sense of the demonstrative *houtos.*" *The Gospel According to Luke X-XXIV*, Anchor Bible Commentary (New York: Doubleday, 1985), p. 1076.

[18]BAGD, p. 596. Other cases of this "connotation of contempt" are found in Mt 13:56; Lk 5:21; 7:39, 49; 19:14; Jn 6:52; 7:15.

[19]*b.t. Kallah Rabbathi* 53a3.

[20]Matta al-Miskin, *The Gospel According to Saint Luke* (Arabic), (Cairo: Dayr al-Qiddis Anba Maqar, 1998), p. 568.

[21]Matta al-Miskin, *Luke*, p. 569 (my translation).

ceptance of them. But he made clear to the Pharisees that the reasons for which they despised him, and for which they complained about him, were the very reasons that led him to come into this world and were the very focus of his ministry. So that which the Pharisees considered shameful for the Messiah, the Christ considered a great honor. And the Pharisees very complaint was proof that Jesus himself was indeed the Messiah.[22]

In addition, Ibn al-Tayyib notes that hostility to Jesus indicates Pharisaic indifference to the plight of the tax collectors and sinners. He writes, "Their words show their lack of compassion for those sinners, and their lack of interest in their salvation."[23] Keeping in mind the first-century context, and Eastern Christian and Jewish reflection on that context, we turn to the two parables before us. The first has to do with a shepherd (see fig. 5.2).

THE RHETORIC

The text of figure 5.2 has three cameos. The first two are a parable. The third is a comment interpreting the parable. Cameo 1 sets out three themes: *You, One* and *Ninety-Nine*. These three themes are repeated in the same order in cameo 3, tying the two cameos together. An Aramaic play on words appears when the Greek text is examined in the light of the Aramaic language behind it. *One* in Aramaic is *hadh*, and the word *rejoice* is *hedhwa*. The text opens with reference to the "one" (*hadh*). Cameo two introduces "rejoice" (*hedhwa*). Then in the third cameo there is joy, *hedhwa*, over the one, *hadh*.[24] This play on words supports Luke's presentation of the parable (and its interpretation) as composed by Jesus.

Cameo 2 is formatted with what I have called the *prophetical rhetorical template*,[25] which means that it is composed of seven inverted themes. A series of ideas is presented and then repeated backwards.[26] This same rhetorical style was observed earlier in Psalm 23. In this second section of the parable there is movement from *lost to found* to *rejoice* and finally to *restore*.

---

[22]Ibn al-Tayyib, *Tafsir*, 2:262 (my translation).

[23]Ibid., p. 261 (my translation).

[24]This play on words (in Aramaic) is observed by Matthew Black in *An Aramaic Approach to the Gospels and Acts* (Oxford: Clarendon Press, 1967), p. 184.

[25]Kenneth E. Bailey, *Paul Through Mediterranean Eyes* (Downers Grove, IL: IVP Academic, 2011), pp. 38-41.

[26]This style is often called *chiasm*. It has also been named *ring composition* or *inverted parallelism*.

So he told them this parable:

1. a. "What man of *you*,   YOU (man)
        having a hundred sheep,

      b. if he has lost   ONE
        one (*hadh*) of them,

      c. does not leave the *ninety-nine*   NINETY-NINE
        in the wilderness,

----------   ------------------

2.   a. and go after the one that is *lost*,   LOST

        b. until he *finds* it? And when he has found it, FIND

           c. he lays it on his shoulders, *rejoicing*.   REJOICE (*hedhwa*)

              d. And when he comes home,   RESTORE
              he calls together his *friends* and neighbors,

           c. saying to them, *'Rejoice* with me,   REJOICE (*hedhwa*)

        b. for I have *found* my sheep   FIND

      a. that was *lost*.'   LOST

----------   -------------

3.   a. Just so, I say to *you*,   YOU
        that thus there will be more *joy* (*hedhwa*) in heaven

      b. over *one* (*hadh*) sinner   ONE
        who *repents*

      c. than over *ninety-nine* righteous persons
        who need no repentance.[a]   NINETY-NINE

---

[a]Bailey, *Jacob and the Prodigal*, p. 65; and Bailey, *Poet and Peasant*, p. 144. Some of this text is my own translation.

Figure 5.2. The parable of the good shepherd and the lost sheep (Lk 15:4-7)

In the third section the *hadh* (the one) is united with *hedhwa* (joy). In the center of section two the shepherd arrives home and calls his "friends" and neighbors to rejoice with him.

Cameo 3 is an "interpretation" of the parable. What can be said about such an interpretation? The parable of the prodigal son has no such interpretation at its conclusion. Why then is there one here and in the parable of the good woman in Luke 15:8-10?

On the rare occasions when Jesus presents a parable and attaches to it some interpretation or application, he is not introducing a new style into the Hebrew tradition. This format is as old as the prophesy of Isaiah 55:10-11, which exhibits such a pattern (see fig. 5.3).

55:10For *as the rain and the snow* come down from heaven,	THE RAIN – comes down
and do not return there but *water the earth,*	Not Return (*shuv*)
making it bring forth and sprout,	Result
giving seed to the sower and bread to the eater,	
11*so shall my word be* that goes forth from my mouth;	MY WORD – goes forth
it shall not return to me empty,	Not Return (*shuv*)
but it shall accomplish that which I purpose,	Result
and shall succeed in the thing for which I sent it.	

Figure 5.3. Text and interpretation (Is 55:10-11)

Verse 10 presents a *parable* and verse 11 offers an *explanation* of it. Without the explanation in verse 11, the reader would be at a loss to understand the intent of the parable. In Hebrew a parable is called a *mashal*, and if there is an explanation attached to parable it is identified as a *nimshal* (both words are built on the Hebrew root *mshl*). Another example of this same style appears in Isaiah's famous account of the vineyard (Is 5:1-7), which when summarized appears as follows (see fig. 5.4 on p. 119).

First is the parable, the *mashal*.

As in Isaiah 55:10-11, the vineyard text presents a *parable* (cameos 1-2) to which is added an *explanation* of its meaning (cameo 3). As noted earlier, this style was in use as early as the eighth century B.C.[27] It continued in use

---

[27]Noting Jacob Neusner, Klyne Snodgrass writes, "They [Jesus' parables] are context-specific and built in relation to their *nimshalim*, the interpretive explanations that follow most rabbinic parables." Klyne Snodgrass, *Stories with Intent* (Grand Rapids: Eerdmans, 2008), pp. 55-56. See

1. [5:1-2] Sparing no effort, a man *plants a vineyard.*
    He expected *good grapes.* It yielded *wild grapes!*

2. [3-6] The man presents his case against his vineyard.
    What will he now do? He will *destroy the vineyard!*

(Then comes the *nimshal*: the explanation of the parable.)

3   [7] The vineyard is Israel/Judah.
    God "the farmer" expected a harvest of justice and *righteousness* (good grapes).
    The vineyard produced *bloodshed* and a *cry of pain* (wild grapes).

Figure 5.4. A parable is told and then explained (Is 5:1-7)

during the exile and on into the extensive rabbinic literature of the early centuries. Commenting on the rabbinic parables, Robert Johnson notes,

> The typical *mashal* includes an application, in most cases introduced by the word כד (kd)[28] which drives home the lesson intended in a quite explicit manner. This application may be regarded as the interpretation on the minimal level.[29]

The above examples show that Luke 15:4-7 follows a literary pattern that was in use for centuries before and after the time of Jesus. Both Isaiah and Jesus usually leave their parables and metaphors without any accompanying interpretation. As noted, this is the case at the end of Luke 15 in the parable of the prodigal son. After the father's final speech in Luke 15:32, the parable falls silent. Not only is there no *nimshal* (explanation) but also the story itself is not finished. The reader does not know how the older son will respond to the father's plea.[30] Clearly Jesus, like Isaiah, is flexible. He can add a brief explanation to the end of a parable (Lk 15:7), or he can leave the conclusion dangling (Lk 15:32) and in addition omit any interpretation of it.

Jacob Neusner, *Rabbinic Narrative: A Documentary Perspective* (Leiden: Brill, 2003), 4:185, 221.

[28]Strangely this same word survives in modern Egyptian colloquial Arabic with the same meaning.

[29]Robert M. Johnson, *Parabolic Interpretations Attributed to Tannaim* (Ph.D. diss., Hartford Seminary, 1977), 1:192.

[30]Bailey, *Cross and the Prodigal*, pp. 75-98; Bailey, *Finding the Lost*, pp. 164-93.

COMMENTARY

The first of the three cameos in this parable is seen in figure 5.5.

	So he told them this parable:	
1.	a. "What man of *you*, having a hundred sheep,	YOU (man)
	b. if he has lost *one* (*hadh*) of them,	ONE
	c. does not leave the *ninety-nine* in the wilderness,	NINETY-NINE

Figure 5.5. The shepherd loses a sheep (Lk 15:3)

Luke writes, "he told them *this* parable," indicating that the three stories in chapter 15 are a single parable. This will become important as on occasion we will note the relationships between the good shepherd, the good woman and the good father (in the parable of the prodigal son). What then is Luke 15:4-7 all about?

When read in isolation from the prophetic accounts of the good shepherd and his sheep, this parable appears to be a simple story about a man who loses something of value and who then quite naturally searches for it until he finds it. In the modern world, such a story can be told about a person who loses their wallet, car keys, datebook or iPhone. Full of self blame, the person then slips into temporary insanity and engages in a frantic search, determined to find the lost item. Once it is found he or she experiences an intense form of joy in finding the lost, and may well choose to share that joy with friends. All of us have gone through this "mad dance" and have known the joy of finding the lost item. On a very basic level, Jesus is saying to his audience,

> You are shepherds of Israel. Let us imagine that you have lost one of your sheep. The natural and expected response to this predicament is that you go after it! You will be thrilled when you find it and may well invite in a few good friends with whom you can share your joy.

Granting the validity of this first level of meaning, we note that Jesus was retelling a classical story that the learned audience before him knew first appeared in Psalm 23 and was revised and retold by Jeremiah, Ezekiel and Zechariah. Therefore they would listen intently to see how "this . . ." was going to shape his version of the sacred sequence, made famous by the psalm, and so must we.

The first cameo begins at a very dramatic point in the life of a shepherd and his flock. They have been through a normal day and, as is customary, the shepherd counts his flock late in the afternoon as he settles them into a secure area for the night. At the end of the count alarm bells start ringing in the back of his head as he realizes that a sheep is missing. The shepherd responds by making the important decision to "leave the flock" exactly where it is there in the wilderness.

In cameo 1 he makes the decision and completes his preparations to "move out." With cameo 2 the action begins. The first question is, who owns the sheep?

Jesus invites his audience onstage to imagine themselves as owners of such a flock. He asks, "What man of you, if he has one hundred sheep and has lost one of them, will he not do so-and-so?" The Greek text is a bit ambiguous about who owns the one hundred sheep, but Semitic languages lack a verb "to have." The text does not read, "What man of you, if he is herding a hundred sheep . . ." or "if he is guarding a hundred sheep . . ." rather it reads, "he has a hundred sheep." Whenever this text was translated from Greek into Hebrew, Syriac or Arabic over the last nineteen hundred years, without exception, the translations read "there is *to/for him* a hundred sheep" using a preposition and a pronoun. These three Semitic language traditions always read לֹה (*lahu*: to/for him). This construction affirms ownership. Indeed ownership of the flock is confirmed later in the story by the shepherd himself, who tells his friends "I have found *my* sheep" (v. 6). Thus Middle Eastern Christians have always understood that the shepherd owns these sheep, even as the woman owns her ten coins and the two sons in the third story are children of the father, not his servants. This clarification is important for interpretation in each of the three parables.

If the shepherd in the parable *owns the flock,* then Jesus is telling the Pharisees that the tax collectors and sinners are *a part of their flock!* The loss of even one of them is *their loss,* and that loss is significant. In the second story the lost coin represents a day's wages, which most families can, with some economic pain, sustain. But the loss of a full-grown sheep represents a much greater loss.

Indeed, a hundred sheep represents considerable wealth. It is no accident that the second parable deals with money. In this first story Jesus is indirectly asking, "Traveling in the wilderness, if you dropped your leather pouch with a large number of gold coins in it, what would you do?" People everywhere generally keep information about their money locked up in a very private place at the back of their minds. Jesus opens the discussion of "lost people" (tax collectors and sinners) by referring to "lost personal wealth." He is thus able to invoke an unvarnished response from deep within the souls of his listeners.[31] Even though "the lost" is only one percent of the herd, it is still very much worth finding. Are lost *people* worth less?

Furthermore, Jesus' creation of a parable about a shepherd is complicated by the fact that the rabbis listed the profession of herding sheep as one of the "despised trades."[32] Jesus deliberately ignored the rabbinic disdain for shepherds as he created this story. He must have had a good reason for doing so. His second story is about a woman, and women were generally seen to be inferior to men! It would have been easy to tell a single story about a *man* who loses a *coin*, like the man in *Midrash Rabbah* for the *Song of Songs* that reads:

> If a man loses a *sela'* or *oblo*[33] in his house, he lights lamp after lamp, wick after wick, tell he finds it. Now does it not stand to reason: if for these things which are only ephemeral and of this world a man will light so many lamps and lights till he finds where they are hidden, for the words of the Torah which are the life both of this world and of the next world, aught you not to search as for hidden treasures?[34]

Had Jesus shaped his parable along these lines he would have avoided any negative complications related to the proscribed trades or women. Knowing the negative vibes that any story about shepherds will generate, Jesus deliberately chooses to tell a story about a shepherd. That choice exposes his intense desire to invoke the well-known string of Old Testament stories about

---

[31] Jesus uses the same psychology in Lk 13:10-17; 14:1-6.
[32] Joachim Jeremias, *Jerusalem in the Time of Jesus* (Philadelphia: Fortress, 1976), p. 304.
[33] These were small coins of uncertain worth. See "Song of Songs Rabbah" 1.1, 9, *Midrash Rabbah*, ed. H. Freedman (New York: Soncino, 1983).
[34] Ibid.

shepherds and lost sheep. How will he begin?

Jesus opens by blaming the shepherd for the loss of the sheep. The phrase "If he has lost one of them" makes this clear. Jesus, like Ezekiel 34:1-10, starts with "bad shepherds." But Jesus' criticism of the shepherd is much milder than Ezekiel's. In verse 4 Ezekiel writes,

> The weak you have not strengthened,
>
> the sick you have not healed,
>
> the injured you have not bound up,
>
> the strayed you have *not brought back*,
>
> the *lost you have not sought*,
>
> and with force and harshness you have ruled them.

Jesus limits himself to a single negative reference, but that is enough to call to mind the prophetic accounts of "bad shepherds." Jesus could have used a passive and said, "If one of them goes astray" instead of "if he has lost one of them." In the Middle East this latter option is not used in everyday speech.

Age-old patterns of speech across the area do not allow the speaker to blame himself. "The dish fell from my hand" (I did not "drop the dish"). "The train left me" (I did not "miss the train"). "The pencil went from me" (I did not "lose my pencil").[35] This idiomatic oral style is universal across the Middle East in Arabic, Spanish and Armenian.[36] It is curious that for more than eighteen hundred years—starting with the Old Syriac, through the Peshitta and the centuries of Arabic versions—Luke 15:4 was (to my knowledge) always translated into some form of "If one of them is lost," thereby avoiding blaming the shepherd. It was not until the second half of the nineteenth century that the culturally awkward "having lost one of them" was introduced into Arabic translations. Tellingly, as the story unfolds (v. 6), when the shepherd returns to his village and has a party with his friends, he exhibits the traditional face-saving pattern of speech and, says, "I have found my sheep, *which was lost* [passive]." His personal honor does not allow him to admit in public that he is the one who lost the sheep in the first place.[37]

---

[35]Revised from Bailey, *Finding the Lost*, p. 65.

[36]I have not managed to check Italian and colloquial Greek.

[37]The woman who loses her coin is more open and honest. She admits to her friends that *she* lost her coin. In Matthew the sheep "goes astray" (Mt 18:12). Cyril of Alexandria (d. 444) left us a

Jesus blames the shepherd, and in so doing he *gently* but *firmly* invokes the long prophetic tradition about bad shepherds.

Reflection on the shepherd and his faults raises the issue of the one and the many. In Psalm 23 David sang about a *single lost sheep* (himself) and a good shepherd (God) who came after him and brought him back. No flock is mentioned. Retelling this story, Jeremiah, Ezekiel and Zechariah all talk about a *lost flock* and how God, the good shepherd, comes to the rescue. No individual sheep appears in any of the three prophetic accounts, only a lost flock. Is Jesus' shift of emphasis from the many back to the one, deliberate? It is, but the lost flock is not eliminated from the story.

With great care and awareness of the good shepherd tradition, Jesus incorporates both the *lost sheep* (Ps 23) and the *lost flock* (Jeremiah, Ezekiel and Zechariah) into a single parable. From its inception, Jesus' story follows the traumas of both of them. The parable begins with a flock of one hundred sheep. The careless shepherd loses one of them and the rest of the flock is left "in the wilderness." Aware of the ways of sheep and of shepherds, the Middle Eastern listener/reader follows the account of the rescue of the one lost sheep and eagerly anticipates the shepherd's immediate return to the wilderness to bring home the ninety-nine! It never happens.[38] (We will return to this aspect of the story.) Jesus skillfully weds the one and the ninety-nine together. He is the only one who does this. "The one" totally dominates Psalm 23, while the focus on "the flock" in Jeremiah, Ezekiel and Zechariah is consistent all through the account. Jesus cares about both of them.

In real life in the Middle Eastern countryside, a responsible shepherd would never leave ninety-nine sheep in the wilderness without an assistant to guide them home or protect them in a cave (or a roughly constructed wilderness enclosure).[39] In order to make a point Jesus "pushes the envelope" of what a village shepherd might do. He uses silence to drive home this

---

commentary on the Gospel of Luke. When Cyril comes to Luke 15, he quotes *the text* accurately as "and having lost one of them." A few lines later he writes, "and of them one has gone astray." Cyril of Alexandria, *Commentary on the Gospel of Saint Luke*, trans. R. Payne Smith (n.p.: Studion, 1983), p. 428.

[38]This does happen in the third story. The father restores the younger son *and* goes out a second time to try to rescue/reconcile the older son. But that is beyond the scope of our inquiry. See Bailey, *Jacob and the Prodigal*, pp. 95-117.

[39]Babylonian Talmud *Baba Kamma* (56a) states, "It is indeed the custom of the shepherd to hand over his sheep to the care of his apprentice."

aspect of his message. But what can we make of Jesus' (gentle) criticism of the shepherd?

The three prophetic accounts of the bad shepherds gradually expand as follows.

In Jeremiah God speaks ominously to the bad shepherds saying, "I will *attend to you* for your evil deeds" (Jer 23:2).

In Ezekiel, after listing the many faults of the bad shepherds, God announces their dismissal! Ezekiel 34:10 reads,

> I am against the shepherds,
> and I will require my sheep at their hand
> and I will put a stop to their tending of the sheep.

Zechariah 10:3 is more pointed and more intense as he writes,

> My anger is hot against the shepherds,
> And I will punish the leaders.

For those shepherds the door to recovery is slammed shut. They failed and they will be punished. Jesus opens that door. How so?

As noted, Jesus does not dwell on the shepherd's faults and deliberately omits any discussion of their fate. Rather he points the way for them to recover their losses. Jesus can be understood to be saying to his audience of scribes and Pharisees,

> Gentlemen, you are not trapped by the past. We all know that the bad shepherds in the writings of the prophets who lost their sheep and failed to even *try* to bring them back were harshly punished for their failures. But you are not trapped into following that path. You are free. I have pioneered a way forward. When a shepherd loses his sheep he naturally goes after it until he finds it. He then carries it home and has a party. It is as simple as that. The lost that I am "bringing home" are sheep that *you yourselves have lost*. I know that you don't like them and that you despise me for going after them. But when they are lost—*you lose* because *they are a part of your flock!* When they are found, it is *your gain!* Can't you see it?
>
> Can you not join me in the great task of restoring the lost sheep of the house of Israel *to God?* Isn't that what the famous suffering servant of Isaiah was challenged by God to do—to "bring Jacob back to him [Is 49:5]"? Actually I am doing your work for you! Never mind, let us move forward. The dinners

that I host welcome all who know that they are lost. This applies to you as well. By the way, I have a story that will clarify all of this. It is about a man who had two estranged sons and tried desperately to get both of them to attend a banquet that he hosted in the family home. Listen carefully while I tell it to you. It goes like this, "A certain man had two sons . . ."

The plot now thickens! As noted, the discovery of the fact that a sheep is missing is a huge crisis. In this case the shepherd decides to leave the flock exactly where it is, which is in the wilderness. So far, all is quiet, but the action is just about to start. The shepherd has a plan that unfolds over the next few hours.

The second cameo flows seamlessly from the first (see fig. 5.6).

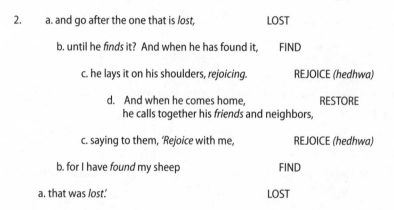

2.   a. and go after the one that is *lost*,   LOST

      b. until he *finds* it? And when he has found it,   FIND

        c. he lays it on his shoulders, *rejoicing*.   REJOICE *(hedhwa)*

          d.   And when he comes home,   RESTORE
           he calls together his *friends* and neighbors,

        c. saying to them, '*Rejoice* with me,   REJOICE *(hedhwa)*

      b. for I have *found* my sheep   FIND

    a. that was *lost.*'   LOST

Figure 5.6. The good shepherd finds and restores the lost sheep (Lk 15:4-6)

The details of the story are authentic to sheep herding in the Middle East in any age. Having created a plan in his mind (cameo 1), the shepherd now acts upon that plan (cameo 2). As light fades he gathers friends (if he can) and tries to retrace the paths he took throughout the day. He needs grit and determination to continue the search. One in a hundred is a small percentage of the herd. The good shepherd ventures out anyway in spite of the fading light, committed to find his sheep alive or dead regardless of how long it takes.

When it realizes that it is lost a sheep runs about, disoriented and terrified. It quickly weakens from heat or is exhausted from its failed attempts to find the herd, but still it bleats. If and when the shepherd approaches and the sheep hears his call, it will summon up any remaining energy to bleat as loudly as it can regardless of how tired it has become. During his search, be it long or short, the shepherd listens eagerly for the sheep's response to his call because that response can guide him to the terrified animal. The magical moment is when the lost sheep first hears and responds to the shepherd's call, guaranteeing the success of the search. The sheep, of course *accepts being found.* That is, it does not struggle against its savior and run yet further away. All of these details were well-known to Jesus' audience. M. P. Krikorian, who herded sheep for years in the hills of southeastern Turkey around the year 1900, records an occasion of losing a goat. Late one afternoon he found that a goat was missing from his herd. His response was:

> I called [over to] my cousin, the village shepherd across the valley, and reported our loss. He was too exhausted to go and search with us but he reported having seen her [the goat] at the foot of Haivali Dagh, the Quincy Mountains. So my brother and I sought for our goat. For four hours we walked in the moonlight over rocks and through thick thorny bushes. We covered every part of the mountain, climbing and then descending again. . . . We imitated the goat's "Baa, baa, hey, hoo!" At last, weary and bleeding from thorns and sharp stones, we gave up hope of finding her. Just then we seemed to hear a faint response in answer to our call. The call was repeated. The answer came again clearer and stronger. Exhausted and perspiring, we kept moving on in the midnight stillness towards the direction of the answer to our calls. To our unspeakable delight we found our blue goat curled against a mossy rock, bathing the latest arrival of her family. I took the pretty kid in my arms close to my bosom, and my brother held the mother goat by the head as we made our way through the thickets to the path to continue homeward. We found our own souls restored as we brought our wandering pet to a place of safety.[40]

When a shepherd finds a lost sheep, he usually needs to carry the animal home, as happens in the story about Moses recorded in *Exodus Rabbah*, which reads:

> Our Rabbis said that when Moses our teacher, peace be upon him, was tending the flock of Jethro in the wilderness, a little kid escaped from him. He ran after it until it reached a shady place. When it reached the shady place,

---

[40]M. P. Krikorian, *The Spirit of the Shepherd: An Interpretation of the Psalm Immortal*, 2nd ed. (Grand Rapids: Zondervan, 1939), pp. 56-57.

there appeared to view a pool of water and the kid stopped to drink. When
Moses approached it, he said: "I did not know that you ran away because of
thirst; you must be weary." So he placed the kid on his shoulder and walked
away. Thereupon God said: "Because thou hast mercy in leading the flock of
a mortal, thou wilt assuredly tend my flock Israel."[41]

This Midrash is attributed to the eleventh or twelfth century and could
record a much earlier story. In any case it demonstrates how good shepherd
stories are deeply embedded in Middle Eastern sacred texts. Like the parable
of Jesus, this story about Moses has an interpretive note at the end. God
walks on the stage and gives a final word. In good Middle Eastern style,
Moses did not *lose* his kid; rather, the kid "escaped from him." Also Moses
carried the kid home.

Returning to the parable of Jesus, the listener fully expects the shepherd,
on arriving home, to secure the animal in the sheepfold and return to the
open pasture lands to bring back the ninety-nine that are still "in the wilderness." The story does not end; it stops. The "unfinished symphony" thus
created is not completed until Jesus tells the story of the prodigal son, where
the father does indeed go out a second time in the hope of bringing the
"righteous" older son (who does not recognize that he is indeed "in the wilderness") into the banquet. To trace that story is beyond the scope of this
book.[42] It is enough to note here that the drama before us has a missing
scene that Jesus has deliberately omitted in the first two parables, only to
include it in the third.

On returning home the shepherd invites his "friends" (*haberim*) to a
party. As noted earlier, the word *friends* (*haberim*) was the Hebrew term
used for the elite guild of Pharisees, who held to the strictest interpretations
of the law of Moses. Jesus now shapes his telling of the story of the good
shepherd by noting that the *haberim come to the party!* They *rejoice* with the
shepherd at the *success of his efforts*. Cannot the audience that is composed
of law-abiding Pharisees (and perhaps members of the guild of "the friends")
do the same with Jesus?[43] As they ponder that question, they and we are

---

[41]Freedman, "Exodus Rabbah" 2.2, *Midrash Rabbah*, p. 49.

[42]See Bailey, *Jacob and the Prodigal;* Bailey, *Finding the Lost;* and Bailey, *Cross and the Prodigal.*

[43]Vatican Arabic Manuscript no. 18 is an Arabic translation of the Gospel of Luke dated A.D. 993.
In the translation of Luke 15:6 (folio 60ʳ) this Hebrew word *habura* appears. The translators
knew that "the friends" were the *habura*.

faced with one of the major concerns of the parable, namely, who does the shepherd in Jesus' story represent?

By retelling the traditional good shepherd story, what is Jesus saying about himself? For hundreds of years in the writings of the psalmist and the prophets, God was the good shepherd who would one day enter history, step into the breach and make up for the failures of the various bad shepherds. Here in Luke 15:4-7 Jesus is clearly talking about himself. Thus the text affirms what can be called "dominical Christology." This affirmation rings many bells. Some of them need to be noted.

Is there any other affirmation of the pre-existence of Christ from the lips of Jesus?

Hints of such an affirmation appear in Mark 1:38, where Jesus tells Peter that he must move on to the next town, "for that is why I came out." In his classical work on the Greek text of Mark, C. E. B. Cranfield argues that the preferred understanding of this text is "that it was for the sake of this preaching ministry that he had come forth from God." For Cranfield, this text is at least a "veiled reference to his coming from God."[44]

Others have already noted that an even clearer affirmation of Jesus' self-identity is available here in Luke 15. Barnett notes that in the parable of the prodigal son, the father's actions mirror what Jesus is accused of doing. Barnett writes, "Jesus' story is asserting a functional sonship of God: the Son [Jesus] welcomes sinners because the Father welcomes sinners."[45] If in Luke 15:4-7 Jesus is offering his version of the classical shepherd story (first told in Psalm 23 and retold in three of the prophets), then the self-affirmed identity of Jesus is clear in this parable as well. In the three prophetic accounts, the good shepherd is God, who pledges himself to come and round up the lost sheep of Israel. By retelling the classical parable of the good shepherd, with himself as its central actor, Jesus is affirming that he is the living incarnation of that centuries-old promise.

Another aspect of the text is that in the prophetic accounts of the good shepherd, the flock was lost *among the nations*. But then God acted in the sixth century B.C. to "bring back" to Jerusalem at least part of the flock that

---

[44]C. E. B. Cranfield, *The Gospel According to St Mark*, Cambridge Greek Testament Commentary (Cambridge: Cambridge University Press), p. 90.

[45]Paul Barnett, *Finding the Historical Christ* (Grand Rapids: Eerdmans, 2009), p. 136.

was scattered across the Babylonian Empire and beyond. But Jesus stands *in Israel* and talks about "the lost sheep of the house of Israel" (Mt 10:6; 15:24). He is not talking about Jews living in Babylon or Alexandria. He is seeking Jews who are lost and who live *in Israel*. In the story of Zacchaeus, Jesus affirmed that his task was to "seek and to save the lost." In Mark Jesus saw the multitude that sought him out "in a lonely place" and understood them to be "like sheep without a shepherd" (Mk 6:34). In John 10:11, 14, Jesus affirms, "I am *the* good shepherd." All through the Gospels Jesus is engaged in "finding the lost sheep." In this parable Jesus declares himself to be the divine shepherd who enters history (as promised by Ezekiel and the others) to make up for the failures of the bad shepherds who lose their sheep.

The study of the identity of Jesus in the New Testament rightly focuses on his *names*.[46] He is called Messiah, Son of God, Son of Man, Savior, Word of God and so forth. A second way to investigate his person is to look at *what he does*. He forgives sin, heals the sick and raises the dead. This parable obliges us to reflect on a third window into an understanding of his person and work. We can discover who Jesus is by looking at how he takes images and stories about God from the Old Testament, retells them and "writes himself into the story." That is, in the retelling of the story he places himself at its center as he acts out the role of God. This can be called *hermeneutical Christology*. This kind of Christology is presented in our text where Jesus starts with Psalm 23 in which God "brings me back," and retells the same good shepherd story with himself as the shepherd who does the finding. In Jesus' version he is the one who finds the lost. In passing we can note that he was not the only Jew of that time to apply divine ascriptions to himself. Rabbi Hillel talked the same way.

The late David Flusser was a distinguished Israeli Jew who for more than three decades was professor of New Testament at Hebrew University in Jerusalem. In 1988 he published a short essay titled "Hillel's Self-Awareness and Jesus."[47] In this essay Flusser discusses how Hillel, a famous founder of rabbinic Judaism who lived one generation before Jesus, used language about God to describe himself. The Teacher of Righteousness in the Dead

---

[46]James D. G. Dunn, *Christology in the Making* (London: SCM Press, 1980).
[47]David Flusser, "Hillel's Self-Awareness and Jesus," *Judaism and the Origins of Christianity* (Jerusalem: Magnes Press, 1988), pp. 509-14.

Sea Scrolls also exhibited "a high self-esteem," as did the author of the Thanksgiving Scroll.[48] In the light of these texts, argues Flusser, is it no longer possible to affirm "the absence of an elevated self-awareness in Jesus."[49] Hillel in particular described himself using language that the Hebrew tradition reserves for God. Flusser argues that Hillel's intent was to "express the sublime dignity of man."[50] Flusser concludes by noting that an elevated self-awareness was thus shared by these Jewish near contemporaries.[51] But Jesus' language is more specific than Flusser allows. "The good shepherd" of the Hebrew Scriptures is God himself, who promises to one day come in person and round up the lost sheep, as we have seen. When Luke 15:4-7 is seen as the fourth retelling of a story created by David and retold by the prophets, it is clear that Jesus is telling his listeners who he is. Jesus is the good shepherd in the parable, and Jesus goes after "the lost" as does God the good shepherd in the earlier biblical accounts of the good shepherd story. Snodgrass affirms that the parable now under study is "both theological and Christological."[52] The story continues.

The shepherd in the parable pays whatever price is required to find the lost. Having *found it*, the task of restoration is only half completed. The shepherd must then *carry it back* to the village. Jesus refers to these two related tasks in the story about Zacchaeus (Lk 19:1-10). The Son of Man must *seek* and also *save* the lost. Accomplishing the first without the second is meaningless. Back in the village the shepherd's friends are happy to attend a party in celebration of the finding of the lost. They do not attack the shepherd for having gotten dirty tramping through the mud to find and restore his lost sheep. Rather they praise him. The Pharisees launch such an attack against Jesus, and at the end of Jesus' parable the Pharisaic audience may be able to see itself in the "ninety-nine" that are "still in the wilderness," or they may identify with the "friends" at the party in the shepherd's home. In either case they are challenged to revise their views of Jesus. That is, Jesus writes them into the parable as the "friends," who support the shepherd and rejoice with him. They do not stand aloof and criticize him.

---

[48]Ibid., p. 509.
[49]Ibid.
[50]Ibid., p. 514.
[51]Ibid.
[52]Klyne Snodgrass, *Stories with Intent*, p. 109. That is, the text tells us about God and about Jesus.

See figure 5.7 for the interpretation of the parable (the *nimshal*).

3.	a. Just so, I say to *you*, that thus there will be more *joy (hedhwa)* in heaven	YOU
	b. over *one (hadh)* sinner who *repents*	ONE
	c. than over *ninety-nine* righteous persons who need no repentance.[a]	NINETY-NINE

[a]Bailey, *Jacob and the Prodigal*, p. 65; and Bailey, *Poet and Peasant*, p. 144. Some of this text is my own translation.

Figure 5.7. Interpretation of the parable (Lk 15:7)

What might the reader of the parable expect as an explanation of Jesus' retelling of such a famous biblical tale? Four themes come quickly to mind. Perhaps the parable is about

1. The *bad shepherd* who loses his sheep.

2. The *good shepherd* who goes after it.

3. The *price paid* by the shepherd to rescue the lost sheep.

4. *Joy in the community* when the sheep is brought home.[53]

To the listener/reader's surprise, the entire emphasis of the interpretation of the parable is on the *return/repentance* of the lost sheep and the resulting joy in heaven. The single lost sheep who "repents/returns" causes that joy. How can this be understood?

The sheep brought back by the shepherd is a *symbol of repentance*, and that repentance brings joy to the sheep, the shepherd, the shepherd's "friends" and to the angels (God) in heaven. This identification electrifies the listeners. Jesus has crossed the Rubicon. As noted, the listeners knew that the prophetic accounts of the good shepherd story present God as one who enters history, finds, gathers and brings back (*shuv*) the lost. No doubt many understood the return under Cyrus in 539 B.C. as at least partially fulfilling those promises even though many had remained in Babylon and elsewhere in the Diaspora.

Now they know that for Jesus the "return to Jerusalem" was not the only

[53]Bailey, *Finding the Lost*, p. 85.

return that mattered. As mentioned, the suffering servant of Isaiah 49:5 was commissioned to "bring Jacob back to *him*," and that "Israel might be gathered to *him*." "Return" in Isaiah 49:1-7 was not focused exclusively on "back to Jerusalem" but included the call to come "back to God." John the Baptist had opened the way. How does Jesus fit into all of this? His listeners now know.

Jesus can be understood to be saying to his audience:

> In my banquets with outcasts, you are witnessing a deeper fulfillment of these great divine affirmations. Who am I? I am the promised presence of God as the good shepherd. What do I do? I round up the lost sheep and bring them home. This is my identity and this is my sacred task. The return to Jerusalem from Babylon was good, but it was not everything. I am engaged, at great cost, in the work of bringing the lost *back to God* as Isaiah affirmed (Isaiah 49:5). You can sit in the shade of the temple and still be lost! Follow me and, in a special way, I will bring you home to God.

Before we can proceed, the word *return/repent* needs clarification. As we have noted, the Old Testament shepherd stories all use the Hebrew word *shuv* (bring back/return). Across the Old Testament the "return" discussed can be to a *place* or a *person* on the one hand or to *the Lord* on the other. Often it is to a place, but "return to the Lord" is a viable option for understanding *shuv* (return). Isaiah 55:7 discusses the wicked person and affirms, "let him return [*shuv*] to the LORD." Moving ahead in history, the translators of the Old Testament into Greek (LXX) consistently translated *shuv* with the Greek word *epistrephō*. Given the fact that our parable about a lost sheep is a story that is told four times in the tradition (using the word *shuv*), we would expect to find the word *epistrephō* in the text of Luke. Rather, the word *metanoeō* (repent) appears. Does this indicate a discontinuity between the Old Testament shepherd texts and the parable before us? It does not, because the two Greek words are synonymous. J. Behm writes, "*Metanoeō* thus approximates to *epistrephō* = *shuv*, the Old Testament technical term for religious and ethical conversion."[54] Earlier in the same larger discussion, Behm also writes, "What the religious language of the Old Testament expressed by *shuv*, and the theological terminology of the Rabbis by *tishuba*, . . . the New Testament, like

---

[54]Ernst Würthwein, "Repentance and Conversion in the Old Testament," *TDNT*, 4:990.

the Jewish Hellenistic writings, expresses by *metanoeō* and *metanoia*."[55] In short, the word *metanoeō* in Luke 15:7 translates the great Hebrew word *shuv* that is behind it. With this in mind, we turn to Luke 15:7.

To understand this "return/repentance" of the sheep we are obliged to start with a review of the active and the passive in the four previous accounts of the shepherd story (Lk 15:4-7). These are as follows:

- David: David affirms, "he brings me back" (God is active as the shepherd; the sheep are passive)

- Jeremiah: God promises "I will bring them back" (God is active as the shepherd; the sheep are passive)

- Ezekiel: God promises: "I, I myself will bring them back" (God is active; the sheep are passive)

- Zechariah: God promises, "I will bring them back" (God is active; the sheep are passive [except as they turn into soldiers and begin fighting])

- Jesus: The shepherd searches, finds, carries home (*shepherd* is *active*). Then in the interpretation of the parable (v. 7) the lost sheep becomes a symbol of *one sinner who repents*. That is, the *sinner* in verse 7 is *active*.

It is amazing to see that the sheep in Luke 15:4-7 become active. Joy in heaven is triggered by "one sinner who repents." As noted, the shepherd does not find and carry home a *carcass*! Rather he shoulders a live sheep who is described in the interpretation of the parable as one who "repents/returns." On the story line, what does that sheep do? Krikorian's realistic and detailed description of his search for his lost goat (quoted earlier) gives important background understood instinctively in Middle Eastern traditional village life. Moghabghab, a Palestinian shepherd, records a similar account from early in the twentieth century. He describes how one evening, during the daily (early evening) count, he found that two sheep were missing, and the following scene unfolded.

> A searching party was soon made up and, each carrying a "*fanous*," or lantern, we set out to seek the lost sheep. The sound of our voices was soon heard ringing among the hills, calling, "Hoo, Hoo! Ta, Ta, Ta!"[56] But there was no

---

[55]J. Behm, "μετανοέω and μετάνοια in the New Testament," *TDNT*, 4:999.

[56]*Ta* is a Palestinian/Lebanese colloquial abbreviation of *ta'alu* (All of you, come here).

trace of the wanderers, no voice to be heard save the prowling of the wolves and jackals. . . . We searched the valleys, the forests, and the hills, feeling our way through the darkness with our staves and partially guided by the dim lights; sometimes falling, sometime straying, sometimes caught in the bushes and tearing our clothes. The rumor of our loss had already been spreading in the village, for the inhabitants had seen our lights wandering on the hills . . . and knew what it meant. . . . At last, after a long and careful search, we discovered a trail of the sheep on the soft sand; and at once we ascended the hill and cried out (again) "He, Hoo! Ta, Ta, Ta!" And after we had listened a while, the faint voices of our sheep were heard on the distant hill "Maaaa!" Poor creatures, they had been wandering blindly on the hills, and had waited long for help to come. . . .We led them home with great joy.[57]

The two sheep at first wandered hoping to find the rest of the flock. Finally they gave up their exhausting efforts and waited for rescue, which after some hours arrived. Moghabghab goes on to describe how on their return the entire family engaged in "great rejoicing" as the searchers were pressed to tell again and again the story of how the "sheep were sought for, found, and saved."[58] This account, like Krikorian's description, highlights the crucial part played by the lost sheep. Because Moghabghab and his friends were not searching for a *dead animal*, he continued to call. On hearing the shepherd's voice (call) one of the two sheep emitted its distress signal in the form of frantic, rapid repetition of its bleats. Without that signal, Moghabghab's night search had little hope for success, and he could have become like the shepherd in Amos's account who "rescues from the mouth of the lion two legs, or a piece of an ear" (Amos 3:12).[59] The searchers however heard a faint bleat that guided them to the living animals. Unspoken but fully understood is the fact that when any rescuer finds a lost sheep, the animal does not struggle against the rescue effort like a deer caught in a wire fence; rather the sheep is *overjoyed* to be found. The sheep *responds to the shepherd's cry* and at the same time it *accepts being found*. The active and the passive blend. So it is with repentance as set forth in this parable.

---

[57]Faddoul Moghabghab, *The Shepherd Song on the Hills of Lebanon: The Twenty-Third Psalm Illustrated and Explained* (New York: E. P. Dutton, 1907), pp. 76-79.

[58]Ibid., p. 79.

[59]The point in Amos 3:12 is that two bones and an ear was all that was left. The shepherd had arrived too late.

No parable is adequate to explain divine mysteries, yet Jesus' brilliant choice of the shepherd image takes us a significant distance along the path toward understanding. The shepherd is the primary figure. At the same time, the lost sheep's actions are critical to the process, a process that creates joy everywhere, even in heaven.

"Heaven" was an early rabbinic way to talk about God without saying the word *God*.[60] The "kingdom of God" and the "kingdom of Heaven" were two titles for the same spiritual reality. "Joy in heaven" means joy in the heart of God. Ibrahim Sa'id thoughtfully remarks, "Jesus concludes the parable with an announcement that he brings news of joy in heaven. And who else is qualified to tell us about heaven?"[61] Then there is the question of order.

T. W. Manson has insightfully observed, "But the characteristic feature of these two parables is not so much the joy over the repentant sinner as the Divine love that goes out to seek the sinner before he repents."[62] Manson affirms rightly that the action of the shepherd represents the movement of divine love in history. He is also correct when he notes the order. First is the offer of divine love acted out in the "search and rescue" operation. Second comes the response of joy on the part of the shepherd, the sheep, the friends and even the angels over the acceptance of that love. But actually three things happen in the parable.

1. *Divine love acts* to search, find and carry home the sheep.

2. The (assumed) *acceptance of the shepherd's efforts* by the sheep, which is their repentance.

3. Finally the *joy in heaven* over that acceptance/repentance.

The sheep's act of *repentance* needs careful scrutiny. Either the interpretation in Luke 15:7 simply does not fit the parable or the assumption of the text is that the action of the shepherd in *finding* along with the participation of the sheep in *being found* together constitute *repentance as redefined by Jesus*. How does the sheep "participate" in this event? The sheep knows it is lost, listens for the shepherd, responds to the shepherd's approach with its

---

[60]They did not want to say "God" lest they use his name in vain and break the Ten Commandments.

[61]Ibrahim Sa'id, *Luqa*, p. 394.

[62]T. W. Manson, *The Sayings of Jesus* (1937; repr., London: SCM Press, 1964), p. 284.

crucial bleating, and accepts the rescue effort rather than running still further away. The success of this full sequence of finding, cooperating and restoring is celebrated back in the village and in the heavenly places. The shepherd acts to find and restore, and the lost sheep participates in the process of being found.

This leaves the question of why this event in particular causes God to rejoice. Throughout the Old Testament the faithful are called on to

1. *Obey* the revealed sacred *law*.

2. *Fulfill* certain *devotional acts* such as prayer, fasting, sacrifices, public reading of Scripture and almsgiving, etc.

3. *Respond* to the *grace of God*. Some of the appropriate responses are listed in Micah 6:8, where doing justice, loving mercy and walking humbly with God, are mentioned.

But in this text a fourth interaction with the divine is discussed. Not only do the faithful relate to God through obedience to *law*, *worship* and appropriate *responses to grace*, but this parable suggests that the faithful are to act in ways that cause *heaven to rejoice*. Yes, on rare occasions God is *pleased* (Ps 105:43; 115:3), but the language used in those texts can usually be compared to the phrase "her majesty's pleasure" (which means her majesty's *will*). The question remains, what brings *joy* to God? The answer of this text is, repentance as defined by Jesus!

The subject of repentance in the Bible and in early rabbinic traditions is central and the literature enormous. Ephraim Urbach dedicates an entire section to it.[63] Montefiore has left us a fine essay that gleans sayings on repentance from the writings of many rabbis.[64] George F. Moore includes an entire chapter on the subject.[65] A few treasures from this vast store may be helpful.

If there is no repentance, none of the sacrifices are valid. Moore writes,

---

[63]Ephraim Urbach, "The Powers of Repentance," in *The Sages: Their Concepts and Beliefs* (Jerusalem: Magnes Press, 1987), 1:462-71.

[64]C. G. Montefiore, "Appendix III: On Repentance," in *Rabbinic Literature and Gospel Teachings* (London: Macmillan, 1930), pp. 377-422.

[65]George F. Moore, "Repentance" and "The Efficacy of Repentance," in *Judaism in the First Centuries of the Christian Era* (New York: Schocken, 1971), 1:507-34; Hultgren lists other very helpful sources (Arland J. Hultgren, *The Parables of Jesus* [Grand Rapids: Eerdmans, 2000], p. 76, n. 26).

"Repentance is the condition *sine qua non* of the efficacy of all the ritual expia-
tions, including those of the Day of Atonement."[66] As observed, Isaiah wrote,

> Let the wicked man forsake his way,
>   and the unrighteous man his thoughts;
> let him *return to the* LORD, [*shuv*]
>   that he may have compassion on him. (Is 55:7)

To "return to the Lord" is literally "repent [*yashov*] to the LORD." The text
then affirms compassion for the one who returns/repents. Without repentance, that grace is not available. Repentance was so essential that it was
created before the world was made.[67] Repentance "brings about redemption,"
and "Great is repentance for on account of an individual who repents, the
sins of all the world are forgiven."[68]

Also in the New Testament period, even before the destruction of the
temple, there was reflection on the fact that many Jews lived at great dis-
tances from Jerusalem and needed atonement for sin apart from pilgrimage
to the holy city. What might they do? The answer was, repentance can substitute for the sacrifices! Moore summarizes rabbinic reflection on repentance
in the early Christian centuries: "To the Jewish definition of repentance
belong the reparation of injuries done to a fellow man in his person, property,
or good name, the confession of sin, prayer for forgiveness, and the genuine
resolve and endeavor not to fall into the sin again."[69]

To summarize, repentance was so powerful that it could substitute for the
atonement sacrifice, but for that to take place, the three components of repentance (noted earlier) were necessary. These are

1. reparations

2. confession of sin

3. resolve not to sin again

When these three were achieved, repentance made it possible for the believer to pierce the heavens and reach to the throne of grace. Moore writes
(referencing *Pesikta* 163b), "An arrow carries the width of a field; but repen-

---

[66]Moore, "Repentance," p. 508.
[67]Moore, "The Efficacy of Repentance," p. 526.
[68]Babylonian Talmud *Yoma* 86b.
[69]Moore, *Judaism in the First Centuries*, 1:117.

tance carries to the very throne of God."[70] Repentance is like the sea in that it is always available for purification.[71]

Into this theological world Jesus interjects a new definition of repentance. Repentance is *responding to a call offering salvation*; it is *accepting to be found*. The sheep is lost. The good shepherd, at great cost, searches diligently for the lost sheep, as noted earlier. The bleating of the sheep communicates "I am over here. I am lost. I cannot find my way home. Please rescue me!" The shepherd comes and carries the sheep home with joy, a joy that he quickly shares with others. That same joy resounds in the heart of God.

If the believer *fulfills the law*, is diligent in *worship* and *responds to grace* with mercy and justice for others, does God rejoice? Or is this a case of "no thanks for duty"? God is often *angry*, and on occasion *compassionate*, but does he express any other emotion? When a person succeeds in the previously mentioned aspects of faithfulness, what is God's reaction? Any cursory review of this topic throughout the Bible brings scant results. As seen in the Old Testament, God is "pleased" with the exodus (Ps 105:43) and at the return of the people from exile (Zeph 3:17). He is also "pleased with"[72] (*ratsah*) the special servant who appears in Isaiah 42:1. That same pleasure is expressed at Jesus' baptism, where God is "well pleased" (*eudokeō*, Lk 3:22). It surfaces again in reference to the giving of the kingdom to the disciples (Lk 12:32). But in the New Testament the word *joy* (*chara*) is *only applied to God* here in Luke 15, where the shepherd, the woman and the father know joy. If for no other reason, the text before us is exceptional. God (heaven/the angels) is full of joy when a sinner *responds to the shepherd/ savior's call offering help* and *accepts to be found*! When Zacchaeus comes down out of the tree, he acts out the two sides of this coin (Lk 19:6). He *responds to* and *accepts the freely offered* grace. These two reactions together become *his repentance.*[73] What then of the ninety-nine "righteous persons who need no repentance"?

---

[70]Ibid., p. 530.
[71]Ibid.
[72]LVTL, *Lexicon*, p. 906.
[73]His speech that evening in his home is *not* his repentance. Rather it is his response to the event of his repentance.

The Prayer of Manasseh 1:8 says,[74]

Therefore thou, O Lord, God of the righteous,
   Hast not appointed repentance for the righteous,
For Abraham and Isaac and Jacob,
   Who did not sin against thee,
But thou hast appointed repentance for me,
   Who am a sinner.[75]

This claim that the patriarchs were sinless is denied by Ecclesiastes 7:20, which reads, "Surely there is not a righteous man on earth who does good and never sins." Yet the Manasseh text has been suggested as a background for Jesus' comment. In the light of this prayer of Manasseh the text in Luke 15:7 could mean, "Heaven rejoices more over a repentant sinner than it does even over the sinless patriarchs who naturally need no repentance!" This possibility is not the full story in Luke 15 because of the fact that in Jesus' parable the ninety-nine are still *in the wilderness* when the parable closes. Many commentators have suggested irony for Luke 15:7. The text would then mean, "the ninety-nine who [only think they] need no repentance." Perhaps both views are correct. It may be that Jesus (using irony) is referring to the audience's assumption that they are sinless like the patriarchs. Much of this is clarified in Luke 15 itself. At the end of the third story (the prodigal son) Jesus elucidates the self-righteousness he has in mind all through the trilogy of parables. The older son *thinks* his brother is a despicable sinner and sees himself as *so righteous* that he can hardly stand it! His prodigal brother needs badly to repent (of course), but he (the older brother) certainly does not! It never occurs to him that (at least) he needs to repent for failing to welcome his brother home and for insulting his father in public by refusing to enter the hall and greet the family's guests![76] Surely Jesus' own picture of the self-righteous older son (who thinks he needs no repentance) represents the audience in front of him.

In conclusion, perhaps it will be helpful to look backwards to summarize how far we have come with the good shepherd tradition before looking forward to the balancing parable of the good woman.

---

[74]The Prayer of Manasseh is one of the shorter works in the Apocrypha (c. first century B.C.).
[75]"Prayer of Manasseh," *The Apocrypha of the Old Testament*, RSV, ed. Bruce Metzger (New York: Oxford University Press, 1965), p. 219.
[76]For a full discussion of this aspect of the parable see Kenneth E. Bailey, *Poet and Peasant and Through Peasant Eyes* (Grand Rapids: Eerdmans, 1980), pp. 195-200.

To do this we turn to an overall glance at the parable of the good shepherd (and the good woman) in the light of the previous accounts of the same story (see fig. 5.8).

Ps 23:1-6 (shepherd)	Jer, Ezek, Zech (shepherd)	Lk 15:4-7 (shepherd)	Lk 15:8-10 (woman)
1. ---	Bad sheep in Jer, Ezek, and Zech	Bad shepherd loses a sheep	Careless woman loses coin
2. Lost **sheep** (no flock)	----- Lost flock	Lost **sheep** + Lost flock	Lost **coin** + Nine coins not lost
3. Good shep. is God	Good shep. is God	Good shep. is Jesus	Good woman is Jesus
4. Good host(ess)?	-----	-----	Good housekeeper + Good hostess
5. Incarnation implied	Incarnation promised	Incarnation realized	Incarnation realized
6. Price paid: bring back	Price paid: search for, save, bring back	Price paid: search for find carry back	Price paid: light lamp sweep, search -----
7. Repentance is **return to God** (*shuv*)	Repentance is return to the land (*shuv*)	Repentance is **return to God** (*metanoeō*)	Repentance is **return to God** (*metanoeō*)
8. -----	Ezek: Bad sheep Good sheep & bad sheep	-----	-----
9. **A celebration**	-----	**A celebration**	**A celebration**
10. Story ends in **house**	Story ends in the land	Story ends in **house**	Story ends in **house**

[a]Revised from Bailey, *Finding the Lost,* p. 68; and Bailey, *Jacob and the Prodigal,* p. 70.

Figure 5.8. The good shepherd and its forerunners (Lk 15:4-10)[a]

The relationships between the six texts are strong, numerous and significant. Following the numbers of figure 5.8 and looking from the perspective of Jesus' new version of the "good shepherd story," we can summarize a few *intertextual observations*.

1. The *good shepherd* in all the previous accounts is God. Here the good shepherd is Jesus. He is thereby affirming his person and ministry to be a fulfilling of the previous promises of divine intervention by God as "the good shepherd."

2. The *bad shepherd* theme is muted and presented by Jesus in a very gentle form. He knows that as he describes the shepherd who loses his sheep, he is metaphorically describing his audience of scribes and Pharisees. The punishments of the bad shepherds are also omitted. He is kind to them.

3. The *lost sheep and the lost flock* are skillfully combined for the first time into a single account. Jesus cares for both the individual and the community. He weeps over Jerusalem and shows profound care for the individuals who cross his path.

4. For the first time in a thousand years the *good host(ess?)* of Psalm 23:5 reappears. Jesus, as it were, resurrects her out of the psalm and creates a full parable to honor her and expand her message.

5. The *incarnation* that is implied (Ps 23) and later promised by Jeremiah, Ezekiel and Zechariah is now *realized*. One of the earliest and most profound declarations of Jesus' identity is thereby set forth. This is of particular significance because it is from Jesus himself.

6. The *price paid* by the good shepherd to search for and to bring back the lost is known, assumed and significant.

7. The *return to God* described by David and redirected by the three prophets is restored to its original intent in the parable that Jesus fashions. Jesus does not deny the value of the prophetic focus of return to the land, nor does he criticize their rewrite. The "ninety-nine" (the community) remain in the story even though they are no longer its central emphasis.

8. The "bad sheep" theme is once again omitted.

9. The *celebration* at the end of Psalm 23 is remembered and restored as the conclusion to the parable.

10. Once again the story ends *in the house* (a theme that has also been missing for a thousand years).

A glance at figure 5.8 makes clear that Jesus has preserved more of Psalm 23 than any of the three prophetic texts. Jesus reintroduces the *single lost sheep*, the *hostess*, the *return to God*, the *celebration* and the *house*.

Finally, it may be helpful to attempt a *theological summary* of the main points of the parable.

THE THEOLOGICAL CLUSTER OF THE PARABLE OF THE LOST SHEEP (LK 15:1-7)

1. *Christology.* Jesus is the good shepherd, the unique presence of God who restores the lost sinner to God. (The joy *in the home* of the shepherd is connected in the parable to joy *in heaven.*) This shepherd must personally make a costly demonstration of love in order to restore the helpless sheep. Four Old Testament texts stand behind the parable; Psalm 23, Jeremiah 23:1-4, Ezekiel 34 and Zechariah 10:2-12. This Old Testament background makes clear that the shepherd is more than merely an agent. He is the one who in his person fulfills the promises of the prophets that God himself will come to his people and seek out his lost sheep.[77]

2. *Failed leadership.* The parable contains criticism of leaders who lose their sheep and do nothing but complain about others who go after them.

3. *Freely offered grace.* The lost sheep does not earn the right to rescue. It is a gift.

4. *Incarnation and atonement.* The shepherd goes out to find the sheep (incarnation) and pays a high price to *restore* it to his home (atonement).

5. *Sin.* Humankind is depicted as unable to find its own way home. This applies both to the one and to the ninety-nine who are last seen while yet "in the wilderness" needing help to return safely home.

---

[77]The reflections in this theological cluster are revised from Bailey, *Finding the Lost*, pp. 91-92.

6. *Joy.* The finding and restoring of even one lost sheep creates joy for all, even for heaven.

7. *Repentance.* Repentance is defined as *responding to the shepherd's call* and as *acceptance of being found.* The sheep is lost, yet it participates with the shepherd in his search. Repentance becomes a combination of the shepherd's act of rescue and the sheep's participation in and acceptance of that act. The ninety-nine "[think they] need no repentance" (as does the older son in Lk 15:25-32), but such a need remains.

8. *The individual and the community.* David tells of a single (lost) sheep. Jeremiah and Ezekiel turn Psalm 23 into a tale of a lost flock (Israel), which God restores to *his land.* Jesus brings together a concern for the individual (the one) *and* the community (the ninety-nine). Returning to the land is not enough, there must be a return to God.

We turn now to the parallel parable of the good woman who loses and then finds her coin (Lk 15:8-19).

The text is displayed in figure 5.9.

1. "Or *what woman,* having ten silver coins,	INTRODUCTION	
2. if she *loses* one coin,	LOST	
3. does not light a lamp and sweep the house and seek diligently until she *finds* it?	FOUND	

4.   And finding it, she calls together
   her friends and neighbors, saying,
   '*Rejoice with me,*
		REJOICE

5. for I have *found* the coin	FOUND	
6. which I had *lost.'*	LOST	
7. Even so, I tell *you,* there is *joy* before the angels of God over one sinner who *repents.*"	CONCLUSION	

[a]Traditional titles for well-known parables often give hints as to how those parables have been understood across the centuries. We traditionally describe Luke 15:8-10 as "the parable of the lost coin," and thereby avoid talking about "the parable of the good woman" and all that such a title implies. More of this follows.

Figure 5.9. The good woman finds a lost coin (Lk 15:8-10)[a]

THE RHETORIC

The seven-cameo structure used here is a further example of what I choose to call the "prophetic rhetorical template." This same rhetorical style was seen in Psalm 23. A further occurrence of the prophetic rhetorical template is in the center of the parable of the good shepherd. Here, four cameos come to a climax in the center at number 4, where the series begins to repeat backwards. As with the story of the shepherd, the middle of the parable focuses on the joy of the community when the woman finds her coin.

COMMENTARY

The most startling aspect of this parable is the fact that the hero of the story is a woman. Women champions were not strange to the Jewish tradition. Deborah the prophetess helped defeat Sisera, and Jael (the wife of Heber) killed Sisera with a tent peg (Judges 4:4-22). The Apocrypha has the heroic story of Judith, who saved her city by killing the opposing general Holofernes (Judith 13). But given the all-male nature of the guild of scribes and Pharisees, it is bold and indeed daring for Jesus to create this story. We are left with two questions: Why did he do so, and what does it mean?

First, then, why does this story appear when the parable of the good shepherd is already in place? A number of reasons surface on reflection. Among them are:

1. Jesus had female disciples. Even though the three parables of Luke 15 are Jesus' reply to complaints from scribes and Pharisees, who were all male, his disciples were also no doubt listening, and some of them were women. Furthermore, Jesus was probably using material that he had created for all his listeners, many of whom were female.[78] He was able to speak to the men on a very deep level by using metaphors and creating stories out of their everyday world. He did the same with the women. On occasion, he told parables in pairs, one part of the pair reflecting the activity of males and the other from the world of females.[79] As noted, male and female are balanced in Isaiah 42:13-14 and in again in Isaiah 51:1-2.

---

[78]Kenneth E. Bailey, "Women in the New Testament: A Middle Eastern Cultural View," *Theology Matters* 6, no. 1 (January-February 2000).

[79]Mt 5:14-15 speaks of "lighting lamps" (the work of women) and "building cities" (the work of men). In Lk 13:18-21 a man plants mustard seed and a woman bakes bread. Jesus likens himself to a shepherd and to a mother hen (Lk 13:34).

Thus Jesus is renewing a prophetic balance, not introducing a new one.

2. Jesus is perhaps reclaiming the long-neglected female component in Psalm 23. God prepares a meal in Psalm 23:5, and as he does so he is fulfilling an important task traditionally carried out by women. As noted, this female component in the good shepherd psalm disappears in Jeremiah, Ezekiel and Zechariah. Jesus reintroduces and reinforces it by telling the story of the good woman and her coin. It will now be more difficult to drop this feminine aspect again because, unlike Psalm 23:5, the woman is the center of the entire parable. The fact of God "preparing a meal" was overlooked by the prophets, as we saw. But if an entire parable focuses on a woman, her story will surely be remembered.

3. Jesus wants to reclaim the equality of male and female that begins with Genesis 1:27 and is not always remembered or honored in ancient or modern times. Jesus does so by using a female metaphor for God. The rabbinic tradition records a parable about a man who loses a coin. This story was told by a second century A.D. rabbi named Phinehas ben Jair (see n. 34 of this chapter and its associated parable).

Ben Jair's parable overlaps with Luke 15:8-10 in a number of ways. Like the parable in Luke, ben Jair's story has an interpretation attached to its end. The man in that parable searches *diligently* "till he finds it." Both accounts take place in a house. Both actors light lamps. But ben Jair tells a story about a *man*, while Jesus chooses a *woman* as the hero of his parable.

4. Finally, there is the consideration of the place where the lost disappears. David is vague on this point. The phrase *He brings me back* does not tell us where he was lost. He is brought back to "the paths of righteousness," which assumes that he was lost in "the paths of unrighteousness." In the three prophetic accounts the flock is lost *among the nations*. The scattered sheep need to be gathered and then brought home. In like manner, in Jesus' first parable the sheep is lost "in the wilderness." But the coin in parable before us is missing *in the house*. More of this follows.

How then are we to understand the parable?

The story itself is deceptively simple and straightforward. A women loses a *drachma* (a days wages for a working man)[80] and turns the house upside

---

[80]Hultgren, *Parables of Jesus*, p. 66 (referencing *Tobit* and Josephus).

down until she finds it. On recovering the coin "that she had lost," she has a joyous party with her (female) friends.[81] The parable does not open with "which one of you," etc. In traditional Middle Eastern culture no one can address a gathering of men, saying, "which one of you," and then tell a story about a woman. This works both ways. Jesus could not have addressed a room full of women with male endings to the verbs. The phrase *Peace be with you my brothers* could be spoken to a mixed gathering, but not to an all female audience. The equality of male and female affirmed in this trilogy of parables is confirmed by the fact that the hero of the story is a *woman* who in the mind of Jesus was a symbol both for God and for himself.

The *drachma* as a coin went out of circulation under Nero (who was emperor from A.D. 54-68) and was replaced with the *denarius*, which had the same value.[82] The word *drachma* occurs only here in the New Testament. It is the word Jesus would have used, and its presence in the text reinforces the assumption of authenticity for the parable as a story told by Jesus. The early tradition remembered the story as Jesus told it.

The most readily available building material at the northern end of the Sea of Galilee is a very black and very attractive basalt. The Israeli department of antiquities has reconstructed a few village homes in the ancient ruin of Chorazin just north of the Sea of Galilee. The windows are about two inches high and perhaps fourteen inches wide. They are positioned on the wall about seven feet from the floor. They look like "rifle slots," and their primary purpose is to provide for the exit of smoke from the family cooking fire. They introduce fresh air but very little light. These simple village homes also used flat basalt stones for flooring. Indeed the poorer homes would have had a floor, walls and arch supports constructed of black basalt. The only significant source of light was the door, if it was open. A coin could easily fall into the cracks between those black flooring stones, and in a semi-darkened room it would be very hard to find. There is no wonder that the woman was obliged to light a lamp and "search diligently." Jesus not only ate with sinners, he *sought diligently* to find them that he might eat

---

[81]This is a touch of authenticity. Socializing in village life is "men with men" and "women with women" unless they are of the same family. As in the mountains of German Switzerland, in church, men and women sit separately. It is the custom.

[82]Joseph A. Fitzmyer, *The Gospel According to Luke* (New York: Doubleday, 1985), 2:1081.

with them. What does this mean? Clearly, the woman is a symbol for Jesus. But furthermore, with the two parables linked together there is no doubt that the *good woman* is a symbol also for God as is the shepherd in the previous parable.

Happily this identification was not completely lost across the history of the church. Ibn al-Tayyib, a Syrian Orthodox monk and scholar writing in Baghdad around the year A.D. 1020, comments on this text, saying, "He [Jesus] uses the woman to refer to *Allah* [God]."[83] It is amazing to find this prominent eleventh-century Christian scholar writing in Arabic while resident in Baghdad, the capital of the Islamic empire that stretched from Spain to India, using this language. Did Jesus really use a *woman* to refer to *Allah* (God)?[84] Yes he did, affirms Ibn al-Tayyib.

Just over a century later another Syriac Orthodox monk, scholar and bishop of Diyarbakir by the name of Dionesius ibn al-Salibi (d. 1164) also produced commentaries on the four Gospels. In reflecting on the parable of the good woman and the lost coin he wrote, "He used the woman to interpret [his] divinity."[85]

These remarks are also astonishing. For a modern author to talk about how Jesus used the symbol of the woman to "interpret his divinity" would be surprising enough! But to read these words from the pen of from a bishop of the Syrian Orthodox church in the East in the twelfth century is startling indeed. Now nearly a thousand years later in the West, Hultgren writes, "The parable is quite remarkable, for it portrays a woman as a metaphor for God. No other parable does so."[86] Sometimes we need to rescue Scripture from traditional, unexamined assumptions regarding its meaning. All three of these scholars are correct. But the truly stunning aspect of all of this is not that such an understanding is embedded in the writings of Ibn al-Tayyib (eleventh century) or affirmed by Ibn al-Salibi (twelfth century), but that this thinking represents *Jesus* and is confirmed by Luke *in the first century!* What else is affirmed in this extraordinary parable?

---

[83]Ibn al-Tayyib, *Tafsir*, 2:265.
[84]*Allah* is the generic Arabic word for *God* and has been used throughout the Arabic Bible for at least twelve hundred years.
[85]Ibn al-Salibi, *Tafsir*, 2:153.
[86]Hultgren, *Parables of Jesus*, p. 64.

We need to return to the setting of "the lost," which shifts from the first parable to the second, as noted. The lost sheep is missing "in the wilderness," and thus the idea of "lost far away" is introduced. Then in the second parable, Jesus could easily have told a story about a woman who goes to the market, buys her groceries and returns home only to discover that a *drachma* is missing out of her coin purse. In desperation she retraces her steps, glues her eyes to the path, cross-examines the shop keepers with whom she did business that day, and after a diligent search, finds her missing coin. Rather, Jesus tells a story of a coin lost *in the house*. Together these two stories represent distinct types of "lostness." This careful distinction is unique to this pair of parables, and it prepares the listener/reader for the parable of the prodigal son, where two sons are "lost." One is lost "in the far country" and the other is lost "in the house." This means that you can be lost in the vastness of the Diaspora. At the same time you can sit in the shadow of the temple studying the Torah *and yet be lost* from the heart of God!

Jesus knows that God is spirit and therefore is neither male nor female. Yet humankind, made up of male and female, is created in the image of God (Gen 1:27). In this trilogy of parables Jesus presents a good shepherd, a good woman and a good father. The church has for centuries rightly seen the shepherd and the father as metaphors for God. But in Luke 15 those two classical symbols have the parable of the good woman in between them. Together the three symbols bear witness to God, whose nature incorporates both genders in unity. Hultgren writes insightfully,

> It is as though God cannot be portrayed simply in terms of the shepherd, a man of daring and energy, but must also be thought of in terms of a woman who is upset by her loss, and who seeks the lost coin with the fastidious, meticulous care that the tradition, androcentric by habit, is apt to forgo.[87]

There is an additional significance to the presence of the parable of the woman and her coin. This stems from the fact that there is a deep relationship between the prodigal son and the story of Jacob as he acquires his inheritance, travels to a far country and returns (Gen 27:1-35). I have found fifty-one points of comparison and contrast between these two stories.[88] For

---

[87]Ibid., p. 68.
[88]Bailey, *Jacob and the Prodigal*.

our interests here, the parable of the prodigal son has a father and two sons but no mother, while the story of Jacob's exile and return includes a father, two sons *and a mother*. However Rebekah, Jacob's mother, has serious faults. She assists Jacob in cheating her older son (Esau) and deceiving her husband (Isaac). After that scene, Rebekah is not mentioned again until she dies (Gen 49:31). In Jesus' parallel story of exile and return (parable of the prodigal son) there is no mother. Perhaps she is omitted because of the negative connotations that remain attached to Rebekah.[89] In her place, Jesus introduces the image of a noble woman who has no marks against her record. Furthermore, the new female image (the good woman) is not simply the mother of a troubled family but is elevated into being (along with the shepherd and the father) a symbol for both Jesus and God.[90]

In the parable of the good woman the coin is inert; it cannot bleat like the sheep and has no way to help the woman in her search. Yet out of the ten dramatic components that we have been tracing through the good shepherd biblical tradition, nine of them are present in the parable of the good woman (see fig. 5.8). At the same time this new parable has its own slant on the theological content that it shares with the other good shepherd parables. The following are worthy of note.

THE THEOLOGICAL CLUSTER OF LUKE 15:8-10

1. *Failed leadership.* The opening verse of the parable of the shepherd affirms the shepherd to be a "bad shepherd." He loses his sheep. (This represents Jesus' audience of Pharisees who have "lost their sheep.") In the middle of the parable the shepherd searches for and finds the lost (this is what Jesus is doing). As noted, Jesus is saying, "You lost your sheep. You refuse to go after them. But I go after them and find them, and you come to me complaining. This is outrageous!"

This same fine tuning on the "bad shepherd and the good shepherd" reappears in the parable of the woman. In the opening statement of the parable,

---

[89]It is also possible that Jesus is preserving his theology of the unity of God. He does not want two symbols for God in one story, particularly one male and one female. Such metaphors would be a return to the worship of the Canaanites.

[90]The father in the parable, in his humiliating and self-emptying love poured out for the prodigal and the older son, becomes a symbol of God in Christ. See Bailey, *Jacob and the Prodigal*, pp. 107-11; and Bailey, *Cross and the Prodigal*, pp. 66-70.

the woman loses her coin (and is thus a bad housekeeper). But in the middle of the parable she becomes the good housekeeper. The first part of the parable tells the Pharisees that they are like the bad housekeeper and the last part presents Jesus as the good housekeeper who finds the lost coin. What he does, they should do, but they refuse. Thus Jesus acts like the good woman and finds the lost coin.

2. *Hints of atonement.* The woman puts out a great deal of time and energy to find her coin.

3. *Joy.* The woman is so delighted that she feels the need to celebrate with her friends. The endings of the Greek words tell the reader that the guests (naturally) are all women, following traditional village custom. This is a blue collar community; the woman has no servant to do the hard work of searching for the coin. For her, the recovery of a day's wages is very much worth celebrating.

4. *The agent of repentance.* The entire action is carried out by the woman, who finds and restores her coin to her purse. She is a symbol of God in Christ, who comes and restores. The lifeless coin, unlike the sheep, cannot respond. Yet the agency of the woman is clear.

5. *Christology.* Jesus is the good woman. The shepherd is a symbol for God and for Jesus. Here the woman, as she searches for and finds her coin, is also a symbol both for God and Jesus. As noted, God is likened to a woman in Isaiah 42:14; 66:13 and in Psalm 131:2. In addition 1 John 3:9 describes the believer as "born of God." New life in Christ that is discussed in the Gospel of John (Jn 3:1-12; see also 1 Pet 1:23) is so radical a reality that John uses the imagery of God giving birth. Jesus describes himself as a mother hen (Lk 13:34). All of this is in harmony with the presence of the good woman with her coin as a part of a trilogy that includes a good shepherd and a good father.

At the same time, this second parable has some unique content. This includes:

1. *The unchanged value of the coin.* When found, the sheep may be sick or injured. But the coin is of undiminished worth while lying on the floor, and when found has lost nothing of its original value. "The lost" often think they are worthless because of their self-destructive choices. This parable denies that false perception.

2. *The worth of women.* In this parable Jesus affirms, "I am like this

woman! I search for the lost. You should do likewise." Jesus elevates the worth of all women by his choice of imagery.

3. *The hope of success in finding the lost.* The outcome of the shepherd's search, in spite of his determination, is somewhat uncertain. The woman's diligence is assured success. The coin is *in* the house. It *can* be found.

4. *Lost at home.* As discussed earlier, in this parable Jesus deliberately creates a parable where the lost coin is "in the house." Thus in the setting of the trilogy of parables the reader can see the prodigal, who symbolizes the "sinners" who are *lost far away*, and the older son, who is like the coin that is lost while *in the house.*

In these two parables Jesus defines himself as the good shepherd and the good woman, both of whom *find the lost* and *host their friends* for a celebration (like God in Ps 23:3, 5, who both *brings back* the lost and also *hosts* the psalmist).[91]

Having seen Jesus' self-understanding as the incarnation of the good shepherd of psalm and of prophecy, we are ready to look closely at how he acts out this good shepherd role in one dense and potentially dangerous incident in his ministry. This appears in Mark 6, to which we now turn.

---

[91]Figure 5.8 examines the ten aspects of the good shepherd tradition and compares the good woman to them. That figure can hopefully contribute to the discussion of the good woman and her lost coin.

6

THE GOOD SHEPHERD
IN MARK 6:7-52

INTRODUCTION

In chapter six Mark records events that use the good shepherd tradition to invoke a rich *past*, create a new *present* and look to an unfolding eucharistic *future*. As Paul Minear has affirmed, "Almost all interpreters of this story find its values not on the surface but beneath it."[1] Continuing, Minear writes, "the story staggers us with its wealth of meanings. . . . We do great injustice to such a story if we reduce its purpose to a single point or a single doctrine."[2]

Furthermore Mark the Evangelist somewhat resembles a modern cameraman and television editor. In order to cover an important event, a cameraman first collects as much footage as possible. He or she will assemble many hours of "takes." As an editor he or she will then reduce the great volume of material collected into an agreed-upon length of time. A voice-over narrator will be needed to tie the various scenes together. The scenes themselves need to be arranged and judiciously edited to communicate their perceived meanings. In like manner Mark 6:7-52 selects a series of interrelated events which he summarizes and presents with extraordinary brilliance.

In this series of events "the flock" is lost and Jesus acts decisively to

---

[1] Paul S. Minear, *Saint Mark* (London: SCM Press, 1962), p. 82.

[2] In her commentary on Mark, Morna Hooker writes that her concern is "with the interpretation of the evangelist himself" (Morna D. Hooker, *The Gospel According to St. Mark* [London: A & C Black, 1991], p. 4).

fulfill a part of his destiny by carrying out the task of a good shepherd who cares for his sheep. Specifically, in Luke 15:4-7 Jesus *describes* himself as the good shepherd of Psalm 23 and the prophets. Here in the Gospel of Mark, Jesus *demonstrates* how *the good shepherd* goes about his task of dealing with a large group of scattered sheep. In addition, this entire chapter of Mark presents a very intense debate, indeed a struggle between the bad shepherd (Herod) and the good shepherd (Jesus). My intent in this chapter is to examine the text in its canonical setting and to reflect on it as a new chapter in the sequence of good shepherd stories we have been studying.

David described God the good shepherd as acting in *the present*, but the action was metaphorical. David was not a sheep and he did not eat grass on the hillsides. The three prophetic accounts of the good shepherd and his lost flock all have to do with *the future*. For the prophets, the flock was scattered and lost. But a bright future awaited them. "The days are coming," they announced, when God himself would enter history, put things right, round up his flock and return the sheep to their own pastures. To summarize, David experiences the good shepherd in the *present*. The three prophets look forward to the coming of the good shepherd in the *future*. Luke 15 is in the *present*, but it is a hypothetical present. If and when anyone loses a sheep or a coin, here is what they should do. In Mark 6, for the first time, the shepherd is fulfilling his task of caring for the flock "live," *in contemporary history*. The actions of the shepherd are neither metaphorical nor hypothetical, they are in real time and very much "on camera." Filled out with more detail this appears as follows.

Psalm 23 has no bad shepherd. Jeremiah, Ezekiel and Zechariah introduce the bad shepherd as a new character in the traditional story of the good shepherd. All three of these prophets affirm the good shepherd to be God, who in time will enter history, dismiss the bad shepherds and take over the flock. Indeed the reader is told that when God, the good shepherd, arrives on the scene, he will "attend" to the bad shepherds (Jeremiah). He will dismiss them as shepherds (Ezekiel) and with "hot anger" he will punish them (Zechariah). In short, in those accounts the bad shepherds were already guilty, weak and powerless, and could only await their judgment. But Mark presents a new aspect of the good shepherd story.

In Mark 6 the bad shepherd (Herod) is powerful, erratic, murderous and publically in charge of what is happening, even though he is open to manipulation. The good shepherd (Jesus) is under enormous pressure to respond to a particular Herodian outrage, as we will see. What will be the nature of that response? In the chapter before us, this dramatic question is answered.

In Mark 1:14 John is imprisoned; Mark 6 is built on the awareness of that fact. The outline of the episodes in this extended account (Mk 6:7-52) is displayed in figure 6.1.

1. Jesus sends out the twelve (6:7-13)
2. Herod and John [and the ministry of Jesus] (6:14-20)
3. Herod the *bad shepherd* feeds the powerful [at a *banquet of death*] (6:21-29)
4. The twelve return to Jesus (6:30-33)
5. Jesus the *good shepherd* feeds his flock [at a *banquet of life*] (6:30-43)
6. Jesus, as shepherd, leads his disciples and creates "still water" for them (6:43-52)

Figure 6.1. The setting of the emergence of Jesus the good shepherd (Mk 6:7-52)

In Mark 6:14-20 the author jumps ahead of his story by shifting to the future after John is killed and Herod is trying to figure out Jesus' identity. Mark then returns to the past to describe the murder. What is clear is that for Mark the recording of the precise time sequence of those dramatic days is not his focus. Rather, Mark selects various scenes and presents them in an order that will best convey the meaning of each event as well as affirm the overarching significance of the sequence as a whole.

That is, Mark 6:7-52 needs to be read on two levels. The first is to reflect on the individual accounts and try to understand them. The second is to see how they fit into a larger section of the Gospel. Mark creates a mosaic. In a mosaic each colored stone has its own beauty and fascination. Then, when placed into the picture under construction, it also contributes to a larger whole. Our goal is to enter into the shorter accounts as best we can. We will also look at those texts in the larger mosaic into which they are placed in the Gospel of Mark. This larger mosaic includes the series of events noted earlier. Throughout all of this, Jesus fulfills the role of the good shepherd. As noted, the sequence opens with the sending out of the Twelve (see fig. 6.2).

1.   ⁶Then he went about among the villages teaching;
      ⁷and he called the twelve   THE TWELVE
      and began to send them out, two by two,   Sent out
      and gave them authority over the unclean spirits.

2.   ⁸And he ordered them to take nothing for their journey
          except a staff;   PRINCIPLE 1
      no bread, no bag, no money in their belts,   Accept to
          ⁹but to wear sandals   Be Served
      and not to put on two tunics.

3.   ¹⁰And he said to them, "Where you enter a house,
      stay there until you leave the place.
          ¹¹If any place will not welcome you   PRINCIPLE 2
      and they refuse to hear you, as you leave   A Sacrament
      shake off the dust of the feet   Of failure
          as a testimony against them."

4.   ¹²So they went out and proclaimed that
      all should repent;   THEY GO
      ¹³and they cast out many demons   Preaching & healing
      and anointed with oil many who were sick and cured them.

Figure 6.2. The mission of the twelve apostles (Mk 6:6-13)

This is the first time that Jesus reaches out beyond the range of his voice. He knows that he personally will not be able to proclaim his message in all the towns and villages of Israel. Perhaps influenced by the difficulties he experienced in Nazareth, he calls the Twelve, gives them authority over the unclean spirits, and sends them out two by two to participate with him in the task of restoring "the lost sheep of the house of Israel." As he sends them out, he annunciates an insightful theology of mission, which includes the following points.

1. He affirms *mission from below*. The apostolic teams go out in a state of powerlessness. They do not follow a victorious army, and there is no military force ready to back them up. With no health coverage and no money or food, the apostles enter the various villages in their path *needing the people to whom they go*. They arrive in each place dependent on the community who receives them. They are allowed to take sandals for the rough paths and a

staff for navigating mountain trails and protecting themselves from the stray dogs that roam the streets of traditional Middle Eastern villages. It is a shepherd's staff.[3] They are to carry nothing else other than a message.

2. Jesus gives them a "theology of failure." He essentially tells them: If you are welcomed into any home—well and good—fulfill your ministry while based in that place and don't move about looking for more comfortable lodgings. If they do not receive you, shake off the dust "under the feet." This refers to the dust stirred up by your feet that permeates your clothing. Shaking it off is a symbolic gesture that means "I am finished with you and am leaving. Furthermore, as I leave, I take nothing from this house, not even its dust" (Acts 13:51; 18:6). This dramatic gesture can help the apostles leave behind them any lingering sense of failure. It frees them to go on (like Paul and his band) to the next home or village "filled with joy and the Holy Spirit" (Acts 13:52). Having tried and failed, they must now move on. It is astounding to see Jesus on this *very first* outreach beyond the range of his voice offering advice on how to deal with failure.[4]

This extraordinary exit strategy also relates to the assumed method of entry into those same homes in the first place. There is no suggestion that they yearned for a conquering army to proceed them or that they felt the need to take with them any form of aid that might assure some kind of a welcome. Jesus' admonition is in harmony with D. T. Niles, the famous Sri Lankan theologian, who is well known for having said, "Evangelism is one beggar telling another beggar where they are passing out free food." Across the centuries, powerful Muslim and Christian communities have often happily followed in the wake of conquering armies.

3. Jesus directed them to engage in holistic mission. The first item on his list of assigned tasks was the proclamation (*kēryssō*) of the need to repent.[5] They were then instructed to cast out demons and to heal the sick.

With these three principles in their "theology of mission" the Twelve set

---

[3]Mt 10:10 specifically mentions "no sandals, nor a staff." T. W. Manson thoughtfully suggests that this is to affirm the mission as a journey into a holy place like the Temple Mount, where no staff or sandals were allowed (Mishnah *Berakot* 9:5, in Herbert Danby, *The Mishnah* [Oxford: Oxford University Press, 1933], p.10; T. W. Manson, *The Sayings of Jesus* [London: SCM Press, 1964], p. 181).

[4]Perhaps this is a result of his reflections on the cool reception he received in his hometown (Mk 6:1-6).

[5]For Jesus "repent" meant "accept to be found." Cf. Luke 15:4-7, discussed previously.

out two by two to fulfill their mandate. Now there were seven preaching voices for the new message rather than one.[6]

HEROD AND THE MURDER OF JOHN THE BAPTIZER (MK 6:14-29)

In the text, the Twelve are sent out, and then Mark pauses to reflect on Herod's complicated relationship with John and his anxieties over the emergence of Jesus (Mk 6:14-20).[7] The next scene is the murder of John, which is followed by the sudden return of the Twelve to Jesus.

John's assassination is not a strange, violent incident that interrupts the flow of the account of the sending out of the apostles.[8] Rather, as we will see, it is a critical key to understanding the entire series of episodes that stretches from Mark 6:7-52. Jesus and the apostles did not carry out their ministry in quiet villages, safe and secure from any harm. On the contrary, they lived and witnessed in the midst of tension and the constant threat of danger and death—as did the Christians in Rome for whom the Gospel of Mark was most probably originally written. How then does this play out?

Jesus the good shepherd engaged in his calling to rescue the lost sheep of the house of Israel. As noted, the mission of the Twelve extended that ministry, and that expansion inevitably attracted attention. Dictators are always anxious about movements they do not control. John the Baptizer was seen and known as the one who started it all, and he was already in prison (Mk 1:14). Herod interviewed John and liked to hear him even though he was perplexed by him. Judging John to be righteous and holy Herod tried to protect him. Perhaps John was the only one around Herod who told him the truth about anything.

One of the stories that circulated around Baghdad before the American invasion was that one afternoon Saddam Hussein had a cabinet meeting that ran late, whereupon he asked one of the ministers, "By the way, what time is it?" The minister dutifully replied, "Whatever time you say, Mr. President." John told Herod the truth.

---

[6]Jesus and six pairs of disciples.

[7]These verses are full of meaning, but they do not apply directly to our focus on the good shepherd. Thus I have chosen to note them in passing rather than to comment on them.

[8]R. T. France calls it a "digression." See R. T. France, *The Gospel of Mark* (Grand Rapids: Eerdmans, 2002), p. 255. Hooker sees it as a "somewhat artificial insertion." Hooker, *St. Mark*, p. 158.

Josephus affirms that Herod arrested John because he was afraid John might use his popularity to instigate a rebellion (*Antiquities of the Jews*, 18.118). Peter (Mark's source) and the "Jesus movement" knew of two additional reasons. These two components of the story came together at a party and triggered the murder of John. The first has to do with the guests.

Herod invited three classes of people that represented his primary local sources of power:

1. Courtiers (his administrative aids)

2. Officers (his top generals)

3. The leading men of Galilee (his appointed village mayors)

If Josephus is correct, this banquet took place in the Transjordan fortress of Machaerus. Mark seems to imply Tiberius. Both are possible. In either case, the banquet hall was full of powerful, important people. Granted, Herod was a dictator, but dictators must continually look over their right shoulder to be sure that the military is pleased, and over the left shoulder to keep an eye on leading citizens to assure their continued loyalty. The dominant culture of the Herodians was Greek. The party was a *symposium*, which was a drinking party. In the Jewish culture of the time, a young female member of the ruler's family would not dance for the guests at such a party. But in Greek culture that was not a problem. Herod Antipas was known for his extravagant parties (Josephus, *Antiquities*, 18:102). Enter Herodias.

Herod's personal honor was at stake when the girl (Josephus calls her "Salome") makes her mother's outrageous request. Herod, who was no doubt drunk, offered her half his kingdom, which was not his to give away. The Romans alone made such decisions. Furthermore, as he gave his grandiose promise he was probably trying to look like King Ahasuerus facing Esther (Esther 5:3). Herod should offer all of this to one young girl after a single dance performance? Only someone who was drunk would be so outrageously irresponsible. No one around the room took him seriously—except Herodias behind the door.

Herodias was angry at John and got her revenge by manipulating a banquet into a murder scene. With diabolic planning she insisted, through her daughter, that John's head be produced—*at once*! This would guarantee that all the guests would be eyewitnesses to the fact that John was actually dead. Soon they would report on the certainty of his death in their home communities. Her insistence on "right now" would also make it impossible for Herod to back down when the guests were gone and he sobered up.[9] Her scheme worked because she understood the cultural pressure she was exerting on her husband. The event would traumatize her daughter for the rest of the daughter's life. It would also irrevocably damage Herodias's relationship to her husband, having humiliated him in public. She didn't care. Personal revenge was for her an overpowering drug. Such was "the kingdom of this world" in which Jesus and his disciples proclaimed "the kingdom of God."

Herod was trapped. His strategic interests were at stake. Should he keep his promises or not? What about the military? At the end of the evening are these powerful guests to conclude that Herod only followed through on his promises if they suited him? What about Herod's pledges to them? Many governments across history have opted for what they perceive to be their "strategic interests" even if their actions in support of those interests violate what they themselves believe to be true and good.

At 8:20 a.m. on Wednesday, January 18, 1984, Dr. Malcolm Kerr, the president of the American University in Beirut, Lebanon, was assassinated in the elevator on his way to his office on the university campus. The seminary where I taught was two blocks away from the university, and Dr. Kerr was a personal friend. The Lebanese civil war had been raging for nine years, and many people mistakenly thought that it was winding down. Kerr's murder signaled to all that such was not the case. This horrifying event divided the school year into two epochs. The first was "before Kerr's murder" and the second was "after his death." A day after he was shot, I recorded in my date book, "Stayed in bed all day—sick in spirit." The next day I noted, "Met with seminary colleagues on the question of leaving." At that meeting we opted to lower our profile and stay, if we could, for the sake of our Lebanese colleagues and our students, national and international. But the concern in the minds of all of us was, *If President Kerr was assassinated despite two levels of security on the university campus, who would be next? Is any Westerner now safe in Beirut?* We had *no* security!

---

[9]He could easily promise, "I'll have him killed tomorrow morning at dawn! Executions are always at dawn." The next day he could back down saying, "The time isn't right. Wait a few days."

As a nation, Lebanon was shaken by Kerr's murder. For weeks it was impossible to discuss anything else with anybody. No thoughtful historian could meaningfully record the events of the city of Beirut that winter without discussing Kerr's murder. His assassination took about two minutes, and it changed *everything!*

The murder of John the Baptist must have been a similar event for Jesus, his followers and the province. This is reflected in the text, where after the account of the murder of John, Mark records, "The apostles gathered around Jesus" (Mk 6:30).[10] The verb used here (*synagō*) is often translated as "returned," but it more specifically means "gathered around."[11] The disciples felt the need to stand with Jesus after the murder of his relative. *Synagō* can also carry the overtones of "gather round in view of frightening signs."[12] John was brutally assassinated and suddenly *the mission of the Twelve was suspended!*

John was a relative of Jesus (Lk 1:36) and in the shame-honor culture of the Middle East, the murder of a relative is a grave concern for all the extended family in that it puts the family under enormous pressure to respond in some dramatic (violent?) way! At a drunken banquet, in order to please a dancing girl, John is assassinated by the direct order of the king (tetrarch) even though Herod feared John and respected him as a righteous and holy man (Mk 6:20)! Really? Unbelievable!

John was popular on the grassroots level of society. This is seen in a dramatic confrontation in the temple between Jesus and a delegation from the Sanhedrin. Jesus was challenged as to why he did "these things" (such as the cleansing of the temple). Jesus replied by asking the delegation what they thought about John. They were afraid to affirm that John's baptism was "from men" lest the people stone them (Lk 20:1-8). Recording the same incident, Mark notes that the people "all held that John really was a prophet" (Mk 11:32). When, therefore, the people of Galilee were in the first flush of their reaction to Herod's murder of a Hebrew prophet, they were inevitably in an extremely volatile state of mind. It would have been serious enough if John had been killed by the Romans—but when the

---

[10]My translation. See BAGD, p. 782.
[11]The Arabic versions of the last eleven hundred years have translated it as *ijtam'u* (gathered together) not *raja'u* (they returned).
[12]BAGD, p. 782.

murder was ordered by a Jewish "king" at a drunken party, a popular powder keg was inevitably lit! When might it go off? What could they do?

THE GATHERING OF THE APOSTLES AROUND JESUS AND ITS AFTERMATH (MK 6:30-32)

The apostles' task was not finished, and Jesus did not send for them, *but they came*—of course! The entire countryside was on fire, and the least the apostles could do was to "gather around him." The meaning of the text is clear when the setting is taken seriously (see fig. 6.3).

1.	The apostles gathered around Jesus	
	and told him all that they had done and taught.	COME AWAY TO
	He said to them, "Come away to a place in the wilderness[a]	The Wilderness
	all by yourselves and rest a while."	
2.	For many were coming and going	MANY COME
	and they had no leisure, even to eat.	No rest
3.	And they went away in the boat	GO AWAY TO
	to a place in the wilderness by themselves.	The Wilderness

[a]My translation. The word *erēmos*, which appears here, is the same word that is used in Lk 15:4, where the ninety-nine are left in "the wilderness."

Figure 6.3. The disciples report to Jesus, who opts for a "quiet day" in the wilderness (Mk 6:30-32)

In January of 1983 in Beirut, we struggled to respond, as did the disciples. They managed to focus on reporting the details of their ministry rather than spending their time in endless discussions of "the situation." The disciples were often thick-headed, and that characteristic reappears before this series of events is over. But as they "gathered round" Jesus (Mk 6:30), they behaved nobly. In any age and place, what do you do when a relative of your leader is murdered? You go to that leader and stand with him, offering as much support as you can. The most important thing is to be there! The disciples accomplished that act of solidarity with courage and singleness of purpose.

After the disciples gave their reports, Jesus ordered a withdrawal to the other side of the lake to some place where only shepherds roam. The text gives the reason for this proposed retreat. "Many were *coming and going* and they had no leisure, even to eat" (v. 31). This is the only instance in the Gospels that speaks of people both "coming and going," and nowhere else is there any mention of Jesus being so pressed that "they had no leisure, even to eat." Why this sudden back-and-forth flow of people? All across Galilee people wanted to know how Jesus planned to respond to this horrifying murder of his relative! They came from across the land to hear from his lips what he intended to do, and some of them then went back to report his initial response. Naturally, there was a huge wave of sympathy flowing to Jesus from the entire province. Perhaps he would lead them? We can almost hear the disciples saying to one another:

> What do we do now? Is it all over? These people are erratic, violent and irresponsible. We have no protection under law! Who is next? Our movement had two leaders, Jesus and John. Long ago Nathan the prophet criticized David's personal life, and Nathan was respected for doing so. But now John criticizes the king's private life, and Herod kills him! But then, this butcher's father killed his favorite wife and three of his sons—for nothing! So what can we expect from a son raised by such a father? Our problem is, can we really proclaim the "kingdom of God" in a world where the "kingdom of Herod" *murders John at a drunken banquet to please a dancing girl?*

Jesus must react. He is allowed some time, but he *must* respond! What are the options? The more obvious alternatives include:

1. Agitate for a regime change.

2. Join the developing messianic resistance movement that would soon be known as the Zealots.

3. Join the group of assassins who arose in response to the census ordered by Quirinius (A.D. 6-9) and later were given the name *sicarii*.[13]

4. Go underground as a movement and stop all public proclamation (at least for a year or two).

5. Complain to the Roman governor in Damascus that Herod has violated Roman law and is bringing shame on the entire Roman occupation.

6. Seek an audience with Herod to point out politely that they are all his loyal subjects and should not be treated this way (Joanna is a disciple

---

[13]Martin Hengel, *The Zealots* (Edinburgh: T & T Clark, 1976), pp. 46-49.

and her husband, Chuza, is a member of Herod's court [Lk 8:3]; maybe he can get an audience for them).[14]

7. Lower their profile; namely, scale back their "seven preaching voices" to one (Jesus) and maybe that would be enough. Perhaps Herod would relax and they could function in a small, quiet way that would not attract attention.

8. Quit and go home.

What was it going to be? Jesus decided that they must withdraw in the wilderness and rest a while to pray and think together about the best of their options given the situation.

They escaped by boat from the highly charged pressures of the crowds hoping to find a quiet, isolated place of rest. But thousands followed them on foot around the lake, and it appears that a wind picked up, slowing the progress of the boat. (Later that night the wind would gather strength.)[15] On arrival, to their dismay, a "great throng" *from all the towns* awaited Jesus and the rowers! Among those in the crowd were Herod's spies (or those who would be interviewed by Herod's security forces). Herod was *very interested* in Jesus' response to the death of his relative. Everything Jesus did and said would be reported to Herod as soon as possible. Having lived for ten years under Middle Eastern military dictatorship, I am deeply convinced that it is much easier to assume the presence of Herod's spies than to imagine their absence. To ignore this consideration is to ignore historical realities. The Preacher of Ecclesiastes wrote,

Even in your thought, do not curse the king,
　　Nor in your bedchamber curse the rich;
For a bird of the air will carry your voice,
　　Or some winged creature tell the matter. (Eccles 10:20)

Kings and dictators are not only interested in what you *do* and what you *say*, but also in what you *think,* as is demonstrated in this text.

As the boat reaches the shore, Jesus sees the unexpected crowd. What will he now do? Get angry and send them away? The text is displayed in figure 6.4.

---

[14]Chuza was most likely present and could have provided the details of the murder to the apostles.
[15]The people on foot had much further to go, but if there was a headwind, those walking would have had time to arrive first.

1. 6:34When he went ashore, he saw a *great crowd,*   A CROWD
   and he had *compassion* for them,   Gathered
   because they were like *sheep without a shepherd.*   (Needed: a good shepherd)
   And he began to teach them many things.

2.   35And when it grew late, his disciples came to him
      and said, "This is a place in the wilderness (*erēmos*),
      and the hour is *now late.*   ALL NEED
      36*Send them away* to go   TO EAT
      into the surrounding country and *villages*   (no food here)
      and buy themselves something to eat."

3.   37But he answered them,
         "You give them *something to eat."*   YOU FEED THEM
         They said to him, "Shall we go,   (we can't!)
         and buy two hundred denarii worth of bread,
         and give it to them to eat?"

4.   38And he said to them,
            "How many loaves do you have? Go and see."   FIVE LOAVES
            And when they had found out, they said,   Two fish
            "Five and two fish."

5.   39Then he commanded them all to   "He makes me
               lie down in companies (*symposia*) *in the green pastures.*   lie down in
               40So they reclined in orderly groups[a] of hundreds and of fifties. green pastures"

6.   41And taking the *five loaves and the two fish,*   FIVE LOAVES
            he *looked up to heaven,*   Two fish
            and *blessed* and *broke the loaves,*

7.   and *gave them to the disciples*
         to set before the people.   YOU FEED THEM
         And he *divided the two fish* among them all.   (they can)

8.   42And *all ate and were satisfied.*
      43And they *took up twelve baskets full*   ALL EAT
      of broken pieces and of the fish.   All filled
      44Those who had eaten the loaves   (food left over)
      numbered five thousand men.

9. 45Immediately he *forced his disciples* to get into the boat   A CROWD
   and go before him to the other side, to Bethsaida,   Dismissed
   while he *dismissed the crowd.*   (the shepherd takes charge)
   46After saying farewell to them,
   he went up on the mountain to pray.

---

[a]This word *prasia* appears only here in the New Testament. It originally means a "garden bed" (BAGD, p. 698). Here it means "orderly groups."

Figure 6.4. The good shepherd spreads a banquet of life (Mk 6:34-44)

THE RHETORIC

This text uses the classical ring composition format that we saw in Psalm 23 and Luke 15. This means that the account has been very carefully recorded. A series of ideas/events are presented, come to a climax and then are repeated backwards. The key words on the right attempt to summarize the main ideas that are presented and then repeated.

COMMENTARY

This text is crucial to our topic and each cameo deserves careful scrutiny (see fig. 6.5).

1. [6:34]When he went ashore, he saw a *great crowd,*	A CROWD
and he had *compassion* for them,	Gathered
because they were like *sheep without a shepherd.*	(Needed: a good shepherd)
And he began to teach them many things.	

Figure 6.5. Jesus becomes a compassionate shepherd (Mk 6:34)

The kings of Israel were always thought of as the shepherds of the flock. Moses and David were the two outstanding past leaders who were especially remembered and honored as shepherds.[16] But Herod, a current Jewish "shepherd of the flock," had just demonstrated some of the worst characteristics of the bad shepherds described in Ezekiel 34:1-10. On seeing the huge press of people awaiting him on the shore, Jesus made the decision to jettison his previous plan. Herod, the bad shepherd, presented a challenge. Something had to be done. Not out of desire for retaliation against Herod but out of *compassion* for the scattered flock, Jesus saw a crowd that to him were "like sheep without a shepherd" and quickly initiated a new plan.[17] He opted to present himself as the long-promised divine good shepherd to this large crowd of common people (who had gathered from across the province). For centuries God had promised to one day come himself and be their shepherd. That day had now arrived.

A full account of those few days would have filled more space than was available to Mark for his entire Gospel. The text offers an inspired summary. How does Jesus begin?

---

[16]Washington and Lincoln hold this honored place in American history.

[17]Note Ezekiel 34:5, where Israel is seen as a flock that is scattered over the mountains with no shepherd.

The text affirms that Jesus' first action was to teach them "many things." Oh that we had recordings of all that he said to them on that occasion! Jesus was a riveting speaker and had a great deal to say. Naturally the focus of his remarks would have been on how to respond to the game-changing tragedy that was heavy on all their hearts. What was the path of his choosing through those deep waters? When called on to deal with great injustice, was there an alternative to retaliation? The law of Moses commanded, "An eye for an eye and a tooth for a tooth," and that legislation was very much in force. No one can take two eyes for an eye, but the injured person has the divine right to gouge out *one eye* in retaliation for the loss of *one eye*. Was there another way?

Jesus' teachings in the light of the tensions of the hour were so totally engaging that no one noticed the passing of time. But the disciples became aware of a looming logistical problem that is described in cameo 2 (see fig. 6.6).

2.   ³⁵And when it grew late, his disciples came to him
      and said, "This is a place in the wilderness (*erēmos*),
      and the hour is *now late*.   ALL NEED
      ³⁶*Send them away* to go   TO EAT
      into the surrounding country and *villages*   (no food here)
      and *buy themselves something* to eat."

Figure 6.6. The disciples' "quick fix" (Mk 6:35-36)

Farmers are always glad to sell their produce, and villages have shops. Furthermore it will take some time to reach the inhabited areas. It seems that no one in the crowd wandered away because of the riveting nature of what they were hearing. But the crowd was huge. *We did not invite them. They totally disrupted our plans and we are not responsible for them. They must take care of themselves*, thought the disciples. But Jesus created another option.

Leading citizens from *across the province* were present at Herod's banquet. They represented the rich and powerful. Now Jesus has before him the poor, the angry and the powerless from "all the towns." The powerful who returned to their villages no doubt reported what happened at Herod's *banquet of death*. Jesus decided to give the poor from those same towns and villages a *different kind of banquet* to talk about. The people could then compare the two banquets and come to their own conclusions regarding them. This can be called "first-century mass communication."

Paul S. Minear of Yale writes,

Jesus had just bestowed the gift of his Kingdom and his power, to the end that
men might be healed. King Herod bestowed a similar gift [to Salome, v. 23],
and it is used in spiteful vengeance to secure a prophet's death. The *banquet
of King Herod* in the palace offers the sharpest contrast to the banquet of *King
Jesus in the wilderness* (vss. 39-44).[18]

The account of the new banquet continues. The carefully constructed
center of the passage needs to be examined as a whole (see fig. 6.7).

3.	[37]But he answered them,	
	"You give them *something to eat."*	YOU FEED THEM
	They said to him, "Shall we go,	(we can't!)
	and buy two hundred denarii worth of bread,	
	and give it to them to eat?"	
4.	[38]And he said to them,	
	"How many loaves do you have? Go and see."	FIVE LOAVES
	And when they had found out, they said,	Two fish
	"Five and two fish."	
5.	[39]Then he commanded them all to	"He makes me
	lie down in companies (*symposia*) *in the green pastures.*	lie down in
	[40]So they reclined in orderly groups of hundreds and of fifties.	green pastures"
6.	[41]And taking the *five loaves and the two fish,*	FIVE LOAVES
	he *looked up to heaven,*	Two fish
	and *blessed* and *broke the loaves,*	
7.	and *gave them to the disciples*	
	to set before the people.	YOU FEED THEM
	And he *divided the two fish* among them all.	(they can)

Figure 6.7. The *symposia* of life (Mk 6:37-41)

As noted, Jesus chose to fulfill his destiny as the good shepherd rather
than rail at Herod for his brutality. In the light of that choice, what will this
good shepherd do? The sheep were lost, wandering with no one to care for
them. Therefore Jesus gathered them up and led them as his flock. Once
gathered, he had them *lie down* in *green pastures* where he *fed them* until
they *wanted no more.* All of this takes place in the extended center of the
text (cameos 3-7). The particulars are as follows:

---

[18]Minear, *Saint Mark,* p. 81; italics added.

Cameo 3. The scene opens with Jesus telling the disciples to feed the hungry themselves. The disciples' response is slightly sarcastic. Jesus had sent them out with *no food* and *no money*. Does he now *really* expect them to feed five thousand people? Even if they could somehow produce two hundred denarii, would that be enough money to feed this throng? A denarius was a day's wages for working man. If a laborer had a family of five and spent half of that amount each day for food, his denarius might feed ten people one meal. Two hundred denarii might feed two thousand, but there were five thousand people (and more). A ninth-century Arabic version of Mark's Gospel adds an insightful interpretive flair to the text: "and give them to eat [that each of them might have a little bit]."[19] In short, the disciples were saying, "Following the commands you gave us as you sent us out, we have nothing! Even if we could somehow gather two hundred denarii, that sum would not buy enough food for this huge crowd. You must send them home while there is still light!"

Usually the center of such a rhetorical ring composition is either the climax of the passage or at least a point of special emphasis. Here that center appears to include three cameos (see fig. 6.8).

4.	[38]And he said to them,	FIVE LOAVES
	"How many loaves do you have? Go and see."	Two fish
	And when they had found out, they said,	*With the Disciples*
	"Five and two fish."	
5.	[39]Then he commanded them all to	"He makes me
	lie down in companies (*symposia*) in the green pastures.	lie down in
	[40]So they reclined in orderly groups of hundreds and of fifties.	green pastures"
6.	[41]And taking the *five loaves and the two fish,*	FIVE LOAVES
	he *looked up to heaven,*	Two fish
	and *blessed* and *broke the loaves,*	*With Jesus*

Figure 6.8. The climax of the cameo (Mk 6:38-41a)

Cameo 4. This center opens with cameo 4. Jesus asks them to find and bring what they have. They obey and produce five loves of flat bread and two small fish. Is this a joke? Jesus the good shepherd then begins to act and Mark records those actions in a pointed manner.

---

[19]The translators of this Greek to Arabic ninth-century version knew that two hundred denarii worth of bread would not begin to feed five thousand people. They confirm this view by adding this interpretive note (*Vatican Borgiano Arabic* 85, folio 66).

Cameo 5. Why is cameo 5 in the very center? The answer can perhaps be found in Psalm 77–78. Psalm 77 recollects the exodus and concludes, "You led your people *like a flock*, by the hand of Moses and Aaron" (Ps 77:20). Thus the psalm invokes "Moses the good shepherd" and the exodus. Psalm 78 continues this theme and focuses on Israel's lack of faith. The text reads,

> They tested God in their heart
> > by demanding the food they craved.
> They spoke against God, saying,
> > "Can God spread a table in the wilderness? . . .
> Can he also *give bread*
> > or *provide meat* for his people?" (Ps 78:18-20)

Faithless Israel, in the psalm, casts a shadow over the disciples in the story before us. The disciples obviously doubt Jesus' ability to produce food. Can he (Jesus) *give bread* and *meat* to the *people* here in the *wilderness*? Of course not! Everyone must be sent home!

The voice of Psalm 23 can also be heard in the background. Jesus is obviously "in the presence of his enemies," and those enemies have just killed John, thereby demonstrating their life and death power over a person like Jesus. The situation appears to be hopeless. What will Jesus do? He begins with a *command* (*epitassō*) addressed to the crowd using the language of a military officer giving orders to his soldiers.[20] Jesus is not making a suggestion—his words are a specific command. In like manner Herod gave a *command* to a soldier to murder an innocent prophet! What will Jesus command? They are to recline in groups of fifties and hundreds.[21] Indeed, they are to "lie down in green pastures."[22] The language is precise. They are to recline "*symposia, symposia*." The word repetition is a Hebrew style, while the word itself is a Greek and Roman word that occurs only here in the entire New Testament. Herod had a *symposia* where everyone was expected

---

[20]The word *epitassō* only appears four times in Mark. Two of them are in this text.

[21]In his commentary on the four Gospels, Dionysius ibn al-Salibi translates "circles" (*halaqa, halaqa*) (Ibn al-Salibi, *Tafsir*, 1:608). This suggestion is probably correct. The Greek text (like the Arabic) uses a Semitic style and literally reads *prasiai prasiai* (group, group). This same linguistic feature is repeated in the next phrase with the word *symposia*. Middle Eastern peoples traditionally sit in circles if possible for all social occasions.

[22]The command is to recline, not to sit. To recline for meals was common.

to get inebriated.[23] Now Jesus creates his banquet, *his symposia*. The good shepherd takes over after the failures of the bad shepherd to care for his flock. Herod fed the rich and powerful while Jesus feeds the common folk. The first became a *banquet of death*; the second turns into *a banquet of life*.

Cameo 6. Jesus took the meager resources his disciples provided and used language soon to reappear in the eucharistic Supper (Mk 14:12-25). He looked up to heaven, blessed, broke and finally gave the bread and the fish to his disciples for distribution. The five loaves and two fish were totally inadequate for the needs of the people. But those meager resources, *with his presence and blessing*, became enough for all and provided an unimagined surplus. "I shall not want" (Ps 23:1) and "my cup overflows" (Ps 23:5) became a present reality for thousands at Jesus' *symposia*. But keeping in mind the good shepherd tradition, there is another nuance in the text.

In some unexplained way Jesus *produces* a meal. In the culture of the day such was the work of women. Thus when Jesus *multiplies the loaves* and the *fish* he is in a profound sense on the same page with a woman who *produces* a meal. We have already noted the female overtones of "You prepare a table before me" (Ps 23:5). Both Psalm 23:5 and Mark 6:41-42 describe a person who provides and offers a meal to other people. In Psalm 23 the one who prepares/provides the food is God. In Mark 6:41-42 the person who provides/offers the food is Jesus. In both texts the task is a traditional female responsibility now assumed by a male. Acting as a *shepherd* Jesus connects with the men in the crowd. As he *produces a meal* he identifies with the women reclining before him.

Across the Middle East, bread is considered sacred. Walking along a busy street it is common to find a small crust of bread on a ledge or on top of a low wall. Someone had found it in the street and rescued it for someone else to eat. Abraham Rihbany grew up in Mount Lebanon in about 1850 when all of what is now Lebanon was a part of Syria. Some fifty years later he wrote,

> As the son of a Syrian family I was brought up to think of bread as possessing
> a mystic sacred significance. I never would step on a piece of bread fallen in

---

[23]John Calvin notes that "the strong wine so excited Herod that he forgot all gravity and common-sense and promised to give this dancing-girl up to half of his kingdom" (John Calvin, *Harmony of the Gospels* [Grand Rapids: Eerdmans, 1970], 2:142).

the road, but would pick it up, press it to my lips for reverence, and place it in
a (stone) wall or some other place where it would not be trodden upon.[24]

Of course the disciples picked up the "broken pieces." It would be unthinkable
not to do so.[25] Only twelve baskets? There were thirteen of them in the apostolic band! Each disciple managed to fill his own basket, and it appears
that no one thought about a basketful for Jesus! The disciples were still frail
human beings and more details of that frailty surfaced a few hours later.

There is no discussion of how the miracle happened and no immediate
reaction from the disciples. But something far more important is built into
the tradition. The exodus story as retold in Psalm 78:29 reads, "And they ate
and were well filled, / for he gave them what they craved." In that account it
was *God who acted* to provide *bread and meat in the wilderness*. In the text
before us Jesus "looked up into heaven," but *he, Jesus*, was the *prime mover*
in the story. The Christological assumptions of the story are clear and
stunning. This is not a Greek overlay placed on the text a generation later.
Rather this powerful Christological affirmation appears here in this early or
perhaps earliest Gospel. It is built on a deep awareness of the Hebrew Scriptures behind the text. But the amazement of the reader is not only engaged
at the display of high Christology in the text, but also on the level of the
historicity of the story itself—how can these things be?

In the recent past an Anglican bishop (and long-time personal friend) related
to me an account that had been reported to him by the sister of the woman in
the story. This event took place in a Middle Eastern country about 2003.

> As a traditional feast day approached, a Christian lady in an upperclass family
> [in the Middle East] invited some of her non-Christian neighbors to assist her
> the morning of the feast in preparing a large pot of rice for distribution to the
> poor [as was their custom]. The women gathered and cooked the rice, and the
> time for its distribution arrived. But before they carried the pot into the street,
> the lady of the house insisted on praying over rice in the name of Jesus, asking
> him to bless it that it might be *enough* for the poor who would come to receive
> this gift of food. She didn't want anyone to leave hungry or humiliated. After

---

[24]Abraham Rihbany, *The Syrian Christ* (Boston: Mifflin, 1916), p. 193.

[25]Hooker thinks that such fragments "would have become stale and inedible." Not so, rather they
would be preserved for others (Hooker, *St. Mark*, p. 167). Such small pieces of bread are a special
ingredient in a variety of traditional Middle Eastern dishes.

the prayer, the ladies carried the very large pot of rice into the narrow street, placed it on a table, and began distributing it to those gathered to receive it. The lady of the house then returned to the kitchen to supervise the clean up. After a few minutes one of the ladies involved in serving came into the kitchen, and with wide eyes and a pale countenance said to her, "We do not understand what is happening! We have been distributing this rice in large bowlfuls for some time and the level of the rice in the pot has not gone down!"

My source for this recent story is impeccable. Not being Christians, the ladies distributing the rice were not familiar with the story of the feeding of the five thousand. Those with ears to hear, let them hear.

With all of this in mind we return to our story of Jesus the good shepherd, who leads and feeds his sheep (see fig. 6.9).

7.	and *gave them to the disciples* to set before the people. And he *divided the two fish* among them all.	YOU FEED THEM (they can)

Figure 6.9. The disciples participate (Mk 6:41b)

Jesus does not expose the disciples' doubts or criticize them for their lack of faith. Rather he feeds the flock and involves the skeptical disciples in the distribution. Yet *he* remains the primary figure. The story continues (see fig. 6.10).

8.	[42]And *all ate and were satisfied.* [43]And they *took up twelve baskets full* of broken pieces and of the fish. [44]Those who had eaten the loaves numbered five thousand men.	ALL EAT All filled (food left over)

Figure 6.10. All are satisfied—in the wilderness (Mk 6:42-44)

There is no record of how this happened; it is simply related as a witnessed event. All were satisfied, as was Israel in the wilderness. But the story was not over. Cameo 9 contains yet more surprises (see fig. 6.11).

9.	[45]Immediately he *forced his disciples* to get into the boat and go before him to the other side, to Bethsaida, while he *dismissed the crowd.* [46]After saying farewell to them, he went up on the mountain to pray.	A CROWD Dismissed (the shepherd takes charge)

Figure 6.11. Disciples are forced to leave and the crowd is dismissed (Mk 6:45-46)

Jesus was an integral part of his community. He grew up among them and naturally could feel the pulse of a crowd of his fellow Galileans. John's account of the multiplication of the loaves records, "they [the crowds] were about to come and take him by force to make him king" (Jn 6:15). Hooker finds in the language of this section "a hint that the crowd could easily become an army prepared to march behind Jesus."[26]

The larger good shepherd tradition includes (as we have seen) the good shepherd account in Zechariah 10:2-12, where the opening verse includes the affirmation "the people wander like sheep; / they are afflicted for lack of a shepherd" (Zech 10:2). This verse is very close to Mark 6:34, which reads, "he had compassion on them, because they were like sheep without a shepherd."[27] Building on the similarities between these two texts, we note that Zechariah alone in the good shepherd tradition predicts a transformation of sheep into victorious soldiers with their battle bows and mighty men who can even defeat "the riders on horses" (Zech 10:5). Their victories will be so comprehensive that they will "trample the foe in the mud of the streets" (Zech 10:5). The five thousand men in front of Jesus would no doubt be pleased if a sudden attack on Herod and his military could achieve such results. Herod deserves it! Perhaps it was time to participate in a fulfillment of Zechariah's prophecy!

Jesus could give riveting speeches and he knew how to command. He had organizational skills and could arrange large groups of people efficiently in "companies" and "orderly groups." How about "platoons and companies"? Would that not also be possible? His ability with logistics was amazing! He could unexpectedly feed five thousand people, a number that in itself was a small army. At least they could march on Herod's new palace in Tiberius and give vent to their anger! Jesus is Joshua, and everyone knew what Joshua accomplished. How about, "Jesus the new Joshua"? Why not?

The disciples were apparently getting swept up into a rising tide of popular expectations. Jesus *forced them* (*anagkazō*) into the boat, and got them away from the misdirected enthusiasm of the crowd. He then dismissed the

---

[26]Ibid.

[27]The text also recalls Num 27:17. However, Numbers states a wish. Zech 10:2 and Mk 6:34 are statements about the condition of the flock in the present. Thus Zechariah appears to be closer to Mk 6:34 than the text in Numbers. See also Mt 9:36.

people. That is, he sent them home. As Jesus did this, he was continuing to interact with Herod. One way or another Herod would hear everything. The message to Herod was,

> You can sleep securely in your bed, Herod! I am not coming after you, nor are any of my followers. There is no need to beef up your body guard. Nor will I try to infiltrate them and have you murdered. I threw away a golden opportunity to make life *very* difficult for you. I sent all the people home. Try to remember this![28]

Psalm 23	Mark 6:7-52
a. *"The Lord is my shepherd"*	(6:34ff.: Jesus had compassion on them, became their shepherd, and the flock followed him.)
b. *"He settles me down in green pastures"*	(6:39: He commanded them to *"recline in green pastures."*)
c. *"He leads me in the paths of righteousness"*	(6:34: "He taught them many things" and demonstrated to them a righteous path of nonviolent response to injustice.)
d. *"I walk through the valley of the shadow of death"*	(6:24-29: John had just been killed. The shadow of death loomed over them.)
e. *"I will fear no evil"*	(6:50: He told them, "Have no fear. I am!")
f. *"...your staff comforts me"*	(6:8: "Take nothing . . . except a [shepherd's] staff.")
g. *"You prepare a table before me"*	(6:41: Jesus prepared a banquet of life in the face of Herod's banquet of death.)
h. *"In the presence of my enemies"*	(6:21-28: Herod, an enemy, was "watching.")
i. *"You anoint my head with oil"*	(6:13: The disciples had just "anointed many with oil.")
j. *"I shall not want"* and *"My cup overflows"*	(6:42: They "were filled" and "they took up twelve baskets full of broken pieces.")
k. He rests me *"beside still waters"*	(6:51: "the wind ceased and they crossed over.")

Figure 6.12. Psalm 23 and its echoes in Mark 6

---

[28]It appears that Herod remembered. When Pilate sent Jesus to Herod for judgment, Herod joined with the soldiers in mocking Jesus but refused to judge him (Lk 23:6-11) or cooperate in any way in his death.

Jesus demonstrated to the five thousand, and to the province, how a good shepherd cares for his sheep. He deliberately set aside all violent options.

As the same time Jesus knew that on the basis of his decision, all Galilee would soon be buzzing as people compared the two banquets and the two shepherds. This was Jesus' response to the murder of his relative. To close the day, after dismissing the crowd, Jesus retreated, *at last*, "up on the mountain to pray" (Mk 6:46). But the story was not over. The coming of night presented new challenges.

Before moving on to Jesus' repetition of the second miracle of the exodus, it may be helpful to review the points at which Mark's presentation of the good shepherd story mirrors Psalm 23. Figure 6.12 includes references from before and after the multiplication of the loaves.

Jesus was taking over leadership of a lost flock and becoming their good shepherd. Peter most likely understood Jesus' intentional dramatic actions and passed on his perceptions to Mark, who faithfully recorded, arranged and edited them for a frightened Roman church. The banquet in the wilderness was over, and it ended with Jesus retreating into the mountains for his much needed time of prayer. The text then moves on.

But before examining the night of storm, it may be useful to summarize the "music in the background" of this dense account. All of the following are involved:

- *word* (he taught them) and *sacrament* (he broke the bread)
- a banquet of death and a banquet of life
- Ezekiel 34 (and the other prophetic accounts of the good shepherd)
- the good shepherd and the bad shepherd
- Psalm 23 with its green pastures in the wilderness
- bread and meat in the wilderness
- a foreshadowing of the Eucharist
- Moses and the exodus

The final theme in this list is so interwoven with the wilderness banquet that it seems right to reflect on it briefly. After some time in prayer, Jesus was ready to rejoin the disciples. Here we continue our story.

There was a strong wind arresting their progress on the lake.[29] Figure 6.13 displays the carefully written text.[30]

1.	[6:47]And when evening came,	
	the *boot* was in the *middle*[a] *of the sea*,	DISCIPLES & JESUS
	and he was alone on the land.	Separated
2.	[48]And he saw that they were making headway painfully,	ADVERSE
	for the wind was against them.	Wind
3.	And about the fourth watch of the night,	
	he came to them,	JESUS
	walking on the sea.	Moves to
	He meant to *pass by them*,	*Lead Them*
4.	[49]but when they saw him walking on the sea	DISCIPLES
	they thought it was a ghost and *cried out*,	see "a ghost"
	[50]for they all saw him and *were terrified*.	All are Afraid
5	But immediately he spoke to them and said,	JESUS
	"Take heart; *it is I.* Do not be afraid."	"I am"
	(ἐγώ εἰμι· μὴ φοβεῖσθε)	Fear Not
6.	[51]And he got into the boat with them,	WIND
	and the *wind ceased*.	Ceased
7.	And they were utterly astounded,	
	[52]for they *did not understand* about the loaves,	DISCIPLES & JESUS
	but their *hearts were hardened*.	Still Separated

[a]The RSV correctly translates *en mesō* as "in the middle."

Figure 6.13. Wind, fear, Jesus and still waters (Mk 6:47-52)

THE RHETORIC

The text is yet another example of ring composition and is constructed using the prophetic rhetorical template. Seven semantic units (cameos) present a series of ideas which are then repeated backwards. Seven is the perfect biblical number, and this format is common to the Old and the New Testaments. Ring composition often relates the center to the outside. This feature also appears here in that the disciples are in focus in the *beginning*, the

---

[29]Moses also faced a strong "wind that blew all night" (Ex 14:21).

[30]The division of the text here at 6:47 agrees with the ancient Greek paragraph divisions (*kephalaia*).

middle and at the *end*. In the beginning (1) they are separated from Jesus. In the center (4) they see him and are afraid. At the end (7) they do not understand and are hard of heart.

COMMENTARY

The account opens (see fig. 6.14).

1. ^{6:47}And when evening came,
        the *boat* was in the *middle of the sea*,   DISCIPLES & JESUS
        and he was alone on the land.   Separated

Figure 6.14. Disciples alone in the middle of the sea (Mk 6:47)

The exodus contains two major miracles. The first is the passage through the *sea of reeds*. The second is the feeding of the people in the wilderness with *bread* (manna) and *meat* (quails). The account of the feeding of the five thousand presents Jesus as more than a new Moses. In the aftermath of John's murder, Jesus *himself* feeds the people "bread and meat" (fish) in the wilderness.

Now a second mighty work is described. Jesus leads the twelve disciples (who represent Israel) through the deep water (see fig. 6.15).

2.   ⁴⁸And he saw that they were making headway painfully,   ADVERSE
        for the wind was against them.   Wind

Figure 6.15. The disciples and the wind (Mk 6:48a)

When this text is compared with the exodus, some of the details are different and some are strikingly similar. In both accounts there is a sea that must be crossed, a problem in crossing it and a threatening political figure (Pharaoh in the first, and Herod in the second). In each story the wind is an important factor. These four components encourage the reader to reflect on the two accounts together. The text continues (see 6.16).

3.   And about the fourth watch of the night,
        he came to them,   JESUS
        walking on the sea.   Moves to
        He meant to *pass by them*,   *Lead Them*

Figure 6.16. Jesus is able to make headway in the sea (Mk 6:48b)

Mark uses the Roman division of the night into four watches. The "fourth watch" is our 3-6 a.m. The disciples had been rowing all night and were unable to make headway against the wind. Jesus overcame the wind and the water as a part of his appearance to the disciples. Hooker writes,

> Jesus has already revealed himself to the disciples as Moses' successor by feeding the people—indeed, as greater than Moses, since he himself provided the people with bread: if he now reveals himself as one who is able to cross the sea, this too would seem to point him out not merely as Moses' successor, but as one who is far greater. . . . Jesus does not come to rescue the disciples from a storm; they are there to witness his epiphany.[31]

Shifting for a brief moment to the present we can note that things now whispered in the ear will one day be "shouted from the house tops." That day has not yet come. For more than two decades I have been privileged to have a Middle Eastern friend who is a leading pastor in his country. I will call him "Pastor Farid." His own spiritual journey led him from a non-Christian background to faith in Jesus the Messiah. In 2005 Pastor Farid described to me an event that had recently taken place in his district. An illiterate fisherman in Pastor Farid's area grew up with no contact with Christians or knowledge of the stories of Jesus. One night while fishing on the large river that runs by his village, the fisherman saw a man clothed in shining white robes approaching him walking on the water. In great fear lest the approaching figure be an evil spirit, the fisherman asked him who he was, and the man in white robes answered, *Ana 'Isa al-Masih* (I am Jesus the Messiah). After a life-changing conversation, the man standing on the water told the fisherman, "You must follow me!" and then faded from sight. In the morning the fisherman, with no idea what to do next, rowed back to the shore, beached his boat, unrolled his prayer rug on the shore and placed an earthenware pitcher of water beside it. The fisherman then knelt down on the prayer rug and bowed his head to the ground. While in that position, he reached over and poured water from the jug over the back of his head. In time the fisherman managed to find local Christians, who took him to talk to Pastor Farid. The good pastor listened to his story with its unique ending and told the fisherman, "I believe you and am thrilled at your story. May the

---

[31]Hooker, *St. Mark*, p. 169.

Lord bless you. But we do not baptize ourselves. Come, let us talk."

In time the fisherman became an informed and committed follower of Jesus the Messiah. He was delighted to find that the original disciples had talked in the night to 'Isa al-Masih in an encounter similar to his own. Over the last generation unknown thousands of people in many parts of Africa, Asia and the Middle East have had epiphanies of Jesus. Only we in the rationalistic West are surprised by such events.

With Saint Mark and Morna Hooker of Cambridge University the text affirms an epiphany of Jesus for all the disciples together. But there is an additional possibility for interpreting the text. Jesus did not originally approach the boat. As observed by Hooker, this was not a rescue operation. Jesus was moving out in front of the boat in the direction in which the disciples were trying to row. We are told in Psalm 77:19-20 that God led his people *through the great waters* "like a flock by the hand of Moses and Aaron." A shepherd can only lead his flock from the front. Like Moses, Jesus the good shepherd was moving to a position in front of the boat in order to lead his frightened disciples through the deep and troubled waters. He only turned aside to talk to them when he heard their fearful cries. Furthermore, the disciples were unable to make any headway in the water. Jesus demonstrated his ability to do so. The text records (see fig. 6.17),

4.	⁴⁹but when they saw him walking on the sea	DISCIPLES
	they thought it was a ghost and *cried out*,	see "a ghost"
	⁵⁰for they all saw him and *were terrified*.	All are Afraid

Figure 6.17. They are afraid (Mk 6:49-50a)

They were already on edge because of the assassination of John. Jesus' bold challenge to Herod was a gauntlet thrown down, and no one could predict how the mercurial Herod might react. Exhausted after hours of unsuccessful rowing against a stiff wind, the disciples now witnessed an "apparition" in the night! There is little wonder that they were afraid! Mark was careful to record that "they all saw him." This was not a private vision to one of the disciples. The *disciples' fear* appears here in the middle of the passage (cameo 4). Jesus heard their cries and his response is recorded in cameo 5 (see fig. 6.18).

5	But immediately he spoke to them and said,	JESUS
	"Take heart; *it is I*. Do not be afraid."	"I am"
	(ἐγώ εἰμι· μὴ φοβεῖσθε)	Fear Not

Figure 6.18. It is I (Mk 6:50b)

The phrase *egō eimi* (it is I) is the Greek translation of what God said to Moses at the burning bush (Ex 3:14). There God identified himself to Moses with the phrase, "I am that I am," and now Jesus is revealing himself to his disciples with the same "I am."[32] Once again the text informs its readers about who Jesus really is. The "I am" has appeared and is talking to them. The two final cameos are displayed in figure 6.19.

6.	[51]And he got into the boat with them,	WIND
	and the *wind ceased*.	Ceased
7.	And they were utterly astounded,	
	[52]for they *did not understand* about the loaves,	DISCIPLES & JESUS
	but their *hearts were hardened*.	Still Separated

Figure 6.19. The wind is conquered, the disciples are hardened (Mk 6:51-52)

The wind and the sea were conquered by Jesus' presence, and the disciples were astounded—because they had not understood "about the loaves." The issue was not that they were too dull to understand that Jesus had performed one miracle and thus, of course, he could perform a second. Rather, they did not understand that in the multiplication of the loaves Jesus had demonstrated himself to be the incarnation of the divine among them. Namely, *God* had fed Israel in the wilderness. Now *Jesus* had fed his followers in another wilderness. Having failed to understand the deeper meaning of *that* event, they could not understand that Jesus, beyond Moses, was controlling the sea and not just leading them through it. All of this was because "their hearts were hardened," and thus they were not able to understand. In the exodus there was a sinister figure whose heart was hardened, namely, *Pharaoh* (Ex 14:8). But now the "bad guy" in the account was no longer Pharaoh or Herod, but, horror of horrors, the opposition had become *the disciples themselves* who like Pharaoh were *hard of heart*!

---

[32]*Egō eimi* means both "I am" and "I am he." With no verb "to be" in Semitic languages, Syriac and Arabic versions read "I [am] he" or "I [am] I."

As mentioned, the wilderness supper has ties to Psalm 23 and to the exodus. The night on the lake has only one passing connection to the psalm (the still waters), but it strongly reflects the story of the exodus. This is seen in figure 6.20.

A *strong wind blows at night.*	(Ex 14:21)
The *disciples are unable to pass through the sea.*	(Ex 14:1-2)
The disciples are in the *middle of the sea.*	(Ex 14:22)
The *disciples are terrified.*	(Ex 14:10, 13)
The disciples are told, *"Be courageous."*	(Ex 14:13 LXX)
I am reveals himself to them.	(Ex 3:14)
They are told, *"Do not be afraid."*	(Ex 14:13)
Jesus helps them *through the sea.*	(Ex 14:6)
The disciples hearts were *hardened* like pharaoh's.	(Ex 14:8)

Figure 6.20. Features appearing in the crossing of the lake and in the crossing of the Sea of Reeds

These nine parallels tie the two accounts together in a profound way.

It remains for us to compare Mark's presentation of the good shepherd with the list of major components in the good shepherd story observed again and again from Psalm 23 to Luke 15.

The sweep of the biblical good shepherd story now appears in figure 6.21.

All ten of the core aspects of the traditional story of the good shepherd appear (in some form) in Mark 6. Using the numbers from figure 6.21, the following can be noted:

1. *The good shepherd.* Jesus accepted that role and fulfilled it.

2. *The lost flock.* On arrival at the distant shore (Mk 6:34), Jesus had compassion on the lost flock who had no shepherd.

3. *The bad shepherds.* The three prophetic texts all criticize the bad shepherds. This theme intensifies here in Mark 6. Few shepherds of Israel were as bad as Herod (perhaps Ahab?).

4. *The good host.* As is clear in Psalm 23:5 and assumed in Luke 15:8-10, so here God/Jesus prepares/provides a meal.

5. *The incarnation.* Jesus takes up and fulfills the long-awaited role of the good shepherd who is described in Luke 15:4-7. Here Jesus, the good shepherd, walks on stage and demonstrates his identity through what he does.

6. *The price paid.* Jesus gathers, teaches, organizes, feeds and leads the flock who is in the wilderness with no shepherd. In the process he proves himself to be the missing good shepherd, and at the same time

Ps 23:1-6	Jer, Ezek, Zech	Lk 15:4-7	Lk 15:8-10	Mk 6:7-52
1. *God* is the good shep.	*God* is the good shep.	*Jesus* is the good shep.	*Jesus* is the good woman	*Jesus* is the good shep. & new Moses
2. Lost sheep (no flock)	----- Lost flock	Lost *sheep* + Lost flock	Lost *coin* -----	----- Lost flock
3. Opponent: death & "enemies"	Bad sheep in Jer, Ezek, Zech	Bad shepherd loses a sheep	Careless woman loses coin	Herod: bad shepherd, murderer
4. A Good host(ess)? and a meal	-----	A good host and (offered food)	A good hostess and (offered food)	Jesus produces a meal[a]
5. Incarnation implied	Incarnation promised	Incarnation realized	Incarnation realized	Incarnation realized
6. Price paid: bring back	Price paid: search for, save bring back	Price paid: search for, find carry back	Price paid: light lamp, sweep, search -----	Price paid: gather, order, feed, lead flock. Confront Herod.
7. Repentance is *return to God* *(shuv)*	Repentance is return to the land *(shuv)*	Repentance is *return to God* *(metanoeō)*	Repentance is *return to God* *(metanoeō)*	The "flock" "accepts to be found."
8. -----	Ezek: bad sheep Good & bad shep.	Good/bad sheep	-----	Disciples: hard-hearted
9. A meal for the psalmist	-----	A celebration with friends	A celebration with friends	A meal for 5,000
10. Story ends in the *house*	Story ends in the land	Story ends in the *house*	Story ends in the *house*	At the end, people *go home*. The boat *arrives*

[a]The disciples *distribute* the food. Jesus *produces* the food. When Jesus multiplies the loaves he is on the same page with God, who prepares a table (Ps 23:5), and the woman who entertains her friends (Lk 15:8-10).

Figure 6.21. Mark and the classical account of the good shepherd (Ps 23 to Mk 6:7-52)

he confronts Herod. Herod's response is unpredictable, and Jesus may pay a high price for this public confrontation. Is Herod retaliating in Luke 23:11?

7. *Repentance.* Neither the Greek word *metanoeō* nor hints of the Hebrew word *shuv* appear in Mark 6. Yet a great crowd of people ran on foot around the northern end of the lake in order too be with Jesus. They were not passive. They came to him, listened to him, followed his commands to divide in groups and recline. At the end of the day they accepted his solution to the crisis with Herod and gave up their desire to "make him King" (Jn 6:15). They remained obedient to the shepherd, who during the day had fed them and demonstrated great compassion for them. At his command they went home. They were "in the wilderness" and they "accepted to be led/found." This acceptance is a crucial component in repentance as defined by Jesus (see Lk 15:4-7).

8. *Bad sheep.* The disciples in the boat reflect the "bad sheep" aspect of the traditional story of the good shepherd. In spite of all that they witnessed, they fail to understand the identity of Jesus that was on display before them.

9. *Celebration.* This aspect of the story is assumed. The five thousand people "ate and were satisfied." Bread and fish constituted a good meal. For hungry Israel, bread and meat in the wilderness was surely a celebratory occasion. Was it any less so for the five thousand who were likewise fed in the wilderness?

10. *The ending.* The account of the great throng in the wilderness and the story of the high wind on the sea end with "goodness and mercy" for all. In the first instance the people go home reinforced by hours of teaching and a good meal. In the second, the wind ceases and the disciples (and Jesus) arrive safely on the distant shore.

The cluster of accounts in Mark 6:7-52 are like a diamond with many brilliant facets. No adequate summary is possible. With the risk of some overlap with the previous list, the highlights appear to fall into five summary categories.

THE THEOLOGICAL CLUSTER OF THE GOOD SHEPHERD AND THE NEW MOSES (MK 6:7-52)

1. *Jesus the good shepherd demonstrates his identity by reenacting Psalm 23.* The multiple themes that connect this account with the long tradition of the good shepherd (previously noted) make clear that Jesus is acting out the psalm and thereby affirming himself to be the long-promised divine presence among the people.

2. *Jesus, the good shepherd, offers a banquet of life to his flock.* Herod had a banquet for the important people across the province. It was a *symposia* (a drinking party) that ended in murder. It became *a banquet of death.*

    Jesus' followers came from "all the towns." Jesus offered them *a banquet of life.* This banquet was Jesus' public response to the murder of his relative. He rejected inevitable cultural pressure to initiate some form of organized resistance. Rather, he reprocessed his own anger into grace and thereby taught the people to do the same. Which banquet would shape the future for the five thousand?

3. *The new Moses feeds the people in the wilderness and brings the disciples through the deep waters.* Moses received bread and meat from God in order to feed the people in the wilderness. Jesus went beyond Moses as he "looked up to heaven" and fed the people *himself.* He was the divine presence among them.

    Jesus, the new Moses, appeared to his disciples in the stormy waters and brought them through the sea.

4. *The Eucharist.* A foreshadowing of the Eucharist is unmistakable. Jesus took the bread and fish, looked up into heaven, blessed, broke it and (through his disciples) distributed it to the now-gathered flock. A part of the meaning of the Eucharist was and is the extending of table fellowship with the Lord to the many.

5. *The disciples do not understand.* In the green pasture the disciples appear to join the crowd with its apparent enthusiasm for some form of political action. They did not understand "about the loaves" or the meaning of the night vision on the water.

An eloquent summary of some of the richness of this passage is provided by Paul Minear:

> The encountering of storms by the Apostles (and later on by the Church)
> is thus seen to be a part of God's plan when he commands the Church to
> take to the boats in order to prove his presence to them in the crises of
> their journey. This "lesson," then, is the same as that taught by the story
> of the wilderness supper. The loaves prove the power of the Lord (Ps 23)
> to sustain and to nourish his people in all situations. But the disciples did
> not understand this, nor did they understand that the Messiah was
> seeking to use the wilderness and the tempest to teach them how to feed
> his sheep and to triumph over their adversities . . . "It is I: have no fear."[33]

The parable of the good shepherd as it appears in Matthew's Gospel now
awaits us.

---

[33]Minear, *Saint Mark*, p. 84.

7

THE DISCIPLES AS GOOD SHEPHERDS IN MATTHEW 18:10-14

The previously examined Old and New Testament texts on the good shepherd have shown a progression in the identification of the shepherd. Initially *God was the good shepherd* (Ps 23). The three prophetic accounts added *bad shepherds* who failed and needed to be replaced by *God, the good shepherd* (Jer 23; Ezek 34; Zech 10). Moving into the New Testament, in Luke 15:4-7 and in Mark 6 *the good shepherd is Jesus*, who incarnates the promise that God himself will come and put things right. Continuing on, here in Matthew the *good shepherd* tradition is expanded further. W. D. Davies and Dale Allison have succinctly and insightfully written about Matthew 18:10-14:

> Throughout Christian history the man with the sheep has been identified with Jesus himself, and our parable has often been conflated with Jn 10. . . . One guesses that the First Evangelist likewise identified the shepherd with Jesus and took the logic of the parable to be this: God (v. 14) approves of the actions of the shepherd Jesus who set out for the lost little ones (vv. 13-14), and those who believe in Jesus must do what he did.[1]

To slightly expand on this, in Matthew 18:14 *God the father* is eager that none of "these little ones" might perish, and in this parable *Jesus* describes

---

[1] W. D. Davies and Dale C. Allison, *The Gospel According to Saint Matthew*, International Critical Commentary (New York: T & T Clark 2004), 2:773.

himself as engaged in rescuing the lost. Finally, *the disciples* are addressed personally in the opening verse with the words, "See that *you do not despise one of these little ones*" (cameo 1; see fig. 7.1 on p. 191). The disciples are to search out the strayed as does the shepherd in the parable. What Jesus is already doing, the disciples are invited to do. The "little ones" referred to (cameo 1) are sheep that went astray (cameos 3-5) and if they are not found, they will perish (cameo 7).

It is often assumed that Luke presents the original parable and that Matthew's Gospel is reshaping it for a new situation.[2] It is also possible to assume, with the Gospel authors, that both accounts of the good shepherd originate with Jesus. Talented preachers are able to remold a good story and use it in different sermons. Jesus can be seen as such a preacher. As Klyne Snodgrass has written, "It is reasonable to think that Jesus told this parable several times and quite possibly for different purposes."[3]

Granting that there are many differences between the two accounts, there is also an impressive list of dramatic components that link them together. These include:

- The flock comprises one hundred sheep.
- One sheep is lost.
- The shepherd searches for the one.
- The shepherd leaves the ninety-nine in the wilderness/on the hills.
- There is joy in finding the one.
- There is more rejoicing over the one than over the ninety-nine.

The overall context in Matthew is the band of disciples from whom one or more sheep have gone astray. The parable confirms that the shepherd goes after the one and strives to find it with the assumed intention of restoring it to the flock. This situation fits the life of the early church, but does it also fit the life and ministry of Jesus? I think it does.

In the first year of his public ministry Jesus was followed by large, adoring crowds. As early as Mark 1:45 we discover that Jesus was so popular that he could not openly enter a town but was obliged to remain in the countryside

---

[2]Joachim Jeremias, *The Parables of Jesus* (London: SCM Press, 1963), p. 40.
[3]Klyne Snodgrass, *Stories with Intent* (Grand Rapids: Eerdmans, 2008), p. 104.

and people came to him. In Mark 3:7 we discover that he was sought out by a great multitude from Galilee, Judea, Jerusalem, Idumea, beyond the Jordan, Tyre and Sidon. In short he achieved "rock star" notoriety. On a wave of international popularity, many decided to follow him. But as time passed they found that his chosen path was a narrow way and that each disciple was expected to carry a cross. Both the "right" (the Pharisees) and the "left" (the Herodians) opposed him (Mk 3:6). Some adherents decided that the price required to follow him was too high and the path too steep. John 6:66 says "that many of his disciples drew back and no longer went about with him." But between those who "followed" and those who "drew back" we can easily assume others who did their best to follow but were not prepared for the rigors of the way and "went astray." They had not rejected him, but had simply fallen behind and lost their way. What then does Jesus do with such followers?

At the end, were not Peter, who denied Jesus, and Thomas, who doubted him, among those who "went astray"? In addition, what about the ten apostles who ran away in the garden and were not heard of again until Easter morning? Did they not also stray from the path? What then can be said about the "Jerusalem street"?

Throughout holy week the "Jerusalem street" was with Jesus. In fact he was so popular that the high priests were obliged to make contact with Judas, who could lead them to Jesus at night when he was not surrounded by a *sympathetic* crowd. Most of those who made up the crowd were likely not disciples but were in some sense supporters. That same crowd followed him to the cross, where they remained standing *quietly* (Lk 23:35). To stand rather than sit was and is a mark of respect. In Mark "those who passed by" railed at him, as did the solders and the high priests. The cry "crucify him" was heard in Pilate's judgment hall, but *not at the cross*. At the cross, *the crowd was quiet.*[4] By the end of the day "all the multitude . . .when they saw what had taken place," became sympathetic and "returned [*hypostrephō*] beating on their chests" (Lk 23:48).[5] To "beat on the chest"

---

[4]This fact is discussed in detail by David Flusser, "The Crucified One and the Jews," *Judaism and the Origins of Christianity* (Jerusalem: Magnes Press, 1988), pp. 575-87.

[5]*Hypostrephō* appears in the Septuagint nineteen times, and sixteen of them translate the Hebrew *shuv* (return/repent). The word "home" is not in the text.

is to exhibit deep remorse and repentance. The very early Old Syriac translation adds a telling interpretive note at the end of Luke 23:48 that reads, "Woe to us. What has happened to us? Woe to us from our sins."[6] The editors who added that early note clearly understood that those who stood all day at the cross were deeply distraught over their sins and were at least on their way to authentic repentance. "Beating on his chest" was what the repentant tax collector did in Jesus' parable (Lk 18:13). This large crowd was now ready to hear Peter's call to repentance at Pentecost (Acts 2:37-38). Even hanging on the cross Jesus, the good shepherd, was still gathering "the lost sheep of the house of Israel."

This becomes even more poignant in John's account of Easter night, when the disciples were gathered in fear. Jesus appeared in their midst, and it is natural to assume that they expected a tongue lashing. From the point of view of their faith, they were "little ones" who "*had gone astray.*" Jesus had every right to despise them. When he needed them the most they had run away, breaking their bold promises of loyalty. Rather than complaining about betrayal, Jesus engaged in a *drama of reconciliation* as he extended his peace to them by saying, "Peace be upon you." After showing them his hands and his side he repeated the ceremony. Once again the good shepherd was finding and restoring wayward sheep. Then came the challenge, "As the Father has sent me, even so I send you" (Jn 20:21). Having seen yet again how he found and restored wayward sheep, Jesus commanded his frightened disciples to follow his example. They, as strayed sheep, were gathered, reconciled, commissioned, empowered and send out to do likewise. Abandoning the faith is not a part of this picture.

An apostate is a person who makes a deliberate choice to discard the faith. There are good reasons for understanding that Matthew 18:12-13 does not discuss such types. The one who "went astray" is simply a sheep who wandered a bit too far up a side path and failed to follow as the rest of the flock moved on. The failure is serious, in that if not found and restored, the straying sheep will die in the wilderness. In short, the parable fits the min-

---

[6]*Evangeleion Da-Mepharreshe, The Curetonian [Syriac] Version of the Four Gospels,* ed. and trans. F. Crawford Burkitt (Cambridge: Cambridge University Press, 1904), 2:413. Note: the Sinai Syriac copy includes the same comment.

istry of Jesus on a very deep level, and at the same time it challenges the leadership of the church in every age. The text is found in figure 7.1.

1. [18:10]See that you do not despise one of *these little ones;*	THESE Little Ones		
2. for I tell you, that in heaven their angels always see the face of *my Father* who is *in heaven.*[a]		MY FATHER In Heaven	
3. [12]What do you think? If a man has a *hundred sheep,* and *one* of them has *gone astray,*		100 SHEEP One Lost	
4. does he not leave the *ninety-nine on the hills* and go in *search* of the one that went astray?			LEAVE & Search
5. [13]And *if he finds* it, truly I say to you, he rejoices over it more than over the *ninety-nine* that never went astray.		ONE FOUND 99 Never Strayed	
6. [14]So it is not the chosen will before[b] *my Father* who is *in heaven*		MY FATHER In Heaven	
7. that one of *these little ones* should perish.	THESE Little Ones		

[a]Some ancient Greek texts add "for the son of man came to save the lost."
[b]The Greek word ἔμπροσθεν does not translate easily. It means "in the presence of, before."

Figure 7.1. Jesus the good shepherd: A model for his disciples (Mt 18:10-14)

THE RHETORIC

Using ring composition this parable presents a *prophetic rhetorical template* composed of seven inverted cameos. The beginning (1), the middle (4) and the end (7) focus on "the little ones." Moving from the outside toward the center, cameos 2 and 6 are a pair that tells of "My father who is in heaven." Cameo 2 mentions seeing the *face* of the Father. Parallel cameo 6 discusses being in the *presence* of my father. The two are closely matched. Cameos 3-5 present a parable on "finding the lost."[7] As noted in the words to the right of

---

[7]Davies and Allison note the chiasm of this passage but see it as a series of five ideas that then repeats backwards. In their analysis "gone astray" appears three times and becomes the center

the text, cameos 3 and 5 focus on "the one and the many" while the climax in the very center (cameo 4) displays the willingness of the shepherd to *risk* leaving the ninety-nine *on the hills* to go after the one what went astray. Without that decision to take a huge risk and go off alone into the mountains/hills, the parable collapses.

Luke 15:4-7 (see chap. 6) is composed of three sections. The first two present the *mashal* (the parable) which is followed by the *nimshal* (the extra information needed to understand and apply the parable).[8] The text here in Matthew 18:10-14 also divides into three sections, which is summarized in figure 7.2.

The *little ones* and *my Father* (cameos 1-2)   (People and God)
   The parable of the good shepherd (cameos 3-5)   (Shepherd and sheep)
My Father and the *little ones* (cameos 6-7)[a]   (People and God)

---

[a]In Luke 15:4-7 the first and second sections tell the parable. The third section provides the application.

Figure 7.2. The three major sections of Matthew 18:10-14

The various pairs of cameos fit together so perfectly that if the parable in the center were missing, cameos 1-2 would connect with 6-7 and together still make sense, even though the passage would be greatly weakened if that were to happen. As is fairly common in Scripture, the center of the ring composition presents a parable.[9] The text with its seven cameos offers a balanced and artistically satisfying verbal picture of a good shepherd in the setting of the love of a divine Father who cares for the "little ones."

INTERPRETATION

The first two cameos are displayed in figure 7.3.

Initially we must answer the question, who are these "little ones"? Matthew 18:1-4 opens with the disciples' question, "Who is the greatest in the kingdom of heaven?" (Mt 18:1). The expected answer is "the rich and

---

of the rhetorical form. The climactic center is perhaps better understood to be the shepherd's *leaving* and *searching* as seen in figure 7.1. See Davies and Allison, *Saint Matthew*, 2:768.

[8]*Mashal* is the Hebrew word for "parable." Using the same Hebrew root (*mshl*), *nimshal* is a Hebrew word for the explanation that is often attached to a parable.

[9]Kenneth E. Bailey, *Finding the Lost* (St. Louis: Concordia Press, 1992), pp. 16-17. A further example is Lk 7:36-50.

powerful." The list of "the greatest" naturally includes people like Joseph of Arimathea, Nicodemus, Johanna, the wife of Herod's minister of finance[10] and the centurion whose slave Jesus healed. These types are surely the kinds of people the movement needs and must cultivate. Not so! Who then was on that special list?

1.[18:10]See that you do not despise one of *these little ones*;	THESE Little Ones	
2. for I tell you, that in heaven their angels always see the face of *my Father* who is *in heaven*.	MY FATHER In Heaven	

Figure 7.3. The little ones and my Father (Mt 14:10)

Jesus' answer is startling. The greatest in the kingdom is like a humble child who obeys the voice of Jesus. Ibn al-Tayyib comments, "Jesus made clear to the disciples in his answer to their question that the attitudes which they demonstrated by asking the question, (if they persisted in those attitudes) would bar them from entrance into the kingdom of heaven."[11]

As Ibn al-Tayyib astutely observes, the disciples are undermining their own credibility with Jesus by even asking this question! But our query remains: Who are these "little ones"? In these same verses (18:1-4) there are three references to a *paidion*, and the word clearly means "a young child." Jesus called a child to him and "stood him up" in the middle of the disciples. The child responded to Jesus' call without fear or hesitation. Jesus then described that particular child by saying, "whoever humbles himself like *this child* is the greatest in the kingdom of heaven" (Mt 18:4). Jesus was not talking about children in general but rather about "this child." Some children, in the presence of a group, realize that they have an audience and start showing off. Such children are neither humbling themselves nor obeying anyone. Others become afraid and run away. It is highly likely that, in his own gentle way, Jesus had already demonstrated kindness to a particular child near him who warmed to him. He then said, "Whoever receives *one such child* in my name receives me"

---

[10]Richard Bauckham, *Gospel Women* (Grand Rapids: Eerdmans, 2002), pp. 135-46.
[11]Ibn al-Tayyib, *Tafsir*, 1:310.

(Mt 18:5). The child Jesus was talking about was the one he had befriended, called, picked up and placed in the center of a circle of disciples. This particular child:

- was not afraid of Jesus

- exhibited unconditional trust in him

- obeyed him instinctively without making a fuss

- humbled himself before all

Jesus was without a doubt talking about a child who exhibited these characteristics. But in Matthew 18:5-6 the language and imagery shift. The "child" in verse 5 is replaced in verse 6 by "one of these *little ones who believe in me.*" The focus of attention is no longer on "a child" (*paidion*) but on "the little one" (*tōn micrōn*). The "little one" in mind is obviously old enough and mature enough to make a faith decision to believe in Jesus. Ibn al-Tayyib, writing in Arabic from Baghdad early in the eleventh century, says about this verse, "He [Jesus] calls them 'little ones' not because they were actually very young, but because of the assumptions of other people regarding them."[12] This view was already affirmed by John Chrysostom in the fourth century, who wrote, "He calleth little ones not them that are really little, but them that are so esteemed by the multitude, the poor, the objects of contempt, the unknown."[13]

Shifting to the twentieth century, Davies and Allison have written regarding Matthew 18:6, "The reference is no longer to literal children (as in vs. 1-5) but to certain members of the Christian community."[14] Which members?

Matthew 10:42 reads, "And whoever gives to one of these little ones (*tōn micrōn*) even a cup of cold water *because he is a disciple*, truly, I say to you, he shall not lose his reward." Here "the little ones" are defined as disciples of Jesus. Gundry translates it as "these little people."[15] William F. Albright calls them, "the common people."[16]

---

[12]Ibid., p. 309.

[13]John Chrysostom, *Homilies on the Gospel of Saint Matthew*, in Nicene and Post-Nicene Fathers (Grand Rapids: Eerdmans, 1983), 10:367-68.

[14]Davies and Allison, *Saint Matthew*, 2:760.

[15]Robert Gundry, *Matthew* (Grand Rapids: Eerdmans, 1982), p. 364.

[16]W. F. Albright and C. S. Mann, *Matthew*, Anchor Bible Commentary (New York: Doubleday, 1971), p. 218.

Societies or self-conscious groups of people naturally include both the strong and the weak. As some wit once said of Marxism, "In Communism all comrades are equal; however, some are more equal than others." Jesus had many disciples. Some of them were women of high rank and others were not well known.[17] Many of the early disciples were simple fishermen and a few of them became prominent. But what about the women and men who did not gain recognition and remained unknown?

Many organizations tend to despise the powerless. Paradoxically, to publically declare an interest in the powerless is one way of attracting attention and thereby gaining more power. In the recent past I was lecturing at an international seminar, and the first evening at dinner I was seated at a table for eight. Eager to get acquainted, we agreed to go around the table and each person give his or her name, country of origin, church tradition and some word about ministry. One person said, "I am so-and-so and I am an information manager." We were puzzled and someone asked, "What is an 'information manager'?" After a bit of clarification we found out that she was a librarian. Surprised, we responded, "*Librarian* is a time-honored title for a noble profession, why don't you call yourself a *librarian*?" She replied, "*Information manger* projects a power image. *Librarian* does not!" She turned out to be a very nice lady.

One is reminded of the numerous television ads (often filmed in a board room) that subtly inform the viewer regarding what clothes to buy, what glasses to acquire and what shoes to wear to appear powerful. Jesus promised the kingdom of God to the "poor in spirit" and announced that "the meek will inherit the earth" (Mt 5:3, 5). Among other things, the powerful tend to marginalize those who do not seek power. If you are not interested in acquiring power, you probably lack initiative!

Most organizations need some form of power (often called "resources") to carry out their goals. When the goals and methods of achieving those goals are noble, such seeking can be admirable. But the down side of that seeking is that the powerful tend to despise the powerless. The word *despise*

---

[17]Richard Bauckham argues cogently that not only were women among Jesus' disciples, but that Joanna of Luke 8:3 and Luke 24:10 is the apostle Junia of Romans 16:7. In any case Junia (female) was an apostle. See Richard Bauckham, *Gospel Women: Studies of the Named Women in the Gospels* (Grand Rapids: Eerdmans, 2002), pp. 109-202.

(*kataphroneō*) involves treating others with "scorn" or "contempt."[18] John
Bengel noted, "They [the disciples] appear to have done so, ver 1, 2."[19]

C. S. Lewis delivered an insightful oration to King's College, London,
titled "The Inner Ring." In it he it talks about the fact that human organizations usually have an inner ring that runs everything but is distinct from the
official board of directors of the organization. Those who yearn to enter that
inner ring will do almost anything to be accepted into its invisible membership. Naturally, those who are "in" subtly *despise* those who remain "out."
Lewis urges his listeners to reject the impulse to join the inner ring. He
suggests rather that they seek to become "sound craftsmen" in their chosen
professions. If they do, he says "other sound craftsmen will know it."[20] As
that takes place, scorn for the powerless usually fades. Jesus in this passage
begins by focusing on the quiet, unnoticed "little ones" in his band of followers.[21] They had special strengths, affirms Jesus, that were not on display.

The following is clear from the text.

First, in cameos 1-2 the "little ones" have "good press." From the earlier
verses it is hinted that such little ones are humble and trusting. Thus far there
is no hint of trouble.

Second, suddenly, in cameo 3, one of the little ones *goes astray*, and in
cameo 5 the reader is told that if that same "little one" is found, the shepherd
"rejoices." The text assumes that the little one who went astray *wants* to be
found! It is impossible to imagine a shepherd rejoicing over a sheep that
refuses to bleat guiding the shepherd to itself, and on being located, struggles
against being picked up and runs further away. The father in the parable of
the prodigal son rejoices over the younger son who clearly *wants to be found*,
even though in the far country he may have thought such an outcome impossible. As the parable stops the father cannot yet rejoice over "finding his
older son," who remains unwilling to accept the father's love. Returning to
Matthew 18, the reader knows that the wayward sheep *wants* to be found
because the shepherd is in ecstasy over its restoration.

---

[18]BAGD, p. 420.

[19]John A. Bengel, *Bengel's New Testament Commentary*, trans. C. T. Lewis and M. R. Vincent (1742;
repr. Grand Rapids: Kregel, 1981), 1:225.

[20]C. S. Lewis, "The Inner Ring," *Screwtape Proposes a Toast and Other Pieces* (London: Collins
Fontana, 1965), p. 39.

[21]Such texts would naturally have become important in the early church as it grew in numbers.

Third, the "little ones" (who are believers) have angels before the face of God who are interested in their welfare (cameo 2). But not only are the "little ones" so blessed.

Scripture assumes that every believer has a special angel assigned to look out for his or her interests. In Jerusalem Peter escaped from prison during the night due to the intervention of an angel. Ibn al-Tayyib thinks it was Peter's angel.[22] When Peter arrived at the house of Mary (mother of John Mark) and knocked on the door, Rhoda the maid answered the door, saw him and ran with joy to tell the household. They replied, "It is his angel!" (Acts 12:15). They did not imagine that it was "*an* angel" but rather "*his* angel." Jacob affirmed the presence of an angel who cared for him. In Genesis 48:16 he speaks of "the angel who has redeemed me from all evil." Paul knew that he lived his life in the presence of angels (1 Cor 4:9) and each of the churches of the book of Revelation had a special angel (Rev 2:1, 8, 12, 18; 3:1, 7, 14). Hebrews 1:14 echoes the same idea. But in Matthew 18 there is a special component. These angels had *access*!

In his concern for "the little ones" Jesus points out that their angels had direct, uninterrupted access to the Father. In Middle Eastern culture any item of business, in any organization, be it important or trivial, must pass the desk of the "big man." To get the electricity switched on in your newly rented apartment you typically need the signature of no less than the director of the department of electricity for the province. On one occasion, I was taking an old, small, well-used computer with me into the (non-Arab) country where I was teaching. It was hardly worth its weight as scrap metal, yet to import that machine (worth about $50), I was obliged to acquire thirty-seven signatures, which included the signature of the head of export and import for the entire country. There was no choice but to hire someone who had "access" to that office. It took us three full days. In the Middle East much of life is affected by such procedures. The key word is *wasta*, which literally means "connections." You need to know people with lots of connections if you want to expedite your business. If this is the way the world goes around in daily life, how much more important is it to have some good *wasta* that will assure you a presence before "my Father who is heaven"? To have a special agent who

---

[22]Ibn al-Tayyib, *Tafsir*, 1:309.

constantly has access to the very presence/face of God is the best *wasta* there is.[23] Such is the position of "the little ones" who are in danger of being despised. Look out, warns Jesus, they are more powerful than you think, they have friends in *very high* places! Furthermore, are such "little ones" only despised because they are powerless, or is there another reason?

Sometimes a "little one" goes astray. When that happens, do such sheep lose their special angelic representative before the Father in heaven? On this question the text is silent, but there is no hint that they do. So far as the reader knows, the mandate for the angel responsible for the strayed little one is not revoked. Thus the natural assumption is that the "little one" who has strayed is a believer who has fallen and needs help to return to the "paths of righteousness."[24] As discussed earlier, this is like Peter and Thomas after the cross.

These three aspects of the text lead the reader to understand the "sheep who has strayed" as a *follower of Jesus* who needs help, not as a *dropout* from the Christian faith who has consciously and deliberately chosen to leave.

Here again the ring composition of the text is important. The "little ones" of cameo 1 are the same little ones who at times go astray (cameo 4) and thereby are at risk of perishing (cameo 7). Apparently some of Jesus' followers were saying, "If they can't keep the pace—too bad! We must press on." It is easy to despise (cameo 1) those who slow you down and need special attention (cameo 4). Not so with Jesus the good shepherd.

This brings us to the parable of the good shepherd at the center of the text (see fig. 7.4).

3.	[12]What do you think?		
	If a man has a *hundred sheep,*	100 SHEEP	
	and *one* of them has *gone astray,*	One Lost	
4.	does he not leave the *ninety-nine on the hills*		LEAVE
	and go in *search* of the one that went astray?		& Search
5.	[13]And *if he finds* it, truly I say to you,		
	he rejoices over it more than over the *ninety-nine*	ONE FOUND	
	that never went astray.	99 Never Strayed	

Figure 7.4. The good shepherd and the wayward sheep

---

[23]In this case, you are not in trouble, and you do not need a lawyer, or an "advocate" (1 Jn 2:1). Rather you need assured access to the "presence."

[24]Like David in Psalm 23, where the text reads "he brings me back."

The metaphor of a flock composed of one hundred sheep, seen in Luke 15:4-7, now reappears. As discussed in our reflections on that text, the absence of a verb "to have" in Semitic languages, along with the wording of the text before us, assures that the hundred sheep mentioned here are the property of the shepherd. One of the sheep, we are told, "goes astray." The verb used is the aorist subjective passive of the Greek word *planaō*, which can mean either "go astray" or "be misled."[25] Is the lostness the fault of the sheep or the shepherd? Is the sheep "misled" or does it "go astray"?

Granting the possible translation of "misled," most certainly the option of "go astray" is correct. The parable has no hint of a bad shepherd who leads sheep astray, and the whole of the Christian tradition, East and West, to my knowledge, has understood the text to mean "go astray." Because the problem is not the shepherd's fault, it would be very easy for him to say, "I am not to blame. There are ninety-nine others. The one that is lost is small and not worth much. We are still in the mountains and for the *sake of the rest the herd*, I must accept this minor loss and use my energies to take care of the rest of the flock."

Add to this the fact that, as noted, the traditional Middle Eastern shepherd counts his flock late in the day. The shepherd in our parable could be sheltering his flock in a cave or in a rough enclosure such as shepherds have for centuries built in the wilderness and mountains of the Holy Land.[26] The details of the parable are tantalizingly brief. The shepherd, we are told, leaves the flock "in the mountains." Did he avail himself of a cave, drive the herd into it, block the entrance with a few large rocks and then set out to find the lost? Did he have an assistant shepherd or a dog like in Job 30:1? Were there other shepherds nearby with whom he could leave his flock? We are not told. As it stands, the text affirms the shepherd's willingness to *endure risk*. Chrysostom comments, "For even He Himself left the ninety and nine sheep, and went after this [lost sheep], and the safety of so many availed not to throw into the shade the loss of one."[27]

---

[25]BAGD, p. 665.

[26]I have seen such enclosures in the wilderness east of Bethlehem. The walls are about four feet high and are built out of rough field stones with thorns held in place by the rocks along the top edge. A single narrow entrance gives the shepherd a chance to count the sheep at the end of the daily grazing.

[27]John Chrysostom, "Homily 49," in *The Gospel of Matthew*, Nicene and Post-Nicene Fathers

Jesus could have very easily told a story about a shepherd who counted his flock on arrival back in the village, and leaving them in the safety of the sheepfold attached to his house, he returned to the mountains to search for the lost, as did M. P. Krikorian (the shepherd, noted earlier).[28] Rather, Jesus deliberately chose to tell a story about *cost* and *risk*.[29]

As the Second World War came to an end in 1945, my late friend Dr. Andrew Roy was serving in China as a professor under the Presbyterian Church. When the communists came to power in China in 1948, Dr. Roy opted to stay. After a few weeks he was placed under house arrest and then interrogated for two years before being allowed to leave. I was privileged to hear him discuss the details of those interrogations. His communist inquisitors kept trying to convince Dr. Roy that the teachings of Jesus were vastly inferior to those of Marx and Chairman Mao Zedong. Jesus' parable of the good shepherd was prominent in those interrogations. The communists insisted that to leave the *ninety-nine* in order to go after the *one* was irresponsible because the individual had value only as he or she contributed to "the people." Jesus left the herd exposed to danger and thereby failed in his primary task. He irresponsibly risked the safety of 99 percent of the herd.

Roy's answer was that the exact opposite was the case. By going after the *one* Jesus gave the *herd* boundless security in that each of them knew "If I get lost he will come after me." A failure to go after the one would leave those same ninety-nine with the ultimate insecurity of realizing "If I get lost, he will leave me to die." Yes, there was risk involved, but undeserved costly love was given to the *one* and thereby assured for the *many*. The radical nature of the shepherd's actions must not be overlooked.

Matta al-Miskin, the learned Coptic Orthodox Egyptian monk, has recently written,

> The church is not a closed and locked society, but rather a coming together of
> individuals. Its ministries and its faithfulness are measured by its concern for
> individuals, and its fidelity in regard to the weak, and the crushed who do not

---

(Grand Rapids: Eerdmans, 1983), p. 368.

[28]M. P. Krikorian, *The Spirit of the Shepherd: An Interpretation of the Psalm Immortal*, 2nd ed. (Grand Rapids: Zondervan, 1939), pp. 57-58.

[29]Matta al-Miskin notes, "He leaves the ninety-nine on the mountains and not in the sheepfold and goes in search of the one sheep that is lost in the mountains" (Matta al-Miskin, *The Gospel According to Saint Matthew* [Wadi Natron, Cairo: Dair Saint Maqar, 1999], p. 531).

exist in the eyes of the world. The world grinds down the individual and crushes the weak. But the church's first message is directed towards those whom the world has pulverized and neglected. Jesus did not compare himself to the priests or the great ones among the people but compared himself to the little ones. . . . [He said,] "whatever you have done to one of these my brethren, the little ones, you have done it to me." (Mt 25:40).[30]

The tension between the need to protect the herd and the importance of seeking the lost sheep is centuries old.

Sophocles's tragedy *Antigone* (composed in Athens in the fifth century B.C.) has been modernized. Some sixty years ago I had the opportunity to attend an unforgettable performance of the modernized version of this classical drama. In the play, two brothers lead separate sides of a civil war in the city-state of Thebes. In the process the two brothers kill each other. Creon becomes king of Thebes and decrees that one brother be buried with honor as a *hero* and the other left to rot in the sun as a *traitor*. Antigone, the sister of the brothers, secretly buries her disgraced brother and is caught and condemned to death. In the play there is a dialogue between Creon the king and Antigone the grieving sister. Creon gives a long speech defending his actions on the basis of society being like a great herd and that on occasion an individual (like her brother) must be sacrificed for the benefit of the society at large. The individual is not nearly as important as the herd, which must always be supreme. Antigone listens silently, and when Creon finished, with great passion she replies,

> Animals! Animals! Oh, what a *king* you would make, Creon,
> if only *men* were *animals*![31]

The twentieth century produced ruthless figures such as Hitler, Stalin and Mao Zedong, who were willing to sacrifice the lives of millions of their own people in order to promote their versions of "the greater good." The parable of Jesus is a bold and daring statement affirming the worth of the one, *even when lost*, and the willingness of the good shepherd to expose the flock to danger in order to seek that flawed "little one." One is drawn to ponder the

---

[30]Ibid., p. 530.
[31]I have not been able to trace the publishing details of this new version of *Antigone*. The line quoted here made such an impression on me that I am confident I have recorded it correctly.

influence this parable has had across history through the witness of the billions who have believed in the creator of the parable and his message.

Cameo 5 closes the parable. "If he finds it" introduces the possibility of failure. The shepherd may not be able to bring the strayed "little one" back to the fold. But if the costly efforts of the shepherd are rewarded, he rejoices more over the one than he does over the ninety-nine. In human terms, the greater the costly love expended, the greater the rejoicing if the lost is found and restored. Ah—but what about the ninety nine?

The critical question is, does the rejoicing focus on *the lost sheep*, or on the *successful efforts of the self-giving shepherd?* The Jesus tradition has an answer. In Luke 15:6-7 the shepherd has a party with his friends to celebrate the *finding* of the lost sheep. The sheep is not the center of attention. The shepherd says, "Rejoice with *me* for *I have found* my lost sheep." The good woman loses her coin, searches diligently and finds it. She also has a party where she tells her friends "Rejoice with *me* for *I have found* my coin." The *coin* is not the center of attention. The party is to honor the *woman*. In the third story the animals (sheep) and the coins (drachmas) turn into people. The prodigal, planning to become a *servant*, is reclaimed *as a son* by his father's costly demonstration of unexpected love. The father orders a party because, "My son was lost and is found." The passive is a "divine passive." The son was lost and the father found him and rescued him from the status of a *hired servant* to that of a *son*. He was so lost at the edge of the village that he thought the issue was the lost money and that he could work, pay and settle his "bill." The real issue was his father's broken heart, and all he could do was *accept to be found*. The young boy in the street tells the older son (Lk 15:27) that the banquet is spread because the father received the prodigal "with peace" (not safe and sound).[32] The community *will come* to congratulate the father, but *not* in order to welcome the prodigal, whom they hate. The older son complains, "You killed *for him* the fatted calf," erroneously thinking that the fatted calf was killed *for the prodigal*. It was not. The party celebrates the success of the father's efforts at reconciling his lost son (as with the shepherd and the woman). The same is true in the parable before us in Matthew. The shepherd "rejoices over it" (the sheep) because the shepherd's

---

[32]Bailey, *Finding the Lost*, pp. 167-70.

costly efforts were not in vain. He succeeded—he found the sheep—and the sheep was eager to be found!

In the summer of 1942, in Egypt, a group of us American Presbyterian missionary families and a number of single women were obliged to evacuate to Sudan in order to escape the approaching German army under Field Marshall Rommel. Some of our party managed to secure passage on a freighter from Port Sudan and sail around Africa across the Atlantic to North America. As they reported to us months later, one night in the middle of the Atlantic a deck hand got drunk and fell overboard. They were within range of German submarines and were observing strict blackout regulations. The chance of finding the sailor was extremely small and any search would endanger the ship. The captain made the courageous and risky decision to turn on the ships powerful spotlights and steer it in a circle hoping against hope that in the dead of night they might spot the tiny speck of a bobbing head among the waves. They circled, shouted and scanned the ocean with their spotlights for about an hour and—to the great joy of all—the man was spotted, retrieved and saved.

As told to me by eyewitnesses, the story does not mention what happened next. But surely there was some kind of a celebration among the officers and crew. Such a party would *not* be in honor of *the drunken sailor*! Rather it would celebrate the courageous captain who risked everything to find his man. Fine speeches would be made by the officers regarding the character of the captain who risked everything for one deck hand, and thereby demonstrated his deep commitment to the welfare of every member of the crew regardless of their rank. On such an occasion the drunken sailor could only apologize for putting all of them at great risk and thank the captain (and everyone else) for saving him.

Of course the shepherd rejoiced over the recovery of the lost sheep. His extraordinary efforts were not in vain. The risk of leaving the herd exposed in the mountains, paid off.

A beloved family pet, when lost and then found after great effort, receives extraordinary love. Jesus loved his disciples and his apostles, but a special reservoir of love was available for believers who strayed and at great cost were found and restored to the flock (like the disciples on Easter night). The shepherd's great love triggered great rejoicing! But a subtle shift takes place in this account.

As indicated previously, the sheep alone is responsible for getting lost. Thus the text is no longer simply discussing powerless and neglected members of the community. The good press that the "little ones" enjoyed earlier in the text shifts as the focus becomes those who have "fallen by the wayside." What was to be done with such cases? Jesus' answer is "the good shepherd goes after them," and if he is able to restore them, he rejoices more over them than over those who never went astray! What the rest of the flock thinks about all of this is not recorded but the mind is stimulated to ask about the ninety-nine.

Moving from sheep to people, not every flock (congregation) is happy to have their shepherd (pastor) spend lots of his or her time searching for the lost (less important) members of the congregation rather than spending it serving them! Sometimes such flocks accuse their pastor of "neglecting them." The older son in Luke 15:11-31 represents their point of view. "You gave him a calf? I didn't even get a goat!" No—the party held in the middle of the Atlantic was *for the captain*, not for the *drunken sailor*. Of course the captain was happy! Of course they all celebrated, but not because of anything the sailor did. They rejoiced over the *success* of the rescue operation!

The two final cameos in this passage are displayed in figure 7.5.

6.	¹⁴So it is not the chosen will before *my Father* who is *in heaven*	MY FATHER In Heaven
7.	that one of *these little ones* should perish.	THESE Little Ones

Figure 7.5. The Father and the little ones (once again) (Mt 18:14)

Yes, some who stray from the flock are not recovered. When this happens, they remain lost, and in fact they may perish. But let there be no confusion about the intent of the Father in heaven, who offers total approval of what the shepherd does. The shepherd does not lock the sheep in individual cages and drop a bit of hay into each cage once a day. Rather he takes them out into the free range of the open mountains, meadows and valleys knowing that some may go astray enticed by other valleys that appear to offer more green grass than those chosen by the shepherd. The shepherd's will (and the Father's will) for all the sheep is that they may heed his call and unfailingly follow where he leads. The fusion between the actions of the good shepherd and the desire of "my Father who is in heaven" is important for the intent of the entire text.

Having chosen the title "Father" as his primary name for God, Jesus is naturally eager to define his term. The parable in Luke 15:11-32 Jesus does so in an unsurpassed way. Our Matthew text contributes to that important effort. Even the weakest has access to "his Father" (cameo 2) and "his Father's will [pleasure]" is that they all be saved (cameos 6-7). He will not deny

Ps 23:1-6	*Lk 15:4-7*	*Mt 18:10-14*
1. Good shepherd is God	Good shepherd is Jesus	Good shepherd is Jesus (and the Father) (a model for Christian leaders)
2. Lost sheep (no flock)	Lost sheep and lost flock	Lost sheep (no flock)
3. Opponents: Death and "enemies"	Opponents: Bad shepherd loses a sheep	-----
4. Good host(ess)?	-----	-----
5. Incarnation implied	Incarnation realized	Incarnation realized
6. Price paid: bring back	Price paid: search for find carry back	Price: risk flock, search (find?)
7. Repentance is return to God *(shuv)*	Repentance is return to God *(shuv)*	Acceptance of being found (implied)
8. -----	Good/bad sheep	Bad sheep goes astray
9. A *celebration*	A *celebration*	Great rejoicing
10. Story ends in *house*	Story ends in *house*	-----

Figure 7.6. Psalm 23, Luke 15 and Matthew 18

their freedom by forcing that salvation on them (there are no cages).

It is now important to reflect on the text as a whole. As observed, the opening cameos (1-2) focus on *people*. The cameos in the center (3-5) introduce the *parable about sheep*. The two concluding cameos (6-7) return the focus to *people*. The close interaction between the two is important to keep in mind in the following discussion.

To recapitulate, the text opens by mentioning "little ones" who are in danger of being "despised." The text closes with a second reference to those same "little ones" and the hope (of the Father) that they will not "perish." The opening and the closing cameos discuss the same "little ones." We now know why some "despise" those little ones. They are not only weak and unnoticed, but in addition some of them have "gone astray." Some voices say, "Let them go! They had their chance and threw it away." The good shepherd chooses another option.

How does the good shepherd here in Matthew compare with the good shepherd tradition we have been tracing across biblical history? Part of that tradition can be seen in figure 7.6.

The Good Shepherd in the Tradition and in Matthew

A few brief reflections on figure 7.6 may be helpful.

1. *The good shepherd.* The good shepherd is God (also assumed to be Jesus). Matthew 18 harmonizes with the good shepherd in Luke and with the good woman. In Matthew 18 the identification of Jesus with the good shepherd is indirect rather than direct. The disciples tend to "despise" the little ones (cameo 1) who have strayed (cameos 3-4). Jesus goes after them (fulfilling the will of "my Father who is in heaven").

2. *The individual lost sheep.* An *individual* lost sheep (without any mention of a *lost flock*) again appears. Matthew 18 has a flock, but it is not lost. Psalm 23 has no flock at all, but it does speak of the psalmist who brings an *individual* back to the "paths of righteousness." This *individual* lost sheep disappears in the three prophetic accounts and now reappears.

3. *The opponents.* Matthew 18 (like Psalm 23) has no hint of any bad shepherd. The bad shepherd theme, which appears in all of the accounts starting with Jeremiah 23, is missing. Its absence is a throwback to Psalm 23, which has "death" and "enemies," but no bad shepherd.

4. *Host(ess?)*. The parable in Matthew has no female component (unlike Luke).

5. *Incarnation realized.* In Matthew 18 the good shepherd (Jesus) is implied as being active in history searching for the strayed sheep. The search may not always succeed, but the shepherd is engaged with the task regardless of potential failure. Jesus fulfills the task knowing that the will of his Father in heaven is the recovery of the lost. The reader knows the good shepherd tradition and thus naturally identifies the good shepherd with God.

6. *Price paid.* The shepherd jeopardizes the safety of the flock (and his own safety) as he searches for the sheep that has gone astray. The shepherd engages in this costly task knowing that there can be no rescue without it.

7. *Repentance.* The word *repentance* does not appear in Matthew 18. But the reader knows that the sheep must be eager to be found or the search is in vain. The projected rejoicing on the part of the shepherd assumes that eagerness. The shepherd is not looking for a carcass. The sheep is alive and must want to be found. The sheep's participation is a critical component of repentance as defined by Jesus in Luke 15:4-7. That same theology of repentance is at the heart of the parable of the prodigal son, where again the word *repentance* is missing even though it is crucial to the story. On the road at the edge of the village the prodigal accepts being found. In the parable the older son does not. This theology is also demonstrated in the story of Zacchaeus in Luke 19:1-10. Again the word *repentance* does not appear. The crowd is angry at Zacchaeus, and Jesus transfers that hostility to himself as he boldly invites himself into Zacchaeus's house for the night. Zacchaeus *accepts being found*, and at the end of the story Jesus says, "Today salvation has come to this house. . . . For the Son of Man came to seek and to save the lost."[33] In like manner, repentance, as defined by Jesus, is an assumed component in the good shepherd account before us. The restoration of the lost sheep fulfills of the will of "my Father."

---

[33]Kenneth E. Bailey, *Jesus Through Middle Eastern Eyes* (Downers Grove, IL: IVP Academic, 2008), pp. 170-85.

8. *Bad sheep.* The theme of bad sheep first appears in Ezekiel. It surfaces again here in Matthew in that the sheep "goes astray."

9. *Celebration.* There is great rejoicing by "my Father," but no hint of any party.

10. *The ending.* Like the parable of the prodigal son, this parable also stops but does not end. Will that anticipated ending take place in the house or the village or the land? We do not know.

In conclusion, the theology of the passage can be summarized in the following theological cluster.

THE THEOLOGICAL CLUSTER OF MATTHEW 18:10-14

1. *The good shepherd is Jesus, whose actions are endorsed by the Father.* The shepherd is also a model for Christian leaders in any age. The parable presents a good shepherd who, like Jesus, searches for the strayed.

2. *Do not despise the "little ones."* Jesus' followers are warned against neglecting/despising the *little ones,* who believe in Jesus (i.e., the humble and powerless), even when they go astray.

3. *Friends (angels) in high places.* Those same "little ones" (among the followers of Jesus) have friends (*angels in high places*) who have unbroken access into the presence *of God.* This by itself gives them importance. The text assumes that those special angels do not abandon them even when they go astray.

4. *Risk taking.* The disciple who goes astray is important enough that *the shepherd leaves the ninety-nine* "in the hills" to go after him or her. He accepts the *risks* involved. The shepherd sees those who go astray as worth those risks.

5. *No salvation without costly love.* The good shepherd chooses to "go in search of the one that went astray." The sheep will not find its way home alone, and its salvation is possible only if the shepherd pays the price (however high) to go after it.

6. *Rejoicing greatly at finding.* If he finds the sheep that strays (a conclusion not assured) the shepherd

a. does *not scold* or *blame* the sheep for wandering away

b. does not regret (at least there is no hint that he does) the expended energy that could have been used caring for the ninety-nine had the strayed sheep but paid attention to his leadership

c. *rejoices more* over this one than over the ninety-nine

7. *Freedom to search.* The shepherd exercises the *freedom* to leave the ninety-nine and go in search of the one.

8. *Failure as a possible outcome.* The shepherd can fail, and the strayed sheep can die as a result. This harsh reality, known to all shepherds, holds true in the community of faith.

9. *The "Father's will."* Jesus further defines the nature of "my Father who is in heaven." The Father does not will the failure of the shepherd's search, and does not choose that any stray sheep should parish. He is not to be blamed for any such tragic outcome. The mystery of the tension between the *will of the Father* and the *freedom* and *responsibility* of people in history is invoked in the parable but not resolved.

Having traced the good shepherd tradition through the Synoptic Gospels, we turn now to the Gospel of John.

8

THE GOOD SHEPHERD
AMID THIEVES AND WOLVES
IN JOHN 10:1-18

To enter the Gospel of John is to enter a world of theological and historical delights. This Gospel was called "the spiritual Gospel" by early church fathers. It records witness to Jesus from "the beloved disciple" and gives us the famous "I am" statements along with the Upper Room discourses. It also includes the unforgettable accounts of the wedding at Cana in Galilee, Jesus and Nicodemus, and Jesus and the Samaritan woman. Many "favorite verses" are included in its pages. This chapter's limited focus is on the presentation of the good shepherd in John 10:1-18. Our goal is to shed some light from the practices of Middle Eastern sheepherding, and from little known Middle Eastern (Arabic) commentaries ancient and modern. I will also seek to place the text into the long biblical tradition of the good shepherd that we have been tracing throughout this study.[1]

This study of the shepherd song in John assumes that the text is *from Jesus* and *enriched and shaped by John.* Jesus' teachings often seem to fuse with John's interpretation of them.[2] Furthermore the text before us demonstrates

---

[1]A thoughtful and insightful summary of the centuries of discussion around the questions of authorship, intent, major themes, and place and time of writing, and so on, are available in Gary Burge, *John,* NIV Application Commentary (Grand Rapids: Zondervan, 2000), pp. 21-50; and *Interpreting the Gospel of John* (Grand Rapids: Baker, 2013); Raymond Brown, *An Introduction to the Gospel of John* (New York: Doubleday, 2003), pp. 26-39, 151-219; and *The Gospel According to John I-XII* (New York, Doubleday, 1966), pp. xxiv-civ.

[2]A classical example of this is the famous John 3:16, which is a comment by John on John 3:1-15.

the use of finely crafted language artistry that is prominent throughout the Bible.[3] The Hebrew origins of that artistry are clear, and the sophisticated use of Hebrew stylistics in John 10:1-18 will be carefully examined to ascertain its theological significance.

Meaning is recovered from *any significant* historical event through authoritative, insider interpretation. The author of John's Gospel (John the apostle [in his community] along with his disciples) pondered the teachings and dramatic actions of Jesus for decades. That process of reflection both preserved and enriched the accounts in the text before us. There is little doubt that the material, guided by the Spirit, passed through a number of editions.[4]

John 10:1-18 is very carefully organized. The shepherd in the Middle East has two types of threats. One is from *thieves* (as individuals and in gangs). The other is from *wild animals*. In the first century these included wolves, lions, panthers, bears and leopards. Up through the nineteenth century panthers and leopards were seen and wolves were numerous.[5] Rarely did these animals enter villages. But thieves were a danger everywhere. They could climb over the wall of the sheepfold in the village in the dead of night, pass an animal over the wall to an accomplice and escape in minutes. Or in the wilderness they often hid near the entrance to a water-cut defile in a narrow valley and waited for a flock moving slowly past, in single file, with the shepherd in the lead. The thieves could then easily snatch a lamb at the end of the line of animals and disappear. Thus the three kinds of threats that are represented in our text are:

- in the village: thieves (vv. 1-6)

- in the wilderness: thieves (v. 10)

- in the wilderness: wild animals (often wolves) (vv. 11-18)

The first strophe takes place in the village (see fig. 8.1).

---

[3]Victor M. Wilson, *Divine Symmetries: The Art of Biblical Rhetoric* (New York: University Press of America, 1997). (Wilson's volume includes a fine bibliography on pp. 321-30.) Extensive use of biblical rhetoric in Isaiah can be seen in Kenneth E. Bailey, "Study Guide to Isaiah 40-66 (A Demonstration and Explanation of its Rhetorical Forms)," *Presbytery of Shenango, 2011,* http://shenangopresbytery.files.wordpress.com/2013/10/isaiah-study-guide-1.pdf.

[4]Brown, *John I-XII,* pp. xxxii-xl.

[5]W. M. Thomson, *The Land and the Book* (1871; repr., New York: Harper, 1958), 1:302.

10:1"Truly, truly, I say to you,

1.   he who does not enter the sheepfold by the door
     but climbs in by another way,   THIEF-ROBBER
     that man is a *thief* and a *robber*.   Climbs in (Violence Assumed)

2.   2but he who *enters* by the door
          is the shepherd of the sheep.   SHEPHERD - Enters
          3To him the gatekeeper *opens*.

3.   The sheep hear his *voice*,   VOICE - HEARD
          and he calls his own *sheep* by name   sheep - called
          and *leads* them out.   shep. leads out
               4When he has brought out all his own,   All Brought Out
          he *goes before* them,   shep. leads out
          and the *sheep* follow him,   sheep - follow
     for they know his *voice*.   VOICE - KNOWN

4.   5A *stranger* they will not follow,
          but they will flee from him,   STRANGER
          for they do not know the voice of *strangers*." Voice not Known (No Violence)

5. 6This figure Jesus used with them, but they did not understand what he was saying to them.

Figure 8.1. With the flock in the village (Jn 10:1-6)

THE RHETORIC

This strophe has four cameos. The two on the outside (1, 4) focus on *thieves* and *strangers*. In the center are two cameos on the *good shepherd* who calls his sheep and they follow him because they recognize his voice (cameos 2-3).

Cameo 3 is a mini-prophetic rhetorical template with seven inverted phrases. The summary words on the right (cameo 3) trace the movement of a special series that is made up of *voice*, *sheep* and *lead*. The climax in the center focuses on bringing out "all his own." Cameo 3 comes to a close with the three introductory themes repeated backwards. Cameo 4 is parallel to cameo 1 in that both of them deal with strangers who are unknown to the sheep. In cameo 1 violence is assumed. The sheep is picked up and carried away against its will. In cameo 4 there is no violence.

Commentary

Each of these cameos deserves a closer look, beginning with the first (see fig. 8.2).

1.	he who does not enter the sheepfold by the door	
	but climbs in by another way,	THIEF-ROBBER
	that man is a *thief* and a *robber*.	Climbs in (Violence Assumed)

Figure 8.2. Morning in the village: the thief and the robber (Jn 10:1)

This scene can be called "morning in the village." In a traditional village, sheep-herding patterns vary based on the size and ownership of the flock. Every family must have a few sheep because they provide wool for winter clothing. But no one can afford the manpower to herd half a dozen sheep. The usual pattern was for a group of families living on the same narrow village street to come together and arrange for one young man (or two young girls) from one of the families to herd the resulting small flock of perhaps twenty to thirty sheep. Palestinian village homes in the past had (and some still have) a lower area in the main family living space. Into that lower area the family donkey, cow and a few sheep were brought each night.[6] The presence of these animals helped heat the house in winter, and while in the house they were secure from theft. In the morning they were taken outside and tied up in the courtyard, and the house was readied for the day.

But if the family had perhaps ten or more sheep, they needed an outdoor walled sheepfold attached to the back (or front) of the house.[7] Its wall was usually five or six feet high with large jagged thorns (or pieces of broken glass) worked into the plaster along the top edge. In the village there was always danger from a thief (an individual sheep stealer) and from robbers. This latter word (*lēstēs*) refers to gangs, and at times is translated "brigands,"[8] who arrived in the middle of the night with a ladder and a plan of operation. Over the wall (or over the housetops) was their only means of entering the sheepfold.[9] These kinds of people came only to "steal, kill and destroy"

---

[6]For a full description (with diagrams) of these simple peasant homes see Kenneth E. Bailey, *Jesus Through Middle Eastern Eyes* (Downers Grove, IL: IVP Academic, 2008), pp. 28-33.

[7]In the Lebanese mountains I have met and talked to shepherds with flocks of more than three hundred sheep.

[8]BAGD, p. 472.

[9]Breaking down the wall would be out of the question because the noise involved would arouse the entire section of the village. Armed men would appear at once and drive them away.

(v. 10). Sadly, those three words have often, across history, described warring religious movements. Such types have always been willing to use any and all violence necessary to achieve their goals. How then does the *shepherd* approach the flock? See figure 8.3 for cameo 2.

2.   ²but he who *enters* by the door
            is the shepherd of the sheep.   SHEPHERD - Enters
            ³To him the gatekeeper *opens*.

Figure 8.3. The shepherd, the gatekeeper and the door (Jn 10:2-3)

The (good) shepherd inevitably calls the gatekeeper by name. Knocking, without calling, would mean that the person seeking entrance is a stranger.[10] A knock on the door without an accompanying voice could frighten the members of the family. But "Good morning, everyone! Hey David! It's Josiah! I'm ready to go!" would guarantee a quickly opened door. The shepherd now has two problems.

The shepherd's first task is to get his flock out the door of the sheepfold and into the street, which is not a problem. He stands in the street and gives his own unique call (a short five-to-ten-second chant or song). Or he may use a village style bamboo flute on which he plays a special tune. A third way to call sheep is simply to cry out "*Haa, haa, taʻo, taʻo.*"[11] From my limited experience, and from numerous nineteenth-century accounts, this third option seems to be the favorite. I have heard all three. What is clear from contemporary shepherding and from the text of John is that *recognizing the voice* of the shepherd is crucial and is mentioned twice in the third cameo examined later. The sheep "know his voice." That is, the timber of the *voice* of the shepherd appears to be more important to the flock than any tune sung by him. I could learn the same tune and sing it in the hearing of the flock and the sheep would pay no attention to me.

While teaching New Testament in Beirut, Lebanon, I once had a class with some students from small farming communities in Syria and Lebanon. We were studying the good shepherd texts that appear in Luke 15,

---

[10]See Kenneth E. Bailey, *Poet and Peasant and Through Peasant Eyes* (Grand Rapids: Eerdmans, 1983), p. 128.
[11]See chap. 5, n. 60 for an explanation of this cry.

Matthew 18 and John 10. I asked the students if in their earlier years they had herded sheep. Some of them had. Their personal experience was a great help to all of us. I asked what was involved when they acquired a new sheep. Avedis Boynerian explained that the new sheep needed to be trained to listen to the new voice. Early each morning the flock starts to get excited because they have had nothing to eat for fourteen hours or more. In addition to being hungry they are restless from being cooped up all night. As daylight increases, they gradually become more and more active and eager. Finally they hear the shepherd's voice outside the barred sheepfold door. As soon as the door is opened by a member of the family, the shepherd calls the animals again and they rush out eagerly anticipating a new day full of lush grass, fresh mountain air, shady trees and rest beside peaceful waters. But for the unfortunate new sheep the voice (or the call) is wrong. *It cannot go to the party!* "What happens to that poor animal?" I asked. "It has a temporary nervous breakdown," replied Avedis as he carefully explained that the new sheep runs around and around banging its head against the rough stone walls of the sheepfold emitting a stream of pitiful, heartbreaking cries. It needs a few days of "therapy" to retrain its ear to recognize the voice of the new shepherd. Such a world of shepherds and their sheep forms the background to the account before us.

Not only in the Middle East are such things true. Recently here in Western Pennsylvania, I was privileged to professionally record a DVD lecture series on the good shepherd. The producers wanted some footage of "real live sheep." A good friend of mine, a sheep farmer and high school teacher, was approached and graciously spent most of a day with the producers and cameramen shooting the needed footage. The producers quickly discovered that their voices only frightened the sheep away, while one call from their shepherd was enough to guide the sheep in the required direction.

Returning to our text, the shepherd, following his morning routine, has thus far effortlessly led his eager herd out of the sheepfold and into the street. There the sheep find themselves in the middle of many other sheep with their shepherds and their unfamiliar voices. Cameo 3 traces their journey (see fig. 8.4).

3.	The sheep hear his *voice*,	VOICE - HEARD
	and he calls his own *sheep* by name	sheep - called
	and *leads* them out.	shep. leads out
	⁴When he has brought out all his own,	All Brought Out
	he *goes before* them,	shep. leads out
	and the *sheep* follow him,	sheep - follow
	for they know his *voice*.	VOICE - KNOWN

Figure 8.4. The shepherd calls, the sheep follow (Jn 18:3-4)

The shepherd's problem is now more complicated. Getting the sheep out of the sheepfold into the street is easy compared to keeping the flock moving through the narrow streets of the village (early in the morning), crowded as it is with sheep from many flocks. This scene is described by a nineteenth-century traveler and author:

> Travelers have noticed the wonderful readiness with which the sheep of a large flock will recognize the shepherd's voice. Though several flocks are mingled they speedily separate at the command of the shepherd, while the word of a stranger would have no effect on them. Porter thus describes a scene he witnessed among the hills of Bashan: "The shepherds led their flocks forth from the gates of the city. They were in full view, and we watched them and listened to them with no little interest. Thousands of sheep and goats were there, grouped in dense, confused masses. The shepherds stood together *until all came out.* Then they separated, each shepherd taking a different path, and uttering as he advanced a shrill, peculiar call. The sheep heard them. At first the masses swayed and moved as if shaken by some internal convulsion; then points struck out in the direction taken by the shepherds; these became longer and longer until the confused masses were resolved into long, living streams, flowing after their leaders."[12]

Such is the ability of sheep to distinguish the voice of their own shepherd from the voices of other shepherds who may be calling at the same time. Whether the shepherd simply calls *ta'u, ta'u* or sings his unique tune, the sheep hear the voice and follow. Dionesius ibn al-Salibi, writing in the twelfth century, observes,

---

[12]James M. Freeman, *Hand-Book of Bible Manners and Customs* (New York: Nelson & Phillips, 1874), p. 429. The quotation in the text is from J. L. Porter, *The Giant Cities of Bashan and Syria's Holy Places* (New York: n. p., 1866), p. 45; italics added.

It is the custom of the shepherd to follow after the flock like a guard to drive away all harm. And the Lord Christ goes before his sheep in order to lead them to the truth and to faith and the right path. But I observe Bishops in our day walking behind the sheep in order to satisfy their filthy desires and to dump dry sticks on the fires of their greediness. O Lord Most High—save thy people from them!![13]

It seems that Ibn al-Salibi (himself a bishop) had a "bad shepherd" problem that approached Ezekiel's description of the bad shepherds (Ezek 34:1-10). Also we can note that when there is the threat of a wolf or some other wild animal following the flock, on the way back to the village the shepherd does indeed follow his sheep, as Ibn al-Salibi has noted. The sheep, once started on the way home, generally know where to go. But in the early morning, and through the day, the shepherd is always in the lead.

The shepherd often develops a special attachment to a few sheep in the flock who follow him closely and become pets. To those few the shepherd gives names, sometimes related to their color. One could be "big red" and another "blackie" and so forth.[14] W. M. Thomson writes, "Some sheep always keep near the shepherd, and are his special favorites. Each of them has a name, to which it answers joyfully, and the kind shepherd is ever distributing to such choice portions which he gathers for that purpose."[15]

Stephen Haboush mentions some of the names he had for his sheep. Those included "Split Ear, Short Tail, Bright Eye, Angel, Lazy and Black Spot."[16] Haboush makes clear that even a named sheep would obey him, "not because of its name being called, but because of the particular sound and nature of my voice. This is the only positive way that the sheep know their shepherd."[17] Obviously no shepherd with a hundred sheep could reasonably be expected to call out one hundred names every time he wants the flock to move in a particular direction. The intent of the text is that the shepherd does indeed call some of his sheep by name and at the

---

[13]Ibn al-Salibi, *Tafsir*, 2:367.

[14]When discussing his lost goat (described earlier), Krikorian refers to it as "our blue goat." See M. P. Krikorian, *The Spirit of the Shepherd: An Interpretation of the Psalm Immortal*, 2nd ed. (Grand Rapids: Zondervan, 1939), p. 56.

[15]Thompson, *Land and the Book*, 1:302.

[16]Stephen A. Haboush, *My Shepherd Life in Galilee: With an Exegesis of the Shepherd Psalm* (Chicago: Merchandise Mart, 1949), p. 16.

[17]Ibid.

same time, all his sheep "know his voice" and follow him.

Every biblical parable or story is like a two-sided coin. On one side is the concrete reality in life; the other side is the application of that concrete reality in the spiritual realm. When Jesus says, "I am the door" he does not mean "I am a number of mute planks of wood nailed together." The listener/reader hearing the metaphor is called on to sort out the aspect of the speaker's teaching that is being clarified with the use of the concrete image invoked. The same is true in this text. Shepherds do indeed, on occasion, give names to some of their favorite sheep. Generally speaking they do not name all of them, especially when the flock is large. But on the "application side" of the use of the parable, it is appropriate for Jesus to say, "he calls his own sheep by name," lest one of the "little ones" among the flock (discussed earlier in Mt 18) think, "I am not important. He probably does not have a name for me, let alone know who I am." Commenting on this verse Ibn al-Salibi writes, "The shepherd expresses his true knowledge of them [the flock] by calling their names. For the one who calls another by name makes clear that he knows him."[18] Indeed, he knows the names of all of us who are among his "little ones." But there is more.

Whenever ring composition is utilized by the author of a biblical text, it is important to examine the pairing of ideas that occurs within it. In this cameo it is possible to see the following parallels:

First pair. In 3a the sheep "*hear* his voice," and in 3g "they *know* his voice." The two are parallel and at the same time there is movement from the first to the second. It is not enough that they "hear his voice." His call will have no effect unless they also "know his voice."

Second pair. In 3b "he *calls.*" Then in 3f "the sheep *follow.*" The first is the *action of the shepherd*, and the second action is the *response of the sheep.* His call (3b) means nothing without their response in following him (3f). The "following" involves a fusion of the action of the shepherd and the action of the sheep. Once again the sovereignty of God and the freedom and responsibility of humankind are placed side by side with no explanation as to how they function in tandem. Yet the parable furthers our understanding of that mystery. He does indeed call, and that call is in vain if the sheep do not follow.

---

[18]Ibn al-Salibi, *Tafsir*, 2:367.

Third pair. The shepherd *leads* (3c) and *goes before* (3e); he does not *drive* his sheep with a stick from the back. He leads from the front. Peter applies this image to church leadership, as we will see later.

The climax of this cameo (with its inverted parallelism) appears in the center (3d) with the phrase "When he has brought out all his own." The flock and the shepherd are by now outside the village and the sheep have chosen to ignore the dozen other calls sounding in the crisp morning air, and are deliberately and purposefully following *their* good shepherd. The shepherd does not start off into the wilderness in his preplanned direction until the morning traffic rush is over and he is sure that he has "all his own" behind him (note the earlier Porter/Freeman eyewitness account). He does not count them. Instead he waits until the entire mixed mass of wooly creatures has sorted itself out and each sheep has heard and followed its own shepherd.

In passing we can observe that this text is extraordinarily contemporary. With the information technology that surrounds us, never in human history have there been as many divergent, strident voices calling loudly for the attention and loyalty of "the flock." Daily the sheep must consciously seek to ignore those noises and listen for the voice of *their good shepherd* and follow it. Jesus has one final comment on the flock at the edge of the village as it stands poised and ready to follow the shepherd into the wide wilderness (see fig. 8.5).

4. ⁵A *stranger* they will not follow,
    but they will flee from him,   STRANGER
    for they do not know the voice of *strangers.*"   Voice not Known (No Violence)

Figure 8.5. The sheep and the voices of strangers (Jn 10:5)

The "stranger" is not a "thief." The thief gives the sheep no choice. He steals the sheep by force. The "stranger" represent voices that call out every morning offering other options to the sheep. In Jesus' day these included the sectarians at Qumran outside Jericho, the high priestly guild in the temple, and the scribes and Pharisees with their more and more precise interpretations of the law. Hellenists sought to modernize the faith to fit the times, while the Herodians were in bed with Rome. Zealots were preparing for a war that (unknown to them) they could not win, and Sadducees in the temple guild clung to power and the past. Many "strangers" called to the faithful, but those who knew the voice of the good shepherd and had the commitment to follow him would ignore all other voices and follow him, come what may. They did not "know" (i.e., recognize the authority of) the voice of strangers. Ah, but did Jesus' listeners understand what he was saying?

The first section of the shepherd songs ends with, "This figure [parable] Jesus used with them, but they did not understand what he was saying to them" (v. 6). The thick-headedness of the disciples that we observed in Mark 6:52 now reappears. So Jesus tries again. Only this time the setting for the text is the open wilderness (see fig. 8.6).

[10:7]So Jesus again said to them, "Truly, truly I say to you,

1. a. I am the door of the sheep.   I AM - DOOR

2.   [8]All who came before me are *thieves* and *robbers*,   THIEVES
        but the sheep did not listen to them.   Robbers

3.   a. [9]I am the door,   I AM - DOOR
            b. If anyone *enters* by me, he will *be saved*,   Enter - Saved
            c. and will go in and out and *find pasture*.   Find pasture

4.   [10]The *thief* comes only to *steal*   THIEF
        and *kill* and *destroy*.   Steal/Kill

5. b. I came that they may have *life*,   I CAME
    c. and have it *abundantly*."   For Abundant Live

Figure 8.6. With the flock in the wilderness (Jn 10:7-10)

THE RHETORIC

This short rhetorical piece on "death and life" is composed of five cameos. Three are on security and life while two focus on thieves and death. These two themes are interwoven as shown in figure 8.7.

1. *Life*/Security (the door)
    2. *Death* (thieves/robbers)
        3. *Life* (the door/salvation)
    4. *Death* (thief, kill, destroy)
5. *Life* (abundance)

Figure 8.7. Life and death (Jn 10:7-10)

The interweaving of these two themes is striking. It would have been very easy to omit the negative theme of "death" and let the passage read

1. I am the door of the sheep.

2. If anyone enters by me, he will be saved,

3. and (he) will go in and out and find pasture.

4. I came that they may have life,

5. and have it abundantly.

In the five lines listed, the ideas flow together seamlessly. If this were the entire text, no reader would sense anything missing. Instead, the text presents a series of jarring contrasts between life and death. In each case "death" is enveloped by "life." That is, the "song" presents *life—death—life—death—life*. The artistically constructed passage presents life dominating death.

Furthermore the center of the five cameos is composed of ideas that appear in the beginning and at the end. The first line of the center (3a) is an abbreviation of the opening line at the beginning (1a). The other two ideas in the center (3b, 3c) repeat ideas that appear again at the end (5b, 5c) using different words. That is "be saved = have life" and "find pasture = abundance." This feature of composing a center out of ideas that also appear at the beginning and at the end is a rhetorical device as old as Isaiah 28:14-18.[19]

Another extraordinary feature of this short rhetorical piece is its "counterpoint." As noted, the reader can hear a pattern of *life—death—life—death—life*. But at the same time a second tune is being played which follows the inverted order of ring composition with its cameos exhibiting: A—B—C—B—A.[20]

COMMENTARY

The good shepherd and his sheep are now in the wilderness. Led by the shepherd, the sheep have spent the day grazing, drinking, gamboling and resting. In the latter months of each year, before the winter rains, the shepherd must lead his flock further and further from the home village to find uneaten

---

[19]Note the discussion of Is 28:14-18 in the introduction.

[20]John 15:7-17 exhibits the same counterpoint. The text uses ring composition, and its eleven cameos alternate between *responsibility* and *privilege* all through the text. 1 Cor 1:17–2:2 open and close with "preaching the cross," and that same theme appears in the center. See Kenneth E. Bailey, *Paul Through Mediterranean Eyes* (Downers Grove, IL: IVP Academic, 2011), pp. 73-76.

grass. Each day more and more time and energy is lost in the endless task of finding pasture. In late summer and early fall it is still hot. For centuries shepherds have constructed round, roughly built enclosures in the wilderness, using uncut field stones. Once again thorns (if available) are worked into the top of the wall, and the herd that arrives first is free to shelter for the night in any one of these freestanding stone structures that have no roofs or doors. The only vulnerable spot, once the sheep are inside the sheepfold, is across the entrance.[21] If there is some dried brush in the area, the shepherd can build a small fire just outside the entrance to help protect the sheep. If he has a dog, he will place it beside the entrance across which he will then sleep. In such a scene the shepherd literally becomes the door. This text exhibits no conflict with the imagery in verses 1-10. In the village there is a well-built walled enclosure with a secure door that must be opened from the inside by a *doorkeeper*. In the open wilderness none of these advantages are available. "I am the door" describes overnight *in the open country*.

When you sit with shepherds, their most exciting and most precious memories of life in the open pastureland often have to do with their battles with wild animals and with thieves. In this case the text focuses again on thieves and robbers. The word for "kill" in verse 8 is "slaughter." The thief (with or without his gang) wants only to "steal and kill [slaughter] and destroy utterly."[22] The thief must first steal his sheep. Sooner or later he will kill it. Finally, he will "destroy utterly," that is, butcher the stolen animal, leaving no traces. There are no extra words in the text, and the verbs in verse 10 are in their proper order. But who are the "thieves and robbers" referred to in the text?

There are many potential candidates. Ibn al-Tayyib, referencing Chrysostom, represents numerous commentators as he writes:

> He [Jesus] is not talking about the prophets whose names appear in the Old Testament, but he refers to those who came before him claiming to be the Messiah such as Judas the Galilean and Theudas [Acts 5:36-37] and others whose voices were not heeded by the sheep. But [he says,] "be assured that I am the door and whoever enters by me, he will be saved."[23]

---

[21]Natural caves in the area are used for the same purpose. The shepherds construct a short wall across the entrance to the cave, leaving a short opening to allow for the movement of the sheep in and out of the cave.

[22]LSJ, *Greek-English Lexicon*, p. 207.

[23]Ibn al-Tayyib, *Tafsir*, 2:551.

The text could refer to other voices from the period. During the three-hundred-year period before the time of Jesus, the history of the Jewish nation was that of wars and rumors of wars with many competing voices for political and religious leadership.[24] The Hasidim in Israel were not always impressed with the Maccabees and their claim to leadership. The devotees of Qumran were sure they were the chosen remnant of the true Israel, not the high priestly guild in Jerusalem. On and on it went. On the Greek side of the first-century world there were what Walter Grundmann calls "the many shepherd gods of Hellenism."[25] These included Attis, Anubis, Dionysus and Hermes,[26] and the affirmation "the sheep did not listen to them" is a challenge to the church in every age.

It is impossible to identify "the thieves and robbers" with any precision. Greek readers and Jewish readers would quickly think of a variety of competing voices. But on the Jewish side, Ibn al-Tayyib and Chrysostom perhaps offer the best option.

The climax appears in the third cameo (see fig. 8.8).

3.		a.	[9]I am the door,	I AM - DOOR
		b.	If anyone *enters* by me, he will *be saved*,	Enter - Saved
		c.	and will go in and out and *find pasture*.	Find pasture

Figure 8.8. Safety and security in the wilderness (Jn 10:9)

This cameo repeats the image of the shepherd and his flock spending the night in a wilderness enclosure, such as is described earlier. "Enters by me" has behind it the picture of night falling and the nervous sheep escaping the boundless wilderness with its lurking dangers into the safety and security of the sturdy stone enclosure with the beloved shepherd becoming the door. Inside they are safe and saved from both thieves and wolves.

To go "in and out and find pasture" tells of both freedom and sustenance. Salvation does not mean that the shepherd places the sheep one by one into wire cages and feeds them in the safety of the barn. Rather, salvation includes the freedom to go *in and out* and *find* pasture. This latter is a challenge because

---

[24]Stewart Perowne, *The Life and Times of Herod the Great* (London: Hodder & Stoughton, 1956); and *The Later Herods: The Political Background of the New Testament* (London: Hodder & Stoughton, 1958). Perowne documents the turmoil of the period with detail and clarity.
[25]Walter Grundmann, "καλός" TDNT, 3:548, n. 43.
[26]Ibid.

by the time the flock needs to spend the night in the wilderness, as noted, most of the year's crop of wild grasses has already been consumed. Flocks often "go in and out" and find nothing. By late summer and fall, it takes an intelligent shepherd to find pasture. There are longstanding agreements between tribes of shepherds regarding grazing rights. This shepherd has picked the right valley where grass is still available and the sheep are free to go in and out. The text uses a singular. It is not a flock that is here described as being on the move in and out, but rather the journey of an individual sheep. On the story line side this would mean that the valley the shepherd has chosen has good grass nearby and he lets the sheep wander in and out of the stone enclosure at will. On the theological side of the text Ibn al-Tayyib understands that the sheep is moving into "a pasture of rich spiritual nourishment" and "he [Jesus] will protect the sheep from the enemies of the soul."[27] Ibn al-Tayyib continues, "John Chrysostom said that the intent of the phrase 'He will go out and in' is that the believer moves with freedom, and in all that he does for the sake of Christ, within the sheepfold or outside of it, he finds sustenance for his own soul."[28] This final phrase is on display in John 4:32, where the disciples return to the well in Samaria with food and Jesus affirms that he has already eaten, saying "My food is to do the will of him who sent me."

Cameo 4 brings the image of the murderous thief to its ultimate expression, as previously noted. This rhetorical piece is not just a picture of a beautiful valley with grass waving in the breeze and a bright sun bringing warmth and light to a tranquil herd grazing contentedly with the good shepherd resting confidently nearby. The thief is not forgotten. Some in every age have managed to turn the sacred foundations of faith into a powerful force that energizes death and mayhem. Jesus wants no part of such things. See figure 8.9 for Jesus' final word in this second section.

| 5. | b. I came that they may have *life*, | I CAME |
| | c. and have it *abundantly*. | For Abundant Live |

Figure 8.9. Life and abundance (Jn 10:10)

[27]Ibn al-Tayyib, *Tafsir*, p. 551.
[28]Ibid.

Strophe A

1a. [10:11]I am *the good shepherd*.   GOOD SHEPHERD
 b.   The *good shepherd lays down his life for the sheep*.

2.   [12]He who is a *hired hand* and not a shepherd,   HIRELING
                Who does not own the sheep,

3.   sees the *wolf*   WOLF - comes
                               coming

4.   and *leaves* the sheep,   HIRELING
                               and *flees*   Flees

5.   and the *wolf snatches* them
                               and *scatters* them.   WOLF - attacks

6.   [13]He flees because he is a *hired hand*   HIRELING
                and cares nothing for the sheep.

7a.   [14]I am *the good shepherd*.   GOOD SHEPHERD
       I *know my own* and *my own know me*,
                [15]just as the *Father knows me* and *I know the Father;*
 b.   and *I lay down my life for the sheep*.

Strophe B

8.   [16]And I have other sheep,   THE VISION
                that are not of this fold.   For evangelism/proclamation

9.   I must bring them also,   THE TASK
                and they will listen to my voice.   Of evangelism/proclamation

10.   So there will be one flock,   THE GOAL
                one shepherd.   Of evangelism/proclamation

Strophe C

11. [17]On account of this the *Father loves me*,[a]   FATHER LOVES ME

12.   because *I lay down my life*,   I LAY DOWN LIFE
       that *I may take it up again*.   & take it up again

13.   [18]*No one takes it from me*,   NO ONE TAKES IT
                but *I lay it down of my own accord*.   I give it freely

14.   I have authority *to lay it down*,   I HAVE AUTH. TO LAY IT DOWN
       and I have authority *to take it up again*.   & authority to take it again

15. This *charge* I have *received* from my *Father*."   FATHER GIVES ME A CHARGE

---

[a]My translation. I have avoided using the word *reason*, which as an English word invokes rational thought rather than an event in history. The King James Version's "therefore" can also sound like the conclusion to a rational argument.

Figure 8.10. The battle with the wolf and its aftermath (Jn 10:11-18)

As noted, the phrase "to have life" (5b) gives further meaning to 3b that reads "to be saved." In the Gospel of John, the two phrases complete each other. Early Arabic versions of the New Testament occasionally call Jesus *al-muhyi* (the one who gives life). Ibrahim Sa'id, a modern Egyptian Protestant scholar, uses that title in discussing this text.[29] Furthermore the third line in the center (3c) about "finding pasture" overlaps in meaning with the last line in cameo 5c with its reference to "abundance." To "find pasture" is to turn the day into a good day that offers "abundance."

This brings the second "poem" to a close with the great struggle against the wolf before us. The text is rich in meaning and the interpreter senses the need to approach it with "fear and trembling." See figure 8.10 for the full text.

This inexhaustible hymn to the cross and the resurrection breaks into three sections[30] which for clarity we will call *strophes*. For ease of reference, the first strophe is as follows.

Strophe A

1a. [10:11]I am *the good shepherd.*   GOOD SHEPHERD
   b.   The *good shepherd lays down his life for the sheep.*

2.   [12]He who is a *hired hand* and not a shepherd,   HIRELING
                   Who does not own the sheep,

3.   sees the *wolf*   WOLF - comes
                                     coming

4.   and *leaves* the sheep,   HIRELING
                                             and *flees*   Flees

5.   and the *wolf snatches* them
                                     and *scatters* them.   WOLF - attacks

6.   [13]He flees because he is a *hired hand*   HIRELING
                   and cares nothing for the sheep.

7a.   [14]I am *the good shepherd.*   GOOD SHEPHERD
                I know my own and *my own know me,*
                [15]just as the *Father knows me* and *I know the Father;*
   b.   and *I lay down my life for the sheep.*

Figure 8.10b. The first strophe (Jn 10:11-15)

---

[29]Ibrahim Sa'id, *Luqa*, p. 418.
[30]Three other texts in this study are also constructed in three parts. See Is 28:14-18; Mt 18:10-14; Lk 15:4-7.

The good shepherd and the flock are still in the wilderness. Having discussed the "thieves" in two parts (vv. 1-6 and vv. 7-10), the text now turns to the other great threat to the flock—the wild animals (in this case, the wolf).

THE RHETORIC

This "poem" (strophe A) uses ring composition and falls into seven inverted cameos. It is thereby a prophetic rhetorical template. In this text, as often occurs, the outside cameos are longer than those in the center.[31] But the most remarkable poetic aspect of this text is the relationship between cameos 1 and 7. As is obvious, cameo 1 (a., b.) is composed of two ideas. Those two ideas are repeated in cameo 7 (a., b.) almost word for word. But cameo 7 adds new material to the center of the cameo. The significance and meaning of this remarkable verbal artistry will be examined shortly.

COMMENTARY

Thus far in the centuries-old biblical tradition the shepherd has been described in many positive ways, but never as the "good shepherd." The word *kalos* (good) that appears here can, as a Greek word, mean "morally good," "noble" or "beautiful." Syriac and Hebrew translation of John 10 have used the word *tov*. As a Hebrew word *tov* includes "(a) *useful/efficient*, (b) *beautiful*, and (c) *right/ morally good*."[32] As an Aramaic word *tov* carries the primary meaning of *morally good*, to which it adds *handsome* along with *happy/blessed*. This last meaning ties this text (through the Aramaic language) to the Beatitudes of Matthew 5 where *tov* appears as the Syriac/Aramaic word for the Greek *makarios*.[33] Our English versions have traditionally translated it as *blessed*. Arabic versions have exclusively translated John 10:11 with the word *salih*, which includes good, pious and fitting.[34] Greco-Roman readers may well have heard the overtones of "noble" and "beautiful." For Hebrew/Aramaic background readers the meanings of *morally good* and *blessed* would likely have dominated. But to these general

---

[31]See the discussion of Isaiah 28:14-18 in the introduction. Also 1 Cor 1:17–2:2. See Bailey, *Paul Through Mediterranean Eyes*, pp. 73-74.

[32]LVTL, *Lexicon*, p. 349.

[33]Marcus Jastrow, *Dictionary of Talmud Babli and Jerushalmi, and the Midrashic Literature*, 2 vols. (New York: Pardes, 1950), 1:521; J. Payne Smith, *A Compendious Syriac Dictionary* (1903; repr., Oxford: Clarendon Press, 1967), p. 167.

[34]Hans Wehr, *A Dictionary of Modern Written Arabic*, ed. J. Milton Cowan (Ithaca, NY: Cornell University Press, 1961), p. 521.

definitions, the text we are now examining adds new meaning.

Two huge theological realities are presented here in cameo 1. First, Jesus affirms "I am *the* good shepherd." Which one is he talking about? David (Ps 23) affirmed "the LORD is my shepherd, I shall not want" (v. 1), and "he brings me back" (v. 3) (when I go astray). Death, sin and enemies were ever present, but he had no fear because "you are with me." But starting with Jeremiah 23, the bad shepherds destroy everything, and the only hope for the flock is the anticipated advent of God himself, who will one day appear as a good shepherd and set things right. This future hope burns brightly in Jeremiah, Ezekiel and Zechariah. After the Babylonians and the Persians came the Greeks and finally the Romans. The hope for divine intervention fulfilling the prophetic promise must have intensified as the centuries passed.

In parable (Lk 15), historical event (Mk 6) and again in parable (Mt 18), Jesus affirms that *in him* such promises are in processes of being fulfilled. Now here in John 10 comes the open declaration "I am *the* good shepherd." The promises of the centuries were at last being realized. But the *manner* of their fulfillment inevitably came as a huge shock. There is cost involved. This in itself is not new, only the intensity of that cost. What we have noted thus far regarding this theme in the long "good shepherd tradition" is found in figure 8.11.

Psalm 23:   The shepherd (God)
                      enters the wilderness, finds me and "brings me back"

Jeremiah 23: The shepherd (God) will one day
                      gather, bring back the sheep and appoint good shepherds over the flock

Ezekiel 34:   The shepherd (God) will one day
                      search for, seek, gather, bring back, lead, feed, judge, rescue the sheep

Zechariah 10: The shepherd (God) will one day
                      care for, strengthen, save, brings back, have compassion on the flock

Luke 15:   The shepherd/woman (God/Jesus)
                      goes after, searches diligently for, finds, carries back and restores the lost

Mark 6:   The shepherd (Jesus)
                      has compassion, teaches, leads, feeds the flock and confronts the enemy

Matthew 18:   The shepherd (God/Jesus)
                      highly values the lost sheep, searches for it, risks failure, and desires its rescue

John 10:   The shepherd (God/Jesus)
                      fights the wolf and dies rescuing the sheep

Figure 8.11. The cost factor in the good shepherd tradition

Clearly the cost factor in the good shepherd tradition is an important part of the story that intensifies as the tradition unfolds. This ancient tradition makes clear that on arrival the expected divine shepherd will engage with evil and is willing to pay a price to restore the lost and scattered flock. But there is no hint of any direct harm to be inflicted on the shepherd in the process. Then come the Gospels.

The Synoptic Gospels include the well known "predictions of the passion" (Lk 9:18-22; 9:43b-45; 18:31-34; and parallels). Here in John those predictions take the form of a statement placed within a song about the good shepherd. That shepherd will not only get hurt, he will be killed. In cameo 1, the good/blessed shepherd "lays down his life for the sheep." Traditional shepherds know the life-threatening dangers of their trade. Wild animals and "wild" people are "out there," and in the open wilderness the shepherd's life is always at risk. All of this applies to the good shepherd song before us.

Not only does cameo 1 bring the long good shepherd tradition to its climax, but that climax is repeated in cameo 7. Cameos 1 and 7 appear at the beginning and at the end of a great battle between the good shepherd and the wolf. The two cameos appear side by side in figure 8.12.

1a.	[10:11]I am the good shepherd.	GOOD SHEPHERD
b.	The good shepherd lays down his life for the sheep.	(Ultimate self-emptying)
7a.	[14]I am the good shepherd.	GOOD SHEPHERD
	I know my own and my own know me,	++
	[15]just as the *Father knows me and I know the Father;*	++
b.	and I lay down my life for the sheep.	(Ultimate self emptying)

Figure 8.12. The death of the shepherd and a vision of its meaning (Jn 10:11, 14-15)

The opening line in each of these cameos (1a, 7a) is identical. Both affirm "I am the good shepherd." The concluding lines of the two cameos are nearly identical (see 1b, 7b). In the first (1b), the good shepherd lays down *his life*. Then in the last (7b), the good shepherd appears on stage and affirms, "*I* lay down *my life*." Third person becomes first person.[35] Furthermore, as noted, there is new material added to the center of cameo 7. If cameo 1 is likened to a bun, then that same bun reappears, sliced in half in cameo 7 and sandwich material is added in the middle.

---

[35]The movement toward the more personal also takes place in Ps 23 as it unfolds.

This precise rhetorical style was noted thirty years ago by David Noel
Freedman in an extended essay introducing a reprint of *The Forms of Hebrew
Poetry* by G. Buchanan Gray.[36] Freedman writes,

> A more complex and less easily recognized form of inclusion (or envelope
> construction) does not involve the repetition of terms, but rather the re-
> sumption or completion of a thought. It is as though the poet deliberately split
> a bicolon or couplet, and inserted a variety of materials between the opening
> and closing halves of that unit to form a stanza.[37]

Freedman further notes,

> It may be added that such a view of poetic structure implies, if it does not
> require, a degree of literary sophistication not usually associated with oral
> composition or the poets of ancient Israel. Nevertheless the subject deserves
> attention, and the isolated example offered here may be a harbinger of others
> not yet detected.[38]

Freedman notes that at times a strophe opens and closes with "the exact
repetition of key words or phrases."[39] This latter is precisely what we find
here in John. Moving on from Freedman's prolegomenon to Gray's introduction to his book, we read about what Gray calls "late Hebrew poetry." He
grants that such poetry may include the Magnificat and other New Testament canticles along with Matthew 25:31-46 and 1 Corinthians 13. Gray
observes, "At the very time that the Rabbis were examining scripture with
eyes blind to parallelism, other Jews were still writing poems that made all
the old use of Parallelism."[40] In regard to the "other Jews" Gray mentions the
Apocalypse of Baruch as an example. We could add that the list of "other Jews"
who were making use of "all the old forms of parallelism" includes Jesus,
Paul and the editors of many sections in the four Gospels.[41] In any case this
is profoundly true of the good shepherd passage before us here in John.

John 10:14-15 (cameo 7), as noted, repeats verse eleven (cameo 1) and adds

---

[36]David Noel Freedman, prolegomenon to *The Forms of Hebrew Poetry*, by G. Buchanan Gray
(1915; repr., Brooklyn, NY: KTAV, 1972), pp. vii-lvi.
[37]Ibid., p. xxxvi.
[38]Ibid. Freedman then discusses examples from Hosea (ibid., pp. xxxvi-xxxvii).
[39]Ibid.
[40]Gray, *Forms of Hebrew Poetry*, pp. 26-27.
[41]Such a list would also include St. Paul in 1 Corinthians. Cf. Bailey, *Paul Through Mediterranean
Eyes.*

two lines to the center creating a sandwich. The end result is found in figure 8.13.

7a.   [14]I am the good shepherd.   GOOD SHEPHERD
          I know my own and my own know me,
          [15]just as the *Father knows me and I know the Father;*
b.   and I lay down my life for the sheep.   (Ultimate self emptying)

Figure 8.13. A Hebrew sandwich on the cross and its meaning (Jn 10:14-15)

The added "center" of the cameo is composed of the three following components: the sheep + the shepherd + the Father. These are like three links of a chain. The verb "to know" in biblical literature is a rich word that refers to personal, indeed, intimate relationships/knowledge. Throughout the Scriptures this verb is used to describe the marital relationship. In Genesis "Adam knew Eve his wife, and she conceived" (Gen 4:1). Clearly this freighted verb means more than objective, rational information. It refers to deep and profound relationships between people. With this in mind, the sandwich material placed into the bun is amazing. It affirms that

1. There is a close, personal relationship between the *shepherd* and the *sheep*.

2. That relationship is *like* the close, personal relationship between the *shepherd* and the *Father*.

3. These two profound, interlocking statements are placed within an *envelope* that describes the shepherd's action in laying down his life for the sheep.

Putting it all together we can understand:

1. The close, personal relationship between the *Father* and the *Son*, in the heart of God, is a model

2. for the potential close, personal relationship between the *good shepherd* and the *sheep*

3. *because of the cross.*

This is astounding! Because the good shepherd lays down his life for the sheep we the believing community are drawn into the heart of the good shepherd who himself dwells within the very heart of God. In commenting on the sandwich material in the center of cameo 7, Ibrahim Sa'id writes,

> The measure of the shared knowledge between Jesus and his flock is the shared knowledge between Jesus and the Father. And this is founded on the

unity of nature, and the sincerity of love and bonding between them. How wondrous is this love by which Jesus has raised us up to himself. Indeed he emptied himself and elevated us to himself by taking on our flesh and blood in order to make us partners with him in the divine nature. Here the interpreter must put aside his pen in order to sit in amazement at the extravagancies of these glories which angels alone are able to penetrate and ponder.[42]

Sa'id captures the sense of awe and the awareness of great profundity that this text inspires, a profundity that reaches beyond our limited ability to fully understand and interpret what is meant. This much is clear. When anyone pays a huge price to save me, that savior thereby creates a special relationship with me. We can think of the American airline pilot, Chesley "Sully" Sullenberger, who recently saved 155 passengers and crew on his plane flying over New York by safely landing it in the Hudson River when the plane's engines were shut down by a collision with a flock of birds. A year later a reunion was held for the passengers and crew of that flight. On that occasion the saved passengers embraced Captain Sully with tears. Those passengers were meeting the captain for the first time. His saving act created a special bond with those he saved. The same is true for us. Yet even more, that special relationship ties us to the third link in the chain, which is the heart of God the Father. All of this is only possible because of the cross.

With this outer frame (cameos 1, 7) in mind we turn to reflect on the fight with the wolf that is placed in the center of this first strophe (see fig. 8.14).

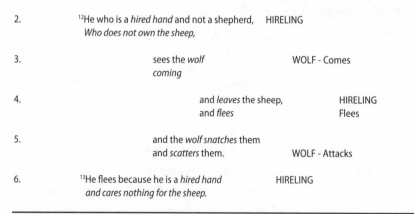

2.   ¹²He who is a *hired hand* and not a shepherd,   HIRELING
            Who does not own the sheep,

3.   sees the *wolf*   WOLF - Comes
                            coming

4.   and *leaves* the sheep,   HIRELING
                                    and *flees*   Flees

5.   and the *wolf snatches* them
                            and *scatters* them.   WOLF - Attacks

6.   ¹³He flees because he is a *hired hand*   HIRELING
            and cares nothing for the sheep.

Figure 8.14. The shepherd, the hired hand and the wolf (Jn 10:12-13)

[42]Ibrahim Sa'id, *Sharh Bisharit Yuhanna* (Cairo: Dar al-Thaqafa, n.d. [c. 1965]), p. 434.

The just-examined outer frame (cameos 1, 7) tells the reader about the shepherd. Now in the center there is a discussion of the other two players in the drama. The *hired hand* appears in the beginning, the middle and the end. The *wolf* is placed in between these three short cameos on the *hired hand*.[43] The hired hand does not own the sheep, and when danger appears he runs away. A Lebanese village proverb says, "When the wolf came, the sheep dog ducked behind a bush to relieve itself." He can then claim, "Wolf? What wolf? I was right here and I didn't see *anything!*" If there is a high price to be paid, the hired hand is certainly not willing to pay it. He is there merely to serve his own interests, not to risk his life fighting a wolf. To what does the text refer?

In a context of powerlessness and oppression, one must often speak in parables. At this distance we cannot be sure what is meant by "the hired hand" and "the wolf." But we can offer suggestions informed by the text itself. It is clear that together the hired hand and the wolf are responsible for the death of the good shepherd—the first by running away and the second by killing the shepherd. It is possible to suggest that the "hired man" is a coded (and gentle) way to talk about the high priestly establishment. The bad shepherds of Jeremiah 23:2, Ezekiel 34:1-10 and Zechariah 10:2-3 most certainly represented the failed leadership of the community. During the last decades of the second temple period the high priestly office was notoriously corrupt, and Jesus may well be criticizing them for being more interested in their own welfare than in the good of the flock they were responsible to lead. In the three prophetic discussions of bad shepherds harsh and pointed language describes their failures and the looming punishments that they will face. Thus when John mentions the *good shepherd*, the reader anticipates some reference to the *bad shepherds*. But the bad shepherd in John morphs into a hired man who does not kill and eat the sheep (Ezek 34:3). Instead, he simply runs away to save his own skin and avoid responsibility. That is, John 10 includes the traditional theme of the bad shepherd but softens it as he applies it to the high priest. Then there is the wolf.

Here in the first strophe (cameos 1-7) of this three-part song, *the good shepherd is killed by the wolf.* Then in the third strophe (cameos 11-15) *death is*

---

[43]This is precisely the same as the previous strophe where the robbers appear in exactly the same two positions.

conquered (by Jesus the good shepherd) *through resurrection.* Thus in some profound sense the wolf must represent the agent of death. And every reader of this great song knew only too well that Rome was the agent of death at the cross.[44] Thus at the cross the wolf may represent death incarnate in the power of Rome. Rome's power over Judea was not defeated Easter morning, but death was. Tellingly it is John who informs us that Rome alone had the legal power to condemn a man to death (Jn 18:31). At the cross the "Jerusalem street" stood silently (in respect), and at the end of the day (Lk 23:26-49) they were sympathetic to Jesus, as previously noted. But the high priests were implicated in his death, and Rome executed him. At the cross the finest system of justice in the ancient world (Rome) combined with the leaders of the finest religion the world had ever known (Judaism) to destroy *this good man.* The hired hand (because he ran away) and the wolf (because he attacked) were co-conspirators in the death of the shepherd and the scattering of the flock. Yet on Easter morning at the empty tomb a far greater victory was won than any the Roman army achieved on any field of battle. In discussing the resurrection Paul writes, "The last enemy to be destroyed is death" (1 Cor 15:26).

But where in the parable of the wolf is the record of the great struggle between the good shepherd and the wolf? Answer: nowhere! The death of the shepherd is affirmed, but there are no details. Dramatically speaking, there is *a missing scene.* Where is the description of "the big fight"? There is no such description—anywhere! This absence of detail is a mirror image of the Gospel accounts of the cross. Mark and Luke state simply, "They crucified him," using two words in Greek (representing two words in Hebrew). Matthew and John are even more reticent in this regard. They flatly refuse to focus their verbal camera on the dreadful moment; instead they skip ahead in time to the casting of lots for his clothes and look back saying, "And when they had crucified him, they . . ." (Mt 27:35; Jn 19:23). Their camera never focuses on the driving of the nails or the raising of the cross.

Even so, here in John the text has no record of the big fight that concludes with the death of the good shepherd. At the end of the great struggle (with the wolf) a person (the shepherd) lies dead on the stage, but the audience does not witness his death. There is no language such as

---

[44]The identification of the wolf as a symbol for death was made by Ibn al-Salibi in the twelfth century (Ibn al-Salibi, *Tafsir*, 2:369).

The powerful wolf quickly dispatched the sheep dog and then threw himself with great speed and power at the trembling flock. Quickly the shepherd blocked his way. The wolf deftly dodged the first blow of the shepherd's heavy rod and managed to tear at the shepherd's leg. The shepherd swung once more striking the wolf on the back. The raging animal momentarily backed away only to lunge again with its full weight trying to knock the shepherd to the ground and tear his throat. The sheep fearfully awaited the outcome of the fearsome battle.

The modern film industry would make this scene the central focus of the story. Not so the authors of the New Testament, who in describing the cross refuse to participate in the "pornography of suffering." The spectacles in the Roman Colosseum reveled in it. But in the New Testament the brutality of the cross is never described. The authors of the Gospels focus on the fact *that it happened* and then turn the reader's attention the question of *what it means*. This is precisely what appears in the good shepherd text before us. The hired hand is described in the briefest of terms and is found wanting. The criticism of the bad shepherds in Ezekiel 34:1-10 is much harsher and more specific than what appears here in John 10:11-14. But the story is not finished. The wolf and the hired hand do not have the final word. In the outer envelope around the account of the attack of the wolf and the death of the good shepherd (cameos 1, 7) there is this stunning affirmation as to its meaning. And there is more.

The song as a whole concentrates on communicating the meaning of *both* the cross and the resurrection. To follow the intent of the author we need an overview of the three strophes together. A summary of the full text is found in figure 8.15.

A. The *cross*: the good shepherd lays down his life for the sheep (vv. 11-14).
B. The *task of evangelism*: attracting other sheep that already belong to the shepherd (v. 16).
C. The *cross* and the *resurrection*: I lay down my life and I take it up again (vv. 17-18).

Figure 8.15. The cross, the resurrection and the resulting task

Summarized even further the outline of this rhetorical section is

    cross
        evangelism/proclamation
    cross and resurrection

The cross and the cross/resurrection are a platform on which the good shepherd stands to announce his vision for the future. To shift to a modern image, the center (strophe B) is a rocket fired from the launching platform constructed out of the cross and the resurrection (strophes A and C). Without that platform there would have been no place for the good shepherd to stand and call "other sheep" to him. For centuries thoughtful commentators have no doubt correctly understood the "other sheep" to refer to the Gentiles. But it is not only here that this threefold structure of cross, resurrection and mission are set forth.

Paul's letter to 1 Corinthians can be understood to be composed of five essays.[45] The first, the third and the fifth of those essays can be summarized as follows:

1.   The Cross (1 Cor 1:10–4:16)
3.   Witness to the Jewish and Gentile worlds (1 Cor 8:1–11:1)
5.   The Cross and the Resurrection (1 Cor 15)

The beginning of the epistle focuses on the cross (1 Cor 1:10–4:16).[46] At the end, in essay 5, Paul reaffirms the cross and adds his most extended discussion of the resurrection (1 Cor 15:1-58).[47] Essay 3 in the center focuses entirely on Christian witness to both Jews and Greeks (1 Cor 8:1–11:1).[48] Granted, essay 3 discusses the topic of food offered to idols. But Paul's declared propose is "That I might win more" and "That I might by all means, save some." This theme is repeated six times in a row in 1 Corinthians 9:19-22 and reappears in the conclusion to his summary of the essay, where he writes, "Indeed I try to please all people in everything . . . that they may saved" (10:33). To this basic structure Paul adds essay 2 on "Men and women in the human family" (1 Cor 4:17–7:40) and essay 4 on "Men and women in the Church" (11:2–14:40), but the concrete and steel structure to which he adds these two related topics is the previous summary.

This deep structural similarity between 1 Corinthians and John 10:11-18 suggests at least that the early church understood fully that without

---

[45]Bailey, *Paul Through Mediterranean Eyes.*
[46]Ibid., pp. 65-152.
[47]Ibid., pp. 419-77.
[48]Ibid., pp. 227-92.

the cross and the resurrection they had nothing to say to Jew or to Gentile. But with full confidence in the authenticity and significance of both of those events they were fired like a rocket into that wider world from a launching pad composed of the very fact of the cross and the resurrection.

Returning to our text, what then does the rocket in John 10:16 look like (see fig. 8.16)?

8.	[16]And I have other sheep, that are not of this fold.	THE VISION For evangelism/proclamation
9.	I must bring them also, and they will listen to my voice.	THE TASK Of evangelism/proclamation
10.	So there will be one flock, one shepherd.	THE GOAL Of evangelism/proclamation

Figure 8.16. The shepherd and the "other sheep" (Jn 10:16)

Cameo 8 reads like Acts 18:10, where Paul, while in Corinth, hears the Lord saying to him in a vision, "I have many people in this city." I am reminded of a story that I read some decades ago of a visitor to a village pastor and his congregation in a small rural community in Asia. The guest told the pastor, "I would very much like to visit some of your people." The round of visits began and the guest noted that all the homes they entered were non-Christian homes. The guest politely commented to the pastor, "I deeply appreciate the visits we are making, but I would still like to meet some of *your* people." With a warm smile on his face the pastor replied, "Oh, they are all my people, it is just that some of them don't know it yet." Paul would have understood.

See figure 8.17 for cameo 9.

I must *bring them also,*
and they will *listen* to my voice.

Figure 8.17. The shepherd "brings" the sheep, and the sheep "listen/obey" (Jn 10:16b)

The action of the shepherd in *bringing* the sheep is placed side by side with the action of the sheep who *listen to/obey* his voice. Once again the text makes no attempt at explaining how these separate realities can take place simultaneously. The mysterious union between the action of the shepherd and the corresponding action of the sheep fuse in ways that can be illuminated in a parable like the one before us, and experienced in daily life, but never fully explained. Projecting this text into the task of Christian preaching it is clear that the preacher must never lose sight of the goal of trying to assure that the "voice of the shepherd" is heard, not solely the voice of the preacher.

Cameo 10 affirms "one flock," but *not* "one sheepfold." Our differing languages, cultures, styles of worship and theological heritages all deserve to be preserved and nourished. Let the Coptic Orthodox rejoice in Athanasius, the Lutherans in Luther, the Latin Catholics in Thomas Aquinas, the Syrian Orthodox in Ephrem the Syrian, the Orthodox in Chrysostom and the Reformed tradition in Calvin and Barth. At the same time, all of these towering figures belong to *all of us*. This text summons "all who call upon his name" to recognize that they are a single flock, even though they dwell in different sheepfolds. In the twelfth century the Armenian Archbishop Nerses Lambronac'i wrote from Cilicia, "For me the Armenian is as the Latin and the Latin as the Greek and the Greek as the Egyptian and the Egyptian as the Syrian."[49] Archbishop Nerses in his *Commentary on the Divine Liturgy* also wrote,

> All we Christians adore in diverse tongues one Jesus Christ and all we Christians are the one Church of Jesus Christ. . . . When Christians in Spain pray, that prayer is for me too, for I am a Christian as they are: and when I am praying in Cilicia, my prayer is for them too, for they too profess the same faith as I. . . . I am united by tradition to whoever bears the name of Christ as a crown of glory. All are in Jesus Christ and Jesus Christ is in all.[50]

Thus more than eight hundred years ago this great Armenian scholar, saint and churchman caught and lived out the essence of the text before us.

This brings us to the final section (see fig. 8.18).

---

[49]Quoted by Anoushavan Tanielian in his translation of *Archbishop Nerses Lambronac'i: Commentary on Wisdom of Solomon* (New York: Skewra Press, 2007), pp. 25-26.
[50]Ibid., p. 26.

11. 17On account of this the *Father loves me,*	FATHER LOVES ME
12. because *I lay down my life,* that *I may take it up again.*	I LAY DOWN LIFE & Take it up again
13. . 18*No one takes it from me,* but *I lay it down of my own accord.*	NO ONE TAKES IT I give it – freely
14. I have authority *to lay it down,* and I have authority *to take it up again.*	I HAVE AUTH. TO LAY IT DOWN & authority to take it again
15. This *charge* I have *received* from my *Father."*	FATHER GIVES ME A CHARGE

Figure 8.18. The cross and the resurrection (Jn 10:17-18)

RHETORIC

This final strophe of the song (as in 1 Cor 15:1-11) picks up the theme of the cross already discussed in strophe A (cameos 1-7), repeats it and moves on to the resurrection. That is, the song before us opens (strophe A) with the shepherd's (offstage) death in his fight with the wolf. Now in strophe C, while on stage, Jesus affirms victory over death through resurrection. Here in John 10:17-18, five cameos are once again presented to the reader using the familiar ring composition.

COMMENTARY

This section on death and resurrection opens with a theological challenge (see fig. 8.19).

11. 17On account of this the *Father loves me,*	FATHER LOVES ME
12. because *I lay down my life,* that *I may take it up again.*	I LAY DOWN LIFE & take it up again

Figure 8.19. Love, death and resurrection (Jn 10:17)

Clearly the cross is profoundly related to the love of God. John has already written, "For God so loved the world that he gave his only son" (Jn 3:16). At the same time, the Bible does not hesitate to describe the anger of God. If by "anger" we mean an irritated sense of self-importance, then God has no anger. But if anger is understood as unflinching opposition to evil, then God has a great deal of anger. Romans 5:6-11 discusses that righteous anger. Here the focus is on God's love. That love is described at the end in cameo 15 as a charge, but there is a problem.

The text seems to say that God loves the Son because the Son was willing to lay down his life. That is, the love of the Father for the Son was withheld until the Jesus earned it through death and resurrection. But this text cannot carry that meaning. Such a possibility is ruled out in John 1:1-18 where "grace and truth" come through Jesus Christ, and by its very nature grace is a gift of love. A very fine discussion of John 10:17 is presented by Gary Burge, who writes, "The Father gives everything into the Son's hands (3:35), shows him everything (5:20), gives him life (5:26), and gives his own glory (17) and name (17:26). Indeed, the Father has loved the Son from the 'creation of the world' (17:24)." Burge astutely concludes, "Jesus' voluntary death therefore is a hallmark of his union with the Father's will and an expression of the love they share together."[51]

John 5:20, noted in Burge's discussion, takes the form of a miniparable. In the Middle East the traditional skilled craftsman and his family take trade secrets very seriously. If the family has developed a particular product in glass, wood, brass, stone, silver, gold and the like, the family that develops it is very reluctant to let anyone outside the family see how it is made.

All my life my major hobby has been woodworking. One of the finest Middle Eastern forms of woodworking is called *mahabbaba*. In this particular style of woodworking, finely fashioned pieces of wood are locked together (without glue or nails) to form intricate geometric designs. This style often appears in door panels and altar screens. For forty years I tried to get someone to show me how these beautiful wooden panels are created— I failed. No one would explain or demonstrate how *mahabbaba* panels were made. The Father "loves the son and shows him . . ." The point being that he does not show anyone else. I am not the son of a master craftsman who works in *mahabbaba*, and so there was no one to reveal to me the secrets of the craft. But with Jesus there is no problem in that "the Father loves the Son and shows him all that he himself is doing."[52] All of this clarifies the fact that in the text of John 10:17 the love of the Father for the Son is not some-

---

[51]Gary Burge, *John*, NIV Application Commentary (Grand Rapids: Zondervan, 2000), p. 292.
[52]C. H. Dodd called this a "hidden parable." See C. H. Dodd, "A Hidden Parable in the Fourth Gospel," in *More New Testament Studies* (Grand Rapids: Eerdmans, 1968), pp. 30-40.

thing earned by Jesus through his willingness to endure the cross. Rather, as Burge noted, Jesus' death is "an expression of the love they share together."[53] In 1742 John Bengel wrote concerning this text, "Love is intimated as something over and above. The love of the Father is to be regarded in Christ's passion not only towards us, but also towards Christ."[54] Here in John 10:17-18 the cross and the resurrection flow with great power from the love of God. This becomes even clearer as the strophe unfolds.

Cameo 12 is carefully balanced with cameo 14. Figure 8.20 presents the two together.

12.   because I lay down my life,
       that I may take it up again.

----

14.   I have authority to lay it down,
       and I have authority to take it up again.

Figure 8.20. Power in death and in resurrection (Jn 10:17-18)

The key word *power/authority* (*exousia*) not only represents *power* but also *legitimate authority*. Imagine the following: I walk into a restaurant and order a large steak. The steak is cooked and brought to me. But before I begin to eat, a full-grown lion walks into the restaurant and with one swipe of his powerful paw drags my steak onto the floor and devours it. I am the *first* to recognize the lion's *power* to eat my steak. I am the *last* to grant to the lion "legitimate authority" to consume my steak. For heaven's sake, *I paid for it!*

Jesus does indeed say, "I lay down my life, that I may take it up again." But this is further clarified and balanced with the addition of cameo 14, which affirms, "I have authority [*exousia*] to lay it down, and I have authority [*exousia*] to take it again." In John "all things" are given into the hands of Jesus before the cross (Jn 13:3), and during Jesus' trial Pilate tries to intimidate him by saying, "Do you not know that I have power [*exousia*] to release you, and power [*exousia*] to crucify you?" (Jn 19:10). Jesus then bluntly tells Pilate that he has no power other than what is given to him from above

---

[53]Burge, *John*, p. 292.
[54]John Albert Bengel, *Bengel's New Testament Commentary* (1742; repr., Grand Rapids: Kregel, 1981), 1:649.

(Jn 19:11). Jesus moves through the passion story in John as the director of the drama, not its victim. Even so, here in John 10:17-18, Jesus has the power/ authority to lay down his life and the power to take it up again. This is surely one of the high points of the entire passion narrative in John and beyond. In our contemporary world, few verses in the entire New Testament are more critical for a variety of reasons.

John 10:17-18 is important for *Christian theology*; it is also of pivotal importance in regard to the interface between *Christianity* and *Judaism*, and again in the dialogue between *Christianity* and *Islam*.

As regards Judaism, if Christians would allow this verse to become the lens through which we look at the rest of the Gospel of John, our traditional reading of John would change. No one takes Jesus' life; he voluntarily lays it down. In short, Christians have no right to blame the Jews for the cross!

The high priests, Judas and Pilate are indeed guilty. Furthermore the crowd in Pilate's judgment hall was made up of "all the chief priests and the elders of the people" (Mt 27:1). It was that same pro–high priestly crowd (in Pilate's judgment hall) who shouted, "His blood be on us and on our children!" (Mt 27:25). Righteous people never take what criminals shout in court as a guide for treating the descendants of those criminals nearly two thousand years later! Finally, the Greek word *oi Ioudaioi* means not only "the Jews" but also *"the Judeans."* Jesus and all his followers were *"Jews."* His problem was with *"the Judeans."* This entire discussion is profoundly connected with the text before us where Jesus says, "No one takes it [my life] from me, but I lay it down of my own accord." Would that this text might be given its appropriate weight in all Christian–Jewish interactions.

John 10:17-18 is also pivotal for the emerging interface with Islam. Kenneth Cragg, across his long life, pointed out that Islam has noble reasons for denying the historicity of the cross.[55] The traditional line of reasoning among Muslims is as follows: God always gives victory to his prophets. Jesus is one of the great prophets. But Christian Scriptures tell a story of the cross in which Jesus is devastatingly defeated! This is impossible. Ergo, "the cross never took place." However, in the Gospels Jesus is given the greatest victory

---

[55]Kenneth Cragg was one of the outstanding Christian scholars of Islam all across the second half of the twentieth century. I am here quoting lectures he delivered in my presence at St. George's College, Jerusalem, July 1957.

of all time. He conquers *death*. Writing in the eleventh century in Baghdad, the capital of the Islamic empire, Ibn al-Tayyib writes,

> "On account of this the Father loves me" throughout all eternity, "Because I lay down my life, that I may take it up again." For I surrender [*aslama*] my human self out of my own free choice and out of my love for the Father who wills that I should die on the cross and after a short time I recover myself and rise from the dead. "No one takes it from me" that is, no one takes life from me by force "but I lay it down of my own accord," for the sake of the salvation of the world. "I have power to lay it down and I have power to take it again." This is the proof of his divinity. No human being has ever demonstrated such power, the power to raise himself while he is dead.
>
> "This commandment I received from my Father" that is the Christ was willing to suffer and die and rise again of his own accord and not from any (human) compulsion or force.[56]

The Arabic verb *aslama* literally means "he surrendered," and for centuries has been used to mean "to become a Muslim," since the word *Muslim* is an Arabic word that means "one who has surrendered." Arabic versions of John 10:17 studiously avoid using the verb *aslama*, probably in order to avoid this Islamic meaning. Ibn al-Tayyib does not use this word *aslama* in his translation of the text, but only in his notes. In the process Ibn al-Tayyib makes two profound theological statements. The first is that Jesus is the one who most fully *aslama*, surrendered himself to the will of God, in that he (Jesus) surrendered his very life. But Jesus also demonstrated his divine identity and power by raising himself while he was dead. No one else in history has possessed and exercised such power. Ibn al-Tayyib is very gently affirming that the cross and the resurrection are evidence of the power of God in Christ and not a sign of Christ's weakness. But Ibn al-Tayyib was not the only Arabic Christian interpreter in the Medieval period who struggled with this rich text.

Bishop Dionesius ibn al-Salibi left us a memorable reflection on John 10:17-18:

> He [Jesus] had been beloved by God from all eternity. Furthermore he [Jesus] revealed that he surrendered himself [*aslama nafsu*] for the sake of his flock out of his own perfect will.

---

[56]Ibn al-Tayyib, *Tafsir,* 2.553-54.

And even if my Father, for whatever reason, empowered any one to kill him [Jesus] the meaning of Jesus' own thoughts are: "I am the Lord. I have power even to go to torment and to death when I so choose, and no one under any circumstance can ever take my life from me or obstruct my way by force. And even if I die, I will arise. And I have power to rise up from the dead and in that [event] my Father wills, as I do, that I die for the world. His will and my will are not in conflict, but are in harmony one with the other." And he had already said, "I accepted the clear sign that the Father gives by means of what the son does, so that none might ever sink so low as to say: 'The Father abandoned him to endure death and never fortified him against its torments.'"[57]

Written while resident near the center of the Muslim empire, these thoughtful reflections from the twelfth century demonstrate not only Ibn al-Salibi's insight and courage but also the open-mindedness of the Muslim leaders of that age that granted Christian theologians the freedom to express themselves on controversial theological topics such as this. The song of the shepherd is now ended.

What remains is the task of examining how this great text compares with the origin of the good shepherd series (Ps 23) and with the parable in Luke (Lk 15:4-7) (see fig. 8.21).

Here in John 10 the traditional account of the good shepherd greatly intensifies the cost to the shepherd for protecting and saving the sheep. It then moves on to the great heights of resurrection. Yet eight out of the ten major components of the traditional story are present in some form. This can be noted as follows:

1. *The good shepherd is Jesus.* In the four Old Testament texts examined earlier, the good shepherd is God. All three of the Synoptic Gospels present Jesus as the good shepherd. The same takes place here in John.

2. *The lost sheep/flock.* John discusses an entire flock, not an individual sheep, but there is a significant change in how the flock in presented. In the previous texts the flock is *scattered and lost.* Here in John the flock is in danger because of thieves and robbers, abandoned by the "hired hand" and under attack from a wolf. Thus the fear and danger that result from being lost (seen in the earlier good shepherd tradition) is

---

[57]Ibn al-Salibi, *Tafsir,* 2.370-71.

Ps 23:1-6	Lk 15:4-7	Jn 10:1-18
1. Good shepherd is God	Good shepherd is Jesus	Good shepherd is Jesus
2. Lost **sheep** (no flock)	Lost sheep & Lost flock	Flock Under attack
3. Opponents: Death, "enemies"	Opponents: Bad shepherd loses a sheep	Opponents: Thieves and robbers, hired hand, wolf
4. Good host(ess)?	Good woman	-----
5. Incarnation implied	Incarnation realized	Incarnation realized
6. Price paid: Bring back	Price paid: Search for, find, carry back	Price paid: Death of good shepherd
7. Repentance is **return to God** (*shuv*)	Repentance is **return to God** (*metanoeō*)	----- Sheep are saved by the death and resurrection of the shepherd
8. ----- (good/bad sheep)	-----	-----
9. **A celebration**	**A celebration**	Resurrection of good shepherd
10. Story ends in **house**	Story ends in **house**	Story ends with resurrection victory over death (a charge of love)

Figure 8.21. The ultimate price paid and the decisive victory won

expanded here in John. John has the same general theme but it is significantly intensified.

3. *The opponents.* In Psalm 23 the opponents are "death," "evil" and "enemies." The prophetic accounts focus on "bad shepherds" and the damage they cause.

In Mark, Herod appears indirectly as an opponent to the shepherd (Jesus) and his flock. John is killed, but Jesus is not attacked. Luke presents a bad shepherd who loses his sheep. Now in John 10 the "enemies" are the "robbers," "thieves" and "the wolf." By his cowardly flight the hired hand joins those enemies.

4. *The good host(ess?).* The good host(ess) theme appears in Psalm 23, as noted, and again in Luke 15:8-10, but not in John.

5. *Incarnation.* Jesus the good shepherd appears clearly in Luke 15 and Mark 6. Now in John 10 the theme of the incarnation comes to its climax. John 10 affirms both the *incarnation* (I am the good shepherd) and the *atonement* (I lay down my life for the sheep).

6. *Price paid.* In Psalm 23 God the shepherd "brings me back." The cost is implied and the reader is expected to add things like scrambling over rough ground in the failing light to find the lost sheep and carrying it back to the village. Here in John the cost involved is the very life of the shepherd in a battle with a wolf.

7. *Repentance.* Repentance/return is an important part of the good shepherd tradition from its beginning. But in Luke 15:4-7 salvation by the action of the shepherd and repentance are profoundly linked. Here salvation is discussed (the good shepherd dies "for the sheep") and repentance is thereby implied.

8. *Good and bad sheep.* As in other good shepherd accounts, so here there is no reference to bad sheep.

9. *A celebration.* John's account does not focus on the joyous celebration such as we saw in the stories of the shepherd and the woman in Luke 15. Rather the "sheep" enjoy "abundant life" as they are caught up into the life of the good shepherd who himself lives in the heart of God. Once again a theme known from the past is taken up, transformed and intensified into a new expression. The freedom to enjoy abundant life (Jn 10) is a glorious form of a continuous joyous celebration (Lk 15).

10. *The ending of the story.* The good shepherd tradition gives significant attention to the ending of the story. The scattered sheep are brought home, the lost are found, the refugees are brought home. But the account in John paints its picture on a wider screen. Here in John sheep daily hear and follow the master's voice. They exercise the freedom to go in and out and find pasture. They know they are loved because the shepherd dies for them and

rises from the dead. The self-seeking hired man is gone and the wolf is overcome. The ending in John is expanded to include a vision of the end of all things where there is one flock and one shepherd.

Having stepped into a theological flower garden full of profound meaning, exquisite beauty and awesome wonder we now have before us the daunting challenge of trying to summarize briefly what we have seen and heard. It seems appropriate to focus on each of the five sections in turn.

THE THEOLOGICAL CLUSTER OF THE SONG OF THE GOOD SHEPHERD IN JOHN 10:1-18

1. Morning in the village (Jn 10:1-5)

   a. The sheep know the voice of the Shepherd who is recognized and followed.

   b. Thieves, robbers and strangers try to take advantage of the sheep but they fail.

2. With the flock in the wilderness (Jn 10:6-10)

   a. Jesus is the door to salvation that offers abundant life.

   b. The shepherd grants his sheep the freedom to go in and out and find pasture.

   c. Thieves/robbers only kill and destroy.

3. The good shepherd and the battle with the wolf (Jn 10:11-15)

   a. Jesus is the good shepherd of Psalm 23, Jeremiah 23, Ezekiel 34 and Zechariah 10:4-6.

   b. He lays down his life for the sheep and he takes it up again.

   c. The intimate relationship between the Father and the Son is a witness to the potential intimacy between the son and the believing community—because of the cross. The intimacy between the Father and the Son is not broken, even by a cross, because of the obedient love demonstrated by the Son (Jn 10:17; Phil 2:8-9).

   d. The good shepherd's willingness to sacrifice himself in his struggle with the wolf inevitably creates a bond between the good shepherd and the sheep for whom he dies.

   e. The good shepherd's motive is love. He "cares for the sheep." His action is the action of the Father.

   f. The hireling (the temple leadership?) has no such love and is not willing to get hurt for the sheep.

   g. The suffering of the good shepherd for the sheep is not described, but simply assumed. There is no "pornography of suffering" in the text. What matters is the *meaning* of the event.

   h. The wolf symbolizes the combination of evil forces (religious and political) that killed Jesus on the cross. Those same forces were conquered through resurrection. The wolf appears to win with his "snatching" and "scattering," but in the end (vv. 17-18) it is defeated by resurrection.

4. The good shepherd and the task ahead (Jn 10:16)

   a. The *vision* of evangelism/proclamation: And I have other sheep
                              that are not of this fold.

   b. The *task* of evangelism/proclamation: I must bring them also,
                         and they will listen to my voice.

   c. The *goal* of evangelism/proclamation: So there will be one flock,
                             and one shepherd.

   d. This threefold task is set in the center between a discussion of the cross and a second discussion of the cross and the resurrection. This task cannot be separated from them. The *vision, task* and *goal* of evangelism are together like a rocket fired from the "launching pad" composed of the cross and the resurrection.

   e. The "other sheep" are best understood to be the Gentiles.

   f. The shepherd "brings" the sheep and they "listen/obey." Both actions are essential for the creation of the "one flock." The shepherd acts and so must the sheep.

5. Through resurrection love triumphs over death (Jn 10:17-18)

   a. *As regards the Jews:* Jesus lays down his life. No one takes it from him. In 1 Corinthians 2:8 Paul affirms that had Herod and Pilate known who Jesus was, they would not have crucified him. John 13:3 affirms that on the eve of the cross, "The Father had given all things into his hands." That is, Jesus was in charge of the drama of the Passion. At the trial Jesus tells Pilot that God is in control.

   b. *As regards Islam*: In Islam God always gives victory to his prophets.

Islam is confident that it is showing honor to Jesus by denying the historicity of the cross. This text affirms for Jesus the greatest victory of all, the victory over sin and death.

c. *The cross is an expression of the love of God.* God does get angry over sin (Rom 5). That anger flows from the betrayal of a covenant of love. At the cross, at great cost, anger at betrayal and injustice is reprocessed into grace that flows from that cross in the form of love. "God so loved the world that he gave . . ."

d. *There is a theology of mission:* Jesus does not surrender his freedom to choose the direction of his servanthood. "I lay down my life" says Jesus.

e. *Salvation flows from the cross and the resurrection.* In regard to the passion of Jesus, traditionally the Latin West has placed great emphasis on the cross, while the Eastern Orthodox tradition has focused on the resurrection. In this text these two great traditions meet. Salvation is through the cross *and* the resurrection. Paul writes in 1 Corinthians 15, "If Christ is not *raised* you are still in your sins."

f. *Paul and John.* Paul writes, "God raised him up." John records, "I have power to take it up again." Both are true. A diamond sheds light in many directions.

g. *Theology of the cross.* At the cross evil is engaged, suffering is endured, costly love is demonstrated and victory is won. "I lay down my life that I may take it again." Why? To demonstrate that sin and death are defeated. The shepherd dies, but in the process, sin and death are overcome. On the cross, evil enacts its horrifying worst, yet it cannot break the will and dignity of the crucified One. Through resurrection that ultimate evil is defeated and redeemed.

At the end of the day one senses the need to return to,

Nothing in my hand I bring,
Simply to thy cross I cling.[58]

Our final question is: How does the good shepherd tradition play out in the life of the early church? To answer this question we turn to 1 Peter 5:1-6.

---

[58]Augustus M. Toplady, "Rock of Ages," 1776.

9

THE GOOD SHEPHERD
AND 1 PETER 5:1-4

In the middle of an epistle filled with reflections on many weighty theological topics, here in 1 Peter 5:1-4 the apostle presents a brief discussion of Christian leadership. In doing so he does not reflect on a centurion and his soldiers, a master builder and his stone masons, a sea captain and his sailors or a governor and his administrative staff. Instead he turns to the picture of a shepherd and his flock. Although the text does not discuss a lost sheep and a shepherd who goes after it, the overlap with the biblical good shepherd tradition is sufficiently extensive that it seems appropriate to include this text in our study of the good shepherd tradition in biblical literature.

The epistle identifies Peter as the author (1 Pet 1:1). Near the end of the letter there is reference to a "brother" by the name of Silvanus who helped him (1 Pet 5:12). No doubt Peter's Greek was not adequate for the composition of such a document. In modern times, voices have been raised claiming that Peter the apostle could not have written such a theologically sophisticated work. Joseph Fitzmyer lists six proposed arguments against Petrine authorship but finds none of them convincing.[1] A reference to the emperor is particularly significant.

In 1 Peter 2:13-17 there is an important discussion of being subject to "every human institution." This includes governors and the emperor, who

---

[1]Joseph Fitzmyer, "The First Epistle of Peter," in *The Jerome Biblical Commentary* (Englewood Cliffs, NJ: Prentice-Hall, 1968), 2.362. The Silvanus mentioned in this text is most likely the Silas of Acts 15:22, 27, 40.

are presented in a positive light. The epistle therefore appears to have been written before Nero began his A.D. 64 persecution of Christians, in which Peter was martyred. Fitzmyer suggests a date of early 64 for the composition of the epistle. John Elliott argues for the authorship of "a circle once gathered around the apostle Peter and now writing in his name." He continues, "Less important than who actually wrote the letter is the fact that 1 Peter represents the witness of the apostle Peter."[2] In either case the epistle offers penetrating insights into Christian leadership under the banner of the good shepherd.

Peter's opening reference to the shepherd and the sheep is in 1 Peter 2:25, which says, "For you were straying like sheep, but have now returned to the shepherd and overseer of your souls." Then in the beginning of chapter 5 Peter returns to the imagery of the shepherd and his flock (see fig. 9.1).

1. [5:1]I therefore[a] exhort the elders among you, as the fellow elder and a *witness to the sufferings of Christ,* as well as a partaker in the *glory* to be revealed.[b]	CHRIST His sufferings & glory
2. [2]Shepherd *the flock of God* that is with you,[c]	SHEPHERD THE FLOCK With you
3. exercising *oversight,* not under compulsion but *willingly,*	WILLINGLY No compulsion
4. as *God* would have you *do it;* not for shameful *gain* but *eagerly;*	EAGERLY No dirty money
5. [3]not domineering over those in your charge, but being *examples to the flock.*	EXAMPLE TO FLOCK In your charge
6. [4]And when the *chief Shepherd* appears, you will receive the unfading *crown of glory.*	CHRIST Chief shepherd & glory

[a]My translation. RSV and ESV translate it as "so."
[b]RSV reading.
[c]BAGD, p. 259. Bauer notes the use of *en* "to introduce the persons who accompany someone: *with."* This shade of meaning seems appropriate. The RSV has "in your charge." The ESV reads "among you."

Figure 9.1. The shepherds and the chief Shepherd (1 Pet 5:1-4)

[2]John Elliott, "Peter, First Epistle of," *Anchor Bible Dictionary,* ed. David Noel Freedman (New York: Doubleday, 1992), 5.227.

As in previous texts, we will once again examine the literary structure and then turn to the theological and ethical content of the passage.

RHETORIC

The rhetorical style of the text is simple and clear. The four verses are composed of six cameos that exhibit ring composition. This ring composition comes to its completion at the end of verse four, and verse five opens a new subject that I have chosen to omit.

COMMENTARY

This brief passage opens with the use of the connective *oun*. The *Bauer New Testament Lexicon* defines this word as introducing something that "is the result of or an inference from what precedes."[3] Bauer translates *oun* as *so, therefore, consequently, accordingly, then*.[4] First Peter uses this word six times (1 Pet 2:1, 7; 4:1, 7; 5:1, 6). In each case the text indicates that what follows is profoundly related to and flows from what precedes. Across the six occurrences of *oun* in 1 Peter, modern translators have commonly used "therefore" and "so," but "therefore" is more prominent. For his famous Latin Vulgate translation Jerome used the word *ergo* (therefore).[5] But therein lies a problem.

The best and the oldest copies of the Greek New Testament include this word in the opening of 1 Peter 5:1. But from about the fifth century onward some texts omit it. The "received text" that was passed down through the centuries and used by the King James translators did not include it. We can only speculate as to why it was occasionally omitted. We know that the early Greek chapter divisions indicate the beginning of a new topic in 1 Peter 5:1.[6] Perhaps some copyists thereby concluded that 1 Peter 5:1-4 was *not* connected to 1 Peter 4:12-19, and so they quietly left the word *oun* (therefore) out of the text. Modern translators appear to be partly influenced by this trend in that they have a tendency to use "so" rather than "therefore." The

---

[3]BAGD, p. 593.
[4]Ibid.
[5]Jerome had slightly different wording in his Greek text with τους rather than *oun*. The Latin text still reads "ergo."
[6]The chapter divisions were called the *kefalaia*.

word *so* in English can be read as a simple connective like "and."[7] "Therefore" makes clear that what follows flows from what comes before. In harmony with Jerome's Latin Vulgate, and the best and oldest of the early Greek texts, I have chosen "therefore" to indicate a connection between 1 Peter 4:12-19 and our text in 1 Peter 5:1-4. What then is the "tie that binds" the two together (see fig. 9.2)?

---

1. [5:1]I therefore exhort the elders among you, as the fellow elder   CHRIST
   and a *witness to the sufferings of Christ,*   His Sufferings & Glory
   as well as a partaker in the *glory* to be revealed.

Figure 9.2. Suffering and glory (1 Pet 5:1)

Peter identities himself as "*the* fellow elder." More than a hundred years ago Charles Bigg noted that Peter is saying, "Not *a* fellow-presbyter, but *the* fellow presbyter whom you know so well."[8] Peter thus assumes some form of leadership over the others. He is "the" elder, but at the same time he is a "fellow elder" in that he is working along side of them.[9] Leadership and collegiality are affirmed together. As "*the* fellow elder" he has the right to offer advice to them regarding the style of leadership appropriate to their calling, and at the same time he is their colleague. He continues with further self identification.

Peter also describes himself as a "witness to the suffering of Christ." In his detailed and thoughtful study of 1 Peter, Edward Selwyn asks, "Why does not St. Peter speak of himself rather as an eyewitness of the resurrection (cf. Lk 24:12, 34; Acts 1:22) or of the passion and resurrection combined (cf. Acts 1:8; 5:32; 10:39)?"[10] Selwyn answers his own question by noting that the theme of suffering and glory is prominent all through the epistle and that in the paragraph just before our text Peter writes, "But rejoice insofar as you share Christ's sufferings, that you may also rejoice and be glad when his glory is revealed" (1 Pet 4:13). In 1 Peter 5:1 Peter continues this topic of suffering and glory, which appears to be the point of connection that joins our

---

[7]"So what happened next?" is fairly close to "And what happened next?"

[8]Charles Bigg, *Epistles of St. Peter and St. Jude,* International Critical Commentary (Edinburgh: T & T Clark, 2002), p. 186.

[9]The word *fellow elder* (*sympresbyteros*) occurs only here in the entire New Testament.

[10]Edward G. Selwyn, *The First Epistle of St. Peter* (London: Macmillan, 1947), p. 228.

text to what precedes it. But before turning to the weighty topic of "suffering and glory," there is a prior question that needs to be asked.

We know that Peter witnessed the resurrection. We also know that he was with Jesus through the experience of his arrest in the garden and remained in the courtyard during Jesus' trial before the Sanhedrin. But did he witness the rest of the events of Good Friday? In short, Peter boasted in the upper room, wounded a man in the garden, denied Jesus during his trial and then disappeared. Can he justly claim to be a "witness to the suffering of Christ"? Strangely, Selwyn does not ask this question.

Furthermore, here in verse 1 Peter is very specific, he was a *martys*, an *eye and ear witness*.[11] He was not simply a member of the apostolic band and thus "in town" at the time of these crucial events. How are we to understand this text? Perhaps the answer is available when we ask the question, is the "suffering of Christ" limited to the last twenty hours of his earthly life, or is more of his life involved?

The deepest pain known to the human spirit is what the late Kenneth Cragg described in my presence as "the agony of rejected love."[12] Surely the reality of "He came to his own and his own received him not" (Jn 1:11 KJV) was not limited to a single experience that began at his arrest on Thursday night of holy week and ended less than twenty-four hours later! Rather, in his home synagogue, at the very beginning of his public ministry (Lk 4:16-30), Jesus' message so enraged his fellow villagers that they drove him out of town determined to kill him.[13] Even though Jesus escaped that attempted assassination, was the event not painful to him? The rude public insults he received in the house of Simon the Pharisee (Lk 7:36-50) were likewise humiliating.[14] There is suffering, too, behind the wistful question in John 6:67, "Will you also go away?" Plans to destroy Jesus surface as early as Mark 3:6, where Pharisees and Herodians join in their determination to kill him. Those two parties were relentless political enemies. Yet their opposition to Jesus was sufficiently intense that it brought them together. Is not

---

[11]BAGD, p. 494.

[12]I heard him use this phrase in lectures he delivered in a study course at St. George's Cathedral in Jerusalem, July 1958.

[13]Kenneth E. Bailey, *Jesus Through Middle Eastern Eyes* (Downers Grove, IL: IVP Academic, 2008), pp. 147-69.

[14]Ibid., pp. 239-60.

all of this and much more a part of the "suffering of Christ"? Was he not "despised and rejected of men; a man of sorrows, and acquainted with grief" (Is 53:3 KJV)? Peter was an eyewitness to this pain even though he was not present during its climax on the cross. Thus can he not truthfully declare himself to be a "witness to the suffering of Christ"? I think he can.

The text continues, "as well as a partaker [*koinōnos*] in the glory to be revealed." Three important questions are raised by this freighted verse. What is the nature of the "glory" here mentioned? Whose glory is the text discussing? And finally, what is the relationship between suffering and glory affirmed by this text?

At the beginning of the twentieth century, commenting on the word *glory*, A. R. Whitham wrote, "There are few commoner words in the English Bible than 'glory,' and few more difficult of definition. . . . Reputation, praise, honor (true and false), splendor, light, perfection, rewards, —all these varying conceptions seem covered by the same word."[15] During the American Civil War (1861–1865) Robert E. Lee, the commander of the southern army, ordered a disastrous frontal assault against the northern army in the pivotal Battle of Gettysburg. Within minutes the Southern charge was repulsed, with thousands dead and wounded. As the remnant of the attacking force fled past him in retreat, Lee tried to console the general who led the catastrophic charge by saying, "General Pickett, you and your men have covered yourselves with glory." Pickett replied, "Not all the glory in the world, General Lee, can atone for the widows and orphans this day has made."[16] Such military use of the word *glory* further confuses the English language reader of the text before us. Lee's use of the word *glory* had to do with winning crucial battles, killing large numbers of people and achieving undying acclaim in the hearts of the supporting community. What then does this key word mean in biblical literature?

The secular Greek word *glory* (*doxa*) means no more than "an opinion" expressed by a speaker or writer. But *doxa* in the Greek Old Testament translates the Hebrew word *kabod*, which has to do with *weight*. *Kabod* (and its

---

[15]A. R. Whitham, "Glory," in *A Dictionary of Christ and the Gospels*, ed. James Hastings (Edinburgh: T & T Clark, 1906), 1.648.
[16]Allen C. Guelzo, *Gettysburg: The Last Invasion* (New York: Knopf, 2013), pp. 428-29.

derivatives) occurs 375 times in the Hebrew Bible.[17] Particularly in Ezekiel that glory (weight) of God "was and will be again (in) the temple."[18] When applied to a person, "a 'weighty' person in society, [is] someone who is honorable, impressive, worthy of respect."[19] As Gary Burge notes, "Few concepts in antiquity were more important than honor, distinction, esteem and glory."[20] The Koehler–Baumgartner lexicon translates *kabod* as, "weight, honor, reputation, splendor, light, and sanctity."[21] Gerhard von Rad notes, "Kabod is something weighty or impressive, a gravitas which constitutes man's place in society."[22]

Furthermore, glory in the Bible has at least five applications. These are:

1. The glory of God

   "The heavens declare the glory of God." (Ps 19:1)

   "Glory to God in the highest." (Lk 2:14)

2. The glory of Jesus

   "We have seen his glory." (Jn 1: 14)

3. The glory to be revealed (at the end of all things)

   "The glory to be revealed . . . the unfading crown of glory." (1 Pet 5:1, 4)

4. Glory and believers

   "A *partaker* in the glory to be revealed." (1 Pet 5:1)

   "that according to the *riches of his glory* he may grant you to be *strengthened with power through his Spirit* in your inner being, so that Christ may dwell in your hearts through faith . . . that you may be filled with *all the fullness of God*." (Eph 3:15-19)

5. Glory and suffering

   "But rejoice insofar as *you share Christ's sufferings*, that you may also rejoice and be glad when *his glory* is revealed. If you are reproached for the

---

[17]John N. Oswalt, "*kābēd*," *Theological Wordbook of the Old Testament* (Chicago: Moody Press, 1980), 1.426.

[18]Gerhard von Rad, "*kābôd* in the OT," *TDNT*, 2.241.

[19]Oswalt, "*kābēd*," 1.426.

[20]Gary M. Burge, "Glory," in *Dictionary of Jesus and the Gospels* (Downers Grove, IL: IVP Academic, 1992), p. 269.

[21]LVTL, *Lexicon*, pp. 420-21.

[22]Von Rad, "*kābād* in the OT," 2:238.

name of Christ, you are *blessed*, because the *spirit of glory and of God rests upon you.*" (1 Pet 4:14)

"I [Peter] . . . as a fellow elder and a witness of the *sufferings* of Christ, as well as a *partaker in the glory* that is to be revealed." (1 Pet 5:1)

"After you have suffered a little while, the God of all grace, who has called you to his *eternal glory in Christ* . . . will himself *restore, establish,* and *strengthen* you." (1 Pet 5:10)

Here in 1 Peter 5:1, 4 we are interested in *glory and believers* particularly in a context of suffering. "Glory" in these texts shines like a diamond that sheds light in a variety of directions. To summarize some of these texts, we can note that the glory of Christ was not only on display at the transfiguration and promised to all believers at his coming. But in addition, those who suffer for Christ are told that they are "*blessed,* because the *spirit of glory and of God rests upon you.*" The glory of God supports and blesses those who suffer *in the now!* Yes, Peter does indeed offer a future glory to his suffering readers. But at the same time "the spirit of glory" is *now* with them and will "restore, establish, and strengthen" them (1 Pet 5:10).

Selwyn notes that the bringing together of suffering and glory "is characteristic of this Epistle."[23] He argues that in 1 Peter 5:1-4 Peter is discussing the transfiguration, where the glory of Christ was revealed to Peter along with James and John.[24] While this certainly forms a part of the background of 1 Peter 5:1, 4, surely there is more.

Here is where the Old Testament Hebrew word for "glory" (*kabod*) is critical. When we discuss "glory" in Scripture (Hebrew or Greek), we are discussing *weight and wisdom,* not *earthly power and wealth.* Both Calvin and Luther affirmed *theologia cruces* (theology of the cross) against what they called *theologia gloriae* (theology of glory). Their choice of vocabulary was appropriate for their time, but not helpful for us. The true glory of God shines forth through the weakness and suffering of the cross. The "glory theology" the Reformers discussed had to do with the wealth, splendor and power of emperors and kings.[25] This they rightly rejected. That same "glory

---

[23]Selwyn, *St. Peter,* p. 228. Selwyn notes 1 Pet 1:11; 3:18-22; 4:13, 14; 5:10, where he rightly observes a link between suffering and glory.

[24]Ibid., pp. 228-29.

[25]I am here deeply indebted to Dr. Bonnie Pattison for sending me her fine lecture "The Suffering

theology" is still with us. Its message now is "if you become a *true* Christian you will acquire wealth." In the circles that endorse this twisted view, such thinking is still popularly called "glory theology," and it takes its definition of *glory* from contemporary (American) culture, not from the *kabod* (weight/ glory) of the Old Testament and New Testaments.

Peter is saying that he was a witness (*martys*) to the suffering of Jesus and a partaker/partner (*koinōnos*) in the glory (of Christ). In short, Peter saw Jesus suffer painful rejection, and also saw how Jesus *responded* to that rejection. As a member of the apostolic band, Peter was united with Christ in that suffering. He watched how Jesus dealt with "the agony of rejected love," and that agony became Peter's agony. In Mark 6 (see chap. 5) Jesus was confronted with the fact of the murder of his relative (John the Baptist). Jesus was under pressure to respond, and a great crowd followed him around the lake to ascertain his response. Jesus opted for neither retaliation nor retreat. Rather he gave a courageous, wise, *glorious* (weighty/wise) response as he fed the five thousand and thus offered "a banquet of life" as a public challenge to the murderous "banquet of death" hosted by Herod. Jesus' response demonstrated gravitas, wisdom and glory. Peter was present witnessing and joining in that glorious response born of suffering. Paul wrote to the Corinthians, "Our inner nature is being renewed every day. For this slight momentary affliction is preparing for us an eternal *weight of glory* beyond all comparison" (2 Cor 4:16-17). We need to retrain our reflexes. When we hear the word *glory* as applied to people, we should instinctively think of *wisdom born of suffering*, not *wealth* or *power*. "Splendor" and "light" are occasionally legitimate options, but never worldly power or acclaim, military or non-military, and there is more.

Human suffering of any kind has a unique potential for good or for evil. As mentioned, in the Hebrew Bible the word *glory* is the word *heavy* (Hebrew, *kabod;* New Testament Greek, *doxa*). When applied to people this weight/ gravitas is of great significance. In the Middle East this biblical definition of glory as gravitas is not unique to Scripture. It applies also to contemporary society all across the area, as my family and I observed it for decades. In Arabic, the title *rajul thaqil* (a heavy man) describes a person who is wise,

---

Church in Calvin's *Se Scandalis:* An Exercise in Luther's *Theologia Crucis*?" (lecture, International Calvin Congress, South Africa, 2010; and Evangelical Theological Society, Atlanta, 2010).

honorable, trustworthy, noble and offers sound advice. When in trouble this person will be able to help you solve your problems. Their thoughts are deep and balanced. When all hell breaks loose he or she will know what to do. In contrast the phrase *rajul khafeef* (a light man) is a person who is scatterbrained, shallow and holds opinions that are of little or no value. He or she is irresponsible and cannot be taken seriously. This person collapses under pressure. One place in English language culture where weight and wisdom are linked is where students, privately discussing the faculty, say, "So-and-so is a *heavy weight* in this faculty, while professor so-and-so is a *light weight*."[26]

Furthermore, in Middle Eastern culture the attaching of "wisdom" to "suffering" reaches as far back as ancient Greece. Aeschylus (an Athenian Greek tragic poet who died c. 456 B.C.) understood this and wrote, "He who learns must suffer. And even in our sleep, pain that cannot forget falls drop by drop upon the heart, until in our own despair, against our will, comes wisdom by the awful grace of God."[27]

But this does not happen automatically. Suffering can lead the sufferer to bitterness, despair, desire for revenge, fear, paralysis and using past suffering (real or imagined) as a club with which to threaten others into bending to the sufferer's will. "Victimism" as a self-serving ideology is alive and well all over the world and continues to fuel unspeakable brutalities. When people suffer profoundly, their suffering becomes an abyss out of which they must climb. Which path will they choose? Will it be the trail that leads to bitterness and revenge, and brings forth death, or will they follow the way into wisdom and weight that can give birth to forgiveness and reconciliation even in the middle of a continuing struggle for justice?

Early in December 2013 Nelson Mandela, the former president of South Africa, died. Imprisoned unjustly for twenty-seven years, Mandela became the first black African president of his country. At the time of Mandela's death, Archbishop Tutu of South Africa wrote regarding him, "I maintain his prison term was necessary because when he went to jail, he was angry. . . . Of course suffering embitters some people, but it ennobles others.

---

[26]This information is not available in the university catalog!

[27]Quoted in Edith Hamilton, *The Greek Way to Western Civilization* (New York: Mentor, 1948), p. 44.

Prison became a crucible that burned away the dross."[28]

Tutu also notes that Mandela, on becoming president of South Africa, invited one of his former prison guards as a VIP guest at his inauguration, and hosted a lunch for the prosecuting attorney who tried very hard at Mandela's trial to have him condemned to death. Mandela invited another of his guards to join the Presidential Security Force, and at the time of Mandela's death that guard said publically that but for Mandela, South Africa would have become another Iraq or Afghanistan. Rather than "justice trials," Mandela set up a "Truth and Reconciliation Commission" chaired by Archbishop Desmond Tutu. In the crucible of his soul, Mandela transformed his suffering into gravitas (kabod). He managed to reprocess his anger into grace, and that grace flowed from his life into the life of his nation and out into the wider world. He was a sterling example of what the Middle East (and the Bible) calls "a heavy man." At the same time, his glory (as wisdom/gravitas) included splendor—a quiet splendor born of suffering that needed no expensive trappings. Mandela's presence was enough. Mandela was educated in Christian schools.

Come with me into the following imaginary scenario. What if during Mandela's term as president in South Africa, serious tribal conflict erupts in Nigeria. The president of America or prime minister of the United Kingdom is invited to fly to Nigeria to assist in achieving a negotiated settlement. Such a world leader would bring economic and military power to the table. Then imagine that Mandela is also invited to join the negotiations. He will not be able to apply large sums of money or military power to the conflict at hand. What will he bring? Only himself. When he walks into the room, everyone present knows that the agenda has changed. Revenge and retaliation, as a method of settling tribal disputes, is by Mandela's very presence powerfully confronted by another option. He is a living witness to the reprocessing of anger into grace! With his presence, his gravitas/glory shines invisibly in the room, and that glory rests on his personal *suffering*.

During the Second World War, Laurens van der Post, the South African author, nearly lost his life in a Japanese prisoner of war camp. After the war, while reflecting on his wartime experiences, he wrote,

---

[28]Desmond Tutu, "Jail Embitters Some but It Ennobled Him," *Guardian Weekly*, December 13-19, 2013, p. 5.

Persons who have really suffered at the hands of others do not find it difficult to forgive, nor even to understand the people who caused their suffering. They do not find it difficult to forgive because out of suffering and sorrow truly endured comes an instinctive sense of privilege. Recognition of the creative truth comes in a flash; forgiveness for others, as for ourselves, for we too know not what we do.[29]

Furthermore, in the epistles we see case after case of suffering that gives birth to wisdom/gravitas.

Paul describes his suffering in 2 Corinthians 11:23-29. Five times he was given the thirty-nine lashes, three times he was beaten with rods, and once he was stoned and left for dead. The list goes on and on. His *glorious* response was, "Who is weak, and I am not weak? Who is made to fall, and I am not indignant?" (2 Cor 11:29). His suffering produced deep sympathy for the weak, and intense indignation against injustice. He was a man of gravitas, a "heavy" man. In his first letter to the Corinthians he wrote, "When reviled, we bless; when persecuted, we endure; when slandered, we try to conciliate" (1 Cor 4:12-13). His suffering produced glory/gravitas.[30]

This same sequence appears in 2 Corinthians 4:6-11:

For God who said, "Let light shine out of darkness," has shone through[31] our hearts to give the light of the knowledge of the *glory of God* in the face of Jesus Christ.

And[32] we have this treasure in jars of clay, to show that the surpassing power belongs to God and not to us. We are afflicted in every way, but not crushed; perplexed, but not driven to despair; persecuted, but not forsaken; struck down but not destroyed; always carrying in the body the death of Jesus, so that the life of Jesus may also be manifested in our body.

---

[29]Laurens van der Post, *Ventures to the Interior* (London: Penguin, 1952), p. 26.

[30]Kenneth E. Bailey, *Paul Through Mediterranean Eyes* (Downers Grove, IL: IVP Academic, 2011), pp. 110-11.

[31]The Greek preposition εν can have a "causal or instrumental" meaning. See LSJ, *Greek-English Lexicon*, p. 552; BAGD, p. 260; F. Blass and A. Debrunner, *A Greek Grammar of the New Testament* (Chicago: University of Chicago, 1962), pp. 117-18 (par. 219). This is where the word εν stands for the Hebrew ב. Blass and Debrunner note the Pauline phrase "in the blood of Christ," that means, "Through the blood of Christ" (Ibid. See Rom 3:25 and elsewhere).

[32]Semitic versions translate the connective word δε as "and," indicating continuity between v. 6 and vv. 7-10. Many of them translate the Greek δε with the Arabic *inna* which means "truly" or "indeed," and indicates both a connection and an emphasis on what follows. The KJV and other English versions have indicated a contrast and translated it as "but."

The "light of the knowledge of the glory of God," writes Paul, has shone "through" our hearts, to others. That glory of God (in the face of Christ) had deeply affected Paul himself. Paul carried the cross (the death of Jesus) with him. The resurrection (the life of Jesus) was also a present power in his life. Once again, suffering and glory are profoundly connected in the present.

To put it another way, "The heavens declare the Glory of God" (Ps 19:1). That glory has to do with the wonder and wisdom of the creation. Not only did God create all that is, but he continues to sustain it. Furthermore God is in control of history and is bringing in his kingdom. This is a glorious part of who he is. The wonder of creation and the overarching control of history are together so astounding as to be beyond our comprehension. Yet in and through suffering we are able to begin to participate in that gravitas, that glory. At the end of all things we will be able to say with Paul, "then I shall know fully, even as I have been fully known" (1 Cor 13:12).

The movement in Scripture from suffering to glory (weight) can be traced as follows. The glory/presence/gravitas of God dwelt uniquely in the temple. Jesus was the new temple and the disciples saw the glory of God shining through his suffering. Through baptism and faith they were united with him, and his life produced in them the power to reprocess their suffering into glory/gravitas. Thus 1 Peter 5:1 points to an open door through which the elders were encouraged to enter. Peter watched how suffering for Jesus evoked grace/glory/gravitas. Indeed, Peter "participated" with Jesus in that suffering. He felt the pain of Jesus at his rejection and knew that through Jesus all believers could transform their suffering as did he. A classical biblical image for this transformation is that of the good shepherd who risks his life daily, enduring many hardships and even losing his life for his sheep. The good shepherd must provide wisdom and fearless leadership for the flock as he faces and overcomes heat and cold, wind and rain, ravenous wolves and ruthless thieves. The end result is a good/beautiful/noble shepherd. It is that image that Peter here invokes. When John wrote "We have seen his glory" (Jn 1: 14) he was not denying the future glory (wisdom/gravitas) to be revealed at the end of history. But his focus was on a present reality in which they had participated.

The text continues (see fig. 9.3).

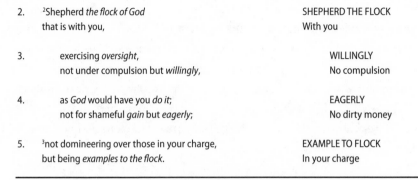

2.	²Shepherd *the flock of God*	SHEPHERD THE FLOCK
	that is with you,	With you
3.	exercising *oversight*,	WILLINGLY
	not under compulsion but *willingly*,	No compulsion
4.	as *God* would have you *do it*;	EAGERLY
	not for shameful *gain* but *eagerly*;	No dirty money
5.	³not domineering over those in your charge,	EXAMPLE TO FLOCK
	but being *examples to the flock*.	In your charge

Figure 9.3. The good shepherd and his leadership style (1 Pet 5:2-3)

Peter calls on the leaders of the church to "herd/shepherd" the flock. The congregations that they led are referred to as "the flock of God." The language is out of the tradition. Psalm 23 does not mention a "flock." The entire psalm is the story of a single lost sheep that is brought back and cared for by the good shepherd. But Jeremiah expands the image and talks of "the sheep of my pasture" (Jer 23:1). The text continues with reference to "my people" who are "my flock" (vv. 2-3). There is no doubt that "my flock" means Israel, and that God is the shepherd. Ezekiel used the same language. The implications of Peter's use of this image are huge. All the promises of God to the "flock of God" in the Hebrew Bible are now promises that can be claimed by the new flock, the church. Peter continues:

3.	exercising *oversight*,	WILLINGLY
	not under compulsion but *willingly*,	No compulsion
4.	as *God* would have you *do it*;	EAGERLY
	not for shameful *gain* but *eagerly*;	No dirty money

Figure 9.4. How the good shepherd must care for his flock (1 Pet 5:2)

The shepherd must lead the flock, but needs to do so willingly, spontaneously, and not because of external pressure. It is not an easy life, but when there is a deep love for the sheep it is a joyful calling. "As God would have you do it" rings with the references to God the good shepherd that appear all through the tradition. How does God the divine shepherd carry out his task? In Psalm 23 the shepherd provides food, water, rest, security and deliverance from fear of evil and death. Central to the "way of God" is incarnation. "You are with me," sings the psalmist in Psalm 23. In Jeremiah, and more so in Ezekiel, God, the good shepherd, promises to come in person to gather and save the sheep. As noted earlier, that promise of incarnation is claimed by Jesus (and the authors of the New Testament) for his ministry. Thus, the good shepherd passages already examined in this study are full of "the way of God" with his flock. Those texts are essential to a biblical understanding of what Peter is here advising.

The final line in cameo 4 uses a rare word (*aischrokerdōs*), which literally means fondness for shamefully acquired profit. The issue is not just "love of money" but rather the love of money *acquired in shameful ways*. There appears to be a special "high" attached to money acquired in underhanded ways. In today's world, the phrase *that's business* is often used to mean "if there is money to be made, all ethical standards are (of course) suspended." Never mind the fact that the drugs I am illegally manufacturing in my basement will ruin the lives of thousands of misguided youth who will buy them—the "profit margin" justifies all things. It is quite amazing to find that the first-century church already had such problems. The rabbinic tradition insisted that no one receive money for teaching the Torah.[33] Jesus allowed his disciples to be paid for teaching the gospel (Lk 10:7; 1 Cor 9:14). This introduced the potential corruption that Mammon brings in its wake. It is an old problem.

The shepherds should lead their flocks eagerly (*prothymōs*) and passionately. Peter was passionate about many things. He wanted the shepherds of God's new flock to engage in leading his sheep with that same enthusiasm. Passion for the gospel was of utmost importance, the compensation package was a minor affair. I wonder what fees Jesus and Paul requested for their lectures? What royalty did Paul receive for writing his epistle to the Romans?

Peter continues:

5.	[3]not domineering over those in your charge, but being *examples to the flock*.	EXAMPLE TO FLOCK In your charge

Figure 9.5. Leading with a gentle call (1 Pet 5:3)

[33]Mishnah' *Abot* 1:13; 3:5.

Peter here uses yet another word that is rare in the New Testament. *Kata-kyrieuō* is to act like a *kyrios* (a master, a lord of the manor). The good shepherd does not direct his sheep with a stick and a bag full of stones gathered to arm his sling and drive them in the desired direction. Rather he leads them from the front with a gentle call, inviting the sheep to follow him. The trail he chooses brings them to green pastures and quiet waters, and provides security even in the valley of death. Paul told the Corinthians to be "imitators of me as I am of Christ" (1 Cor 11:1).

Peter concludes this brief rhetorical strophe:

6. ⁴And when the *chief shepherd* appears,	CHRIST
you will receive the unfading *crown of glory*.	Chief shepherd & glory

Figure 9.6. The crown of glory (1 Pet 5:4)

The "chief shepherd" is Jesus. He was their shepherd, and as such provided a model for Christian leadership in every age. The text now associates glory with the end of all things. When the race is over, the chief shepherd distributes crowns of glory as prizes to the believers who endured to the end. The Greeks gave crowns to the winners of the various international competitions that they organized. The Olympian Games offered crowns of olive leaves. The Isthmian Games awarded crowns of celery. (Sorry, no gold, silver or bronze medals available!) Naturally the crowns made of olive twigs and celery greens quickly faded and wilted.[34] Peter talks of a "crown of glory" that *never fades*. Peter had already told his readers that they had an inheritance that was "imperishable, undefiled, and *unfading*, kept in heaven" for them (1 Pet 1:4). That inheritance included "praise and *glory* and honor at the revelation of Jesus Christ" (1 Pet 1:7). Paul used the same image with the Corinthians who were promised an "imperishable" wreath (1 Cor 9:25).[35]

Paul also told the Corinthians of a "wisdom of God" that was decreed before the ages for "our glorification." This glorification was not built on splendor and acclaim, but on "the wisdom of God" that will be revealed to believers at the end (1 Cor 2:7). He goes on to point out that the "rulers of

---

[34]Otto Meinardus, a German specialist in Eastern Orthodox studies, affirms that the Isthmian crown was "not made of fresh, but of withered wild celery" (Otto Meinardus, *St. Paul in Greece* [Athens: Lycabettus Press, 1972], p. 85).

[35]Paul here uses a different word but is building on the same athletic metaphor.

this age" did not understand any of this "for if they had, they would not have crucified the *Lord of glory*" (1 Cor 2:8). This Corinthian passage makes clear that when Paul thinks "glory" he thinks of the *weight*, indeed of "the wisdom of God," and not of fame and acclaim. This wisdom of God flows from the crucified "Lord of glory" (1 Cor 2:8). Once again we have the wrong reflexes.

For years, this text greatly puzzled me. I could not understand the nature of the "glorification" that Paul was discussing. It was obviously of great importance because it was "decreed before the ages" (1 Cor 2:7). But does not glory have to do with splendor and fame? Was Lee not promising Pickett fame and praise when he tried to assure him of "glory"?[36] How then could popular acclaim be a worthy goal for a believer in any age? But if glory has to do with imparting the gift of the wisdom of God, the entire text takes on a radically different meaning. Paul is talking about the fact that on that great day "I shall know fully even as I have been fully known" (1 Cor 13:12), and this has to do with *glory* understood as gravitas. The very wisdom/gravitas of God will no longer be a mystery to believers, but will be an imperishable, glorious inheritance which they understand and in which they share.

What then of the time-honored tradition of the good shepherd that we have tried to trace for a thousand years from Psalm 23 to the text before us? Which parts of that tradition appear in Peter's reflections on the shepherd leader? The list, as it relates to Peter's text, is as follows:

1. The *good shepherd and his identity*. For Peter, there are three kinds of shepherds. Much of the text focuses on the "elders," who are the shepherds of the sheep under their care. Peter is "the fellow elder," which indicates a leadership role within the framework of a shared task. Finally comes Jesus the "chief shepherd," whose life and ministry is the ideal model for all the shepherd elders.

2. A *lost sheep/a lost flock*. There is no specific reference to any sheep that are lost. However some are treated badly by inadequate shepherds who love money and use a domineering style.

3. The *opponents*. The opponents are offstage. Two types of enemies of the flock appear. (1) The *enemies of Christ* who are persecuting the church. First Peter 5:1-4 does not name these enemies. It was probably not safe to do so.

---

[36]See p. 255, note 16.

However the suffering of the faithful is mentioned again and again throughout the first four chapters. Then in verse 4 the faithful are offered a "crown of glory," which assumes steadfastness in the face of oppression. (The good shepherd tradition is full of enemies that oppose the faithful.) (2) The *bad shepherds* who serve unwillingly. Or they do not follow the pattern of the divine shepherd. These shepherds are "in it for the money" and bully the sheep rather than lead them by example. (These are like the "hirelings" of John 10 and the bad shepherds in Jeremiah, Ezekiel and Zechariah.)

4. The *good shepherd* and the *good host(ess?)*. The good shepherd is the ideal set before them, but his female counterpart is missing.

5. The *incarnation of the shepherd*. Peter writes this epistle in the interim between the first appearance of Jesus, the divine, suffering shepherd and his future arrival as the "Chief-shepherd." Thus the incarnation is both past and future.

6. The *shepherd restores the lost at significant cost*. Peter tells of the "suffering of Christ" that he witnessed, and of the "glory" in which he, Peter, had already partaken. The redemptive nature of the suffering of Christ is assumed although never directly stated or explained.

7. *Repentance/return* (and the use of the verb *shuv*). Bad shepherds are called on to abandon their shameful, domineering ways and to become examples to the flock. Obviously, without repentance those unacceptable leadership patterns would not change. However the verb *shuv* does not appear.

8. The *bad sheep*. This theme is not discussed in 1 Peter 5:1-4 but is covered earlier in 1 Peter 2:25 that reads, "you were straying like sheep." The focus in the Old Testament texts is usually on the faults of the bad shepherds who scattered the sheep that God must gather. Here, as in Ezekiel 34:17-22, the sheep are blamed.

9. A *celebratory meal*. Once again evolution appears in the tradition. The table that appears in Psalm 23:5 and reappears three times as a joyous party in Luke 15 is transformed into an awards ceremony. There may again be overlap with the popular athletic events of the first century. At the Olympian and Isthmian Games there were inevitably some kind of appropriate occasions for the crowning of the winners with their crowns of olive leaves or celery. Peter projects a far grander ceremony in which the faithful will each receive "unfading crowns of glory."

10. The *location of the ending* of the story (in the *house* or in the *land*).

Once again Peter knows and reflects the classical tradition even as he surpasses it. His version of the story does not end in the house or in the land but in the courts of heaven at the end of history.

Remarkably, in one way or another, Peter reflects or reshapes eight out of the ten elements that appear in the long tradition of the good shepherd.

Finally, what ethical and theological content shines forth out of this final telling of the story of the good shepherd?

The Theological Cluster of 1 Peter 5:1-4

1. *Christology.* The Christology of the passage is seen in Jesus the (divine) good shepherd who dwelt among his flock in suffering in the incarnation and who is coming with crowns of glory at the end of history.

2. *Leadership and collegiality.* Peter calls himself "the fellow elder" and thereby affirms collegiality as well as the right to a position of leadership among the elders (pastors).

3. *Suffering and glory.* Suffering in the name of Christ can lead to "glory," which has to do with weight and wisdom, not wealth and fame. That glory is a present potential and a future hope.

4. *The church and the promises of God to Israel.* The "flock of God" through all of the Old Testament texts examined refers to Israel. That same language is here applied to the church. Thus the promises and blessings for Israel apply to the "flock of God," that is the church.

5. *The elder and the shepherd.* The basic model for Christian leadership is the shepherd. That image is then refined with the directive, "Tend the flock of God as God would have you do it." This language assumes that the reader knows all about "God the good shepherd" in the tradition. It is that prophetic pattern of leadership that is here recommended.

6. *Leadership that is neither domineering nor corrupted by money.* Corrupting mammon and oppressive leadership is an ever-present danger to the health of the church.

7. *Leadership style.* The question is, will the shepherd drive or lead?

8. *The ending.* The elders/shepherds are told that they will receive the unfading crown of glory when the "chief shepherd" appears. This promise

is not conditional. The elders (pastors) are not promised, "*if you follow my advice*, you will receive a crown." Rather the crown of glory is promised unconditionally. This is a healing word of encouragement for all pastors.

Our journey with the good shepherd has taken us over high mountains and through deep valleys. The green pastures and quiet waters have refreshed us on our way. All that remains is to reflect briefly about a few of the major high and deep places through which we have traversed.

POSTSCRIPT

After completing a journey of a thousand years from Psalm 23 to 1 Peter 5, what can be said as we meditate on what we have seen and heard in the texts examined? Each of the passages studied has its own setting and focus, and a summary of the whole does not seem appropriate. Yet some reflection on a few high points may be worth recording. At the end of the pilgrimage my mind turns to the following five themes.

1. *The good shepherd tradition.* Initially we can note the fact that there *was a path for the journey.* The ten aspects of the good shepherd tradition that tie the nine texts together do provide continuity between the various expressions of the good shepherd tradition (while allowing for flexibility). I submit that the modern reader can with confidence assume that the ancient readers/ listeners knew the basic flow of the good shepherd story, and that those readers/listeners listened to each fresh telling of the story in the light of what was remembered from what preceded it in the tradition. Each text in the series we have examined is enriched by the good shepherd texts that come before it. This awareness opens new possibilities for us as we attempt to retread and learn afresh from the ancient paths that lead from one account to the next.

2. *Christology from the mouth of Jesus.* Of all the varied themes that the good shepherd tradition presents, perhaps the most significant of all has to do with *the identity of the good shepherd.* The movement from "the good shepherd is God" to "the good shepherd is Jesus" and finally "the good shepherd is a model for church elders" is clear and unmistakable. All three items in this short list of three are well known. Thanks to the unfading popularity of Psalm 23, "The Lord is my shepherd" is familiar to all. The last of this short list is also well known in that many modern churches call the ordained leader of the local

congregation "pastor," that is, "shepherd." Thus, both our understanding of God and of the leader of the local congregation has for centuries been informed by reflection on the good shepherd texts here studied. "Jesus the good shepherd" is even better known because of the two parables that Jesus told about the good shepherd (Mt 18; Lk 15). But "Jesus the good shepherd" has not always been studied in the light of the good shepherd tradition that informs it.

As is known to all, the book of Acts traces the spread of the church from Jerusalem to Rome. This is well and good. But what if Paul (with Luke) had chosen to take the gospel to Babylon and India rather than to the West? Had that happened, the book of Acts would have told a very different story, and Paul would have formulated his understanding of the Messiah of God using different language.[1] The average Middle Easterner does not "illustrate ideas"; he or she "thinks in pictures." One point of reference for this basic approach to reflection and communication is their extensive use of proverbs.[2] A Westerner may say, "Interpretation of the Bible helps the reader understand the text." An Easterner will tell you, "Midrash [interpretation] is the hammer which awakens the slumbering sparks in the anvil of the Bible." Had he traveled east, Paul would have found appropriate ways to communicate his theology to his listeners and readers.

In regard to the Greco-Roman world, the church's understanding of the person of Jesus was crystallized in A.D. 325 in the Nicene Creed, which reads,

> We believe in one Lord, Jesus Christ,
> the only Son of God,
> eternally begotten of the Father,
> God from God, Light from Light,
> true God from true God,
> begotten not made,
> of one being with the Father.

I confess this creed with a good heart and with no disclaimers or footnotes. At the same time, in Luke 15, when Jesus is challenged as to why he welcomes

---

[1]Such a divide took place within Judaism. The authoritative *Babylonian Talmud* and the *Midrash Rabbah*, written in Aramaic, are distinctively different from the works of Philo of Alexandria (and others), who wrote and thought in Greek. Jerusalem and the West was different from Jerusalem and the East.
[2]Anis Freyha made a limited collection of proverbs known and used in his village of Ras al-Metan. He went to press when his assembled list reached 4,248 proverbs. I have similar collections from Egypt, Yemen and Palestine. See Anis Freyha, *A Dictionary of Modern Lebanese Proverbs* (Beirut: Librairie du Liban, 1995).

"sinners" and eats with them, he tells the three parables of a good shepherd, a good woman and a good father. Christology has been seen in each of those parables, and, in a special way, in the first of them Jesus was unmistakably talking about himself as he connected with the good shepherd tradition of the Hebrew Bible. This Christology affirmed by Jesus is Jesus telling us who he understands himself to be, using the metaphorical language available to him in the Hebrew Scriptures. And does not the Christology of the Nicene Creed overlap profoundly with Jesus' parable of the good shepherd in Luke 15 when it is seen in the light of the good shepherd tradition?

In the inevitable coming theological interface with Islam, surely this Christology from the mouth of Jesus has the potential to bypass centuries-old roadblocks to understanding and authentically communicate afresh, without compromise of meaning, the biblical understanding of who Jesus affirmed himself to be. He was *the good shepherd* who was promised in Jeremiah 23, Ezekiel 34 and Zechariah 10, and who appeared in Luke 15, Mark 6, Matthew 18 and John 10.

3. *Salvation.* The lens of the doctrine of salvation is a third aspect of the good shepherd tradition that is especially significant. In one way or another, in all of the texts examined in this study, the good shepherd pays a price "to seek and to save the lost" (Lk 19:10). Thus the good shepherd tradition invokes reflection on the meaning and the means of that salvation.

4. *Christian leadership.* The texts here studied offer a matchless window into a biblical vision for *Christian leadership* in every age. The good shepherd from Psalm 23 to 1 Peter 5 is a guide for good shepherds in every generation.

5. *Jesus as a theologian.* Jesus is the central figure in each of the four Gospel accounts of the good shepherd. His teachings and dramatic actions do not simply promote a series of values or ethical standards, but they surface as profound theological affirmations of the deep things of God as expounded by Jesus of Nazareth. His parables and dramatic actions studied here, edited as they are by the Gospel authors, present Jesus as a thinker, not merely as a doer; a theologian as well as an ethicist.

Hopefully the above study of the good shepherd biblical tradition will help us to follow more perfectly the one who is able to "bring out of his treasure what is new and what is old" (Mt 13:52).

Soli Deo Gloria

BIBLIOGRAPHY

General Bibliography

Albright, William F., and C. S. Mann. *Matthew*. Anchor Bible Commentary. New York: Doubleday, 1971.

Badr, Habib, ed. *Christianity: A History in the Middle East*. Beirut: Middle East Council of Churches Studies & Research Program, 2005.

Bailey, Fred, ed. *Mark I Manuscript Study Manual*. Revised and abridged by Andrew T. Le Peau. Unpublished manual, InterVarsity Christian Fellowship/USA, July 2010.

Bailey, Kenneth E. *Finding the Lost: Cultural Keys to Luke 15*. St. Louis: Concordia Press, 1992.

———. *Jacob and the Prodigal: How Jesus Retold Israel's Story*. Downers Grove, IL: IVP Academic, 2003.

———. *Jesus Through Middle Eastern Eyes: Cultural Studies in the Gospels*. Downers Grove: IVP Academic, 2008.

———. *Paul Through Mediterranean Eyes: Cultural Studies in 1 Corinthians*. Downers Grove: IVP Academic, 2011.

———. *Poet and Peasant Through Peasant Eyes*. Grand Rapids: Eerdmans, 1980.

Barclay, William. "The Good Shepherd," in *Jesus As They Saw Him*. New York: Harper & Row, 1962.

Barnett, Paul. *Finding the Historical Christ*. Grand Rapids: Eerdmans, 2009.

Bauckham, Richard. *Gospel Women: Studies of the Named Women in the Gospels*. Grand Rapids: Eerdmans, 2002.

Bauer, Walter. *A Greek-English Lexicon of the New Testament and Other Early Christian Literature: A Translation and Adaptation of the Work of Walter Bauer.* Edited by William F. Arndt, F. Wilber Gingrich and Frederick W. Danker. Chicago: University of Chicago Press, 1959.

Bengel, John A. *Bengel's New Testament Commentary.* Translated by C. T. Lewis and M. R. Vincent. 2 vols. Grand Rapids: Kregel 1981.

Bigg, Charles. *Epistles of St. Peter and St. Jude.* International Critical Commentary. Edinburgh: T & T Clark, 1902.

Billard, Jules, ed. *Ancient Egypt: Discovering its Splendors.* Washington, D.C.: National Geographic Society, 1978.

Bishop, Eric F. F. *Jesus of Palestine: The Local Background to the Gospel Documents.* London: Lutterworth, 1955.

———. *Prophets of Palestine: The Local Background to the Preparation of the Way.* London: Lutterworth, 1962.

Black, Matthew. *An Aramaic Approach to the Gospels and Acts.* Oxford: Clarendon Press, 1967.

Blass, F., and A. Debrunner. *A Greek Grammar of the New Testament.* Chicago: University of Chicago Press, 1962.

Borger, Joyce, ed. *Lift Up Your Hearts: 2013 Calvin Symposium on Worship Sampler.* Grand Rapids: Faith Alive Christian Resources, 2013.

Broadt, Lawrence. "Ezekiel, Book of." In *Anchor Bible Dictionary.* Vol. 2. New York: Doubleday, 1992.

Brown, Raymond. *The Gospel According to John.* Vol. 2. Anchor Bible Commentary. New York: Doubleday, 1966.

———. *An Introduction to the Gospel of John:* Edited by Francis J. Moloney. New York: Doubleday, 2003.

Bultmann, Rudolf. "ελεος: The OT and Jewish Usage." In *Theological Dictionary of the New Testament.* Edited by Gerhard Kittel and G. Friedrich. Grand Rapids: Eerdmans, 1964.

Burge, M. Gary. "Glory." In *Dictionary of Jesus and the Gospels.* Downers Grove, IL: IVP Academic, 1992.

———. *Interpreting the Gospel of John.* Grand Rapids: Baker 2013.

———. *John.* NIV Application Commentary. Grand Rapids: Zondervan, 2000.

Calvin, John. *A Harmony of the Gospels.* Translated by T. H. L. Parker. Vol. 2. Grand Rapids: Eerdmans, 1972.

Chrysostom, John. *Homilies on the Gospel of Saint Matthew*. Nicene and Post-Nicene Fathers 10. 1851. Reprint, Grand Rapids: Eerdmans, 1983.

Cranfield, C. E. B. *St. Mark*. Cambridge Greek Testament Commentary. Cambridge: University Press, 1963.

Cyril of Alexandria. *Commentary on the Gospel of Saint Luke*. Translated by R. Payne Smith. N.p.: Studion, 1983.

Dahood, Mitchell. *Psalms I, 1-15*. Anchor Bible Commentary. New York: Doubleday, 1965.

Davies, W. D., and Dale C. Allison. *The Gospel According to Saint Matthew: A Critical and Exegetical Commentary*. Vol. 2. London: T & T Clark, 2004.

Dodd, C. H. *More New Testament Studies*. Grand Rapids: Eerdmans, 1968.

Elliott, John H. "Peter, First Epistle of." In *Anchor Bible Dictionary*. Vol. 5. New York: Doubleday, 1992.

Fitzmyer, Joseph A. "The First Epistle of Peter." In *Jerome Biblical Commentary*. Vol. 2. Englewood Cliffs, NJ: Prentice-Hall, 1968.

———. *The Gospel According to Luke X-XXIV*. Vol. 2. New York: Doubleday, 1985.

Flusser, David. *Jesus*. 2nd ed. Jerusalem: Magnes Press, 1997.

———. *Judaism and the Origins of Christianity*. Jerusalem: Magnes Press, 1988.

France, R. T. *The Gospel of Mark*. Grand Rapids: Eerdmans, 2002.

Freedman, David Noel. Prolegomenon to *The Forms of Hebrew Poetry*, by G. Buchanan Gray. 1915. Reprint, Brooklyn, NY: KTAV, 1972.

Freyha, Anis. *A Dictionary of Modern Lebanese Proverbs*. Beirut: Librairie du Liban, 1995.

Gillihan, Yonder M. "Associations." In *The Eerdmans Dictionary of Early Judaism*. Edited by John J. Collins and D. C. Harlow. Grand Rapids: Eerdmans, 2010.

Glueck, Nelson. *Hesed in the Bible*. Translated by Alfred Gottshalk. 1927. Reprint, Eugene, OR: Wipf & Stock, 2011.

Gray G. Buchanan. *The Forms of Hebrew Poetry: Considered with Special Reference to the Criticism and Interpretation of the Old Testament*. 1915. Reprint, Brooklyn, NY: KTAV, 1972.

Guelzo, Allen C. *Gettysburg: The Last Invasion*. New York: Knopf, 2013.

Gundry, Robert H. *Matthew: A Commentary on His Literary and Theological Art*. Grand Rapids: Eerdmans, 1982.

Harris, R. Laird. "ḥsd." In *Theological Wordbook of the Old Testament*. Vol. 1. Chicago: Moody Press, 1980.

Hamilton, Edith. *The Greek Way to Western Civilization*. New York: Mentor, 1948.

Hengel, Martin. *The Zealots: Investigations into the Jewish Freedom Movement in the Period from Herod I until 70 A.D.* Edinburgh: T & T Clark, 1976.

Hill, David. *The Gospel of Matthew*. London: Oliphants, 1972.

Holladay, William L. *A Concise Hebrew and Aramaic Lexicon of the Old Testament Based upon the Lexical Word of Ludwig Koehler and Walter Baumgartner*. Grand Rapids: Eerdmans, 1971.

Hooker, Morna D. *The Gospel According to Mark*. London: A & C Black, 1991.

Hultgren, Arland J. *The Parables of Jesus*. Grand Rapids: Eerdmans, 2000.

Ibn al-Salibi, Dionesius. *Kitab al-Durr al-Farid fi Tafsir al-'Ahd al-Jadid* [The Book of Precious Pearls in the Interpretation of the New Testament]. 2 vols. Cairo: 'Abd al-Masih al-Dawlayani, 1914. Note: Ibn al-Salibi wrote in Syriac and died in 1164 A.D. This commentary was translated into Arabic in the Monastery of Za'farani (Southeast Turkey) in 1728.

Ibn al-Tayyib, Abdallah. *Tafsir al-Mishriqi*. 2 vols. Cairo: Tawfiq Press: 1910.

Jastrow, Marcus. *Dictionary of Talmud Babli and Jerushalmi, and the Midrashic Literature*. 2 vols. New York: Pardes, 1950.

Jeremias, Joachim. *The Eucharistic Words of Jesus*. New York: Scribner's, 1966.

———. *Jerusalem in the Time of Jesus*. Philadelphia: Fortress, 1976.

———. *The Parables of Jesus*. London: SCM Press, 1963.

Johnson, Robert M. *Parabolic Interpretations Attributed to Tannaim*. Vol. 1. PhD diss., Hartford Seminary Foundation, 1977.

Khalil, Samir. "The Role of Christians in the Abbasid Renaissance in Iraq and in Syria (750-1015)." In *Christianity: A History in the Middle East*, ed. Habib Badr. Beirut: Middle East Council of Churches Studies & Research Program, 2005.

Keller, Phillip. *A Shepherd Looks at Psalm 23*. Grand Rapids: Zondervan, 1970.

Koehler, Ludwig, and Walter Baumgartner. *Lexicon in Vetris Testamenti Libros*. Leiden: E. J. Brill, 1958.

———. *Supplementum ad Lexicon in Veteris Testamenti Libros*. Leiden: E. J. Brill, 1858.

Lewis, C. S. "The Inner Ring." In *Screwtape Proposes a Toast and Other Pieces*. London: Collins, 1965.

Lund, Nils W. *Chiasmus in the New Testament*. 1942. Reprint, Peabody, MA: Hendrickson, 1992.

Manson, T. W. *The Sayings of Jesus*. 1937. Reprint, London: SCM Press, 1964.

McVey, Kathleen. *Ephrem the Syrian: Hymns*. New York: Paulist Press, 1989.

Meinardus, Otto. *St. Paul in Greece*. Athens: Lycabettus, 1972.

Meyendorff, John. Preface to *Ephrem the Syrian: Hymns*, by Kathleen McVey. New York: Paulist Press, 1989.

Midrash Rabbah. Edited by H. Freedman. 10 vols. New York: Soncino Press, 1983.

Minear, P. S. *Saint Mark*. London: SCM Press, 1962.

Montefiore, C. G. *Rabbinic Literature and Gospel Teachings*. London: Macmillan, 1930.

Moore, George Foot. *Judaism in the First Centuries of the Christian Era*. 2 vols. 1927. Reprint, New York: Schocken, 1971.

Neusner, Jacob. "Pharisaic Law in New Testament Times." *Union Seminary Quarterly Review*, 26 (1971).

Oppenheimer, Aharon. *The 'Am ha-Aretz: A Study in the Social History of the Jewish People in the Hellenistic-Roman Period*. Leiden: Brill, 1977.

———. "People of the Land." In *The Eerdmans Dictionary of Early Judaism*. Edited by John J. Collins and Daniel C. Harlow. Grand Rapids: Eerdmans, 2010.

Oswalt, John N. "*kābēd.*" *Theological Wordbook of the Old Testament*. 2 vols. Chicago: Moody Press, 1980.

Peck, William H. "The Constant Lure." In *Ancient Egypt: Discovering Its Splendors*. Edited by Jules B. Billard. Washington, D.C.: National Geographic Society, 1978.

Perowne, Stewart. *The Later Herods: The Political Background of the New Testament*. London: Hodder & Stoughton, 1958.

———. *The Life and Times of Herod the Great*. London: Hodder & Stoughton, 1956.

Petersen, David L. "Zechariah, Book of." In *Anchor Bible Dictionary*. Vol. 6. New York: Doubleday, 1992.

Rad, Gerhard von. "*kābôd* in the OT." *Theological Dictionary of the New Testament*. Vol. 2. Grand Rapids: Eerdmans, 1964.

Selwyn, Edward G. *The First Epistle of St. Peter*. London: Macmillan, 1947.

Simpson, William. "The Gift of Writing." In *Ancient Egypt: Discovering Its Splendors*. Edited by Jules B. Billard. Washington, D.C.: National Geographic Society, 1978.

Smith, J. Payne. *A Compendious Syriac Dictionary*. 1903. Reprint, Oxford: Clarendon Press, 1967.

Tanielian, Anoushavan. "Biographical Introduction (to the life and ministry of Archbisop Nerses Lambronacʻi)." In *Archbishop Nerses Lambronacʻi: Commentary on Wisdom of Solomon*. Introduction, Translation, and Diplomatic Edition of the Armenian Text by Bishop Anoushavan Tanielian. New York: Skewra Press, 2007.

Thompson, W. M. *The Land and the Book: Biblical Illustrations Drawn from the Manners and Customs, the Scenes and Scenery of the Holy Land*. 2 vols. 1871. Reprint, New York: Harper & Row, 1958.

Trench, Richard C. *Notes on the Parables of Our Lord*. 7th ed. London: John W. Parker, 1857.

Tutu, Desmond. "Jail Embitters Some but It Ennobled Him." *Guardian Weekly*. December 13-19, 2013, p. 5.

Urbach, Ephraim. "The Powers of Repentance." In *The Sages: Their Concepts and Beliefs*. Vol. 1. Jerusalem: Magnes Press, 1987.

Volf, Miroslav. *The End of Memory: Remembering Rightly in a Violent World*. Grand Rapids: Eerdmans, 2006.

Weatherhead, Leslie D. *A Shepherd Remembers: Studies in the Twenty-Third Psalm*. New York: Abingdon, 1938.

Wehr, Hans. *A Dictionary of Modern Written Arabic*. Edited by J. Milton Cowan. Ithaca, NY: Cornell University Press, 1961.

Weiser, Artur. *The Psalms*. Philadelphia: Westminster Press, 1962.

Whitham, A. R. "Glory." In *A Dictionary of Christ and the Gospels*. Edited by James Hastings. Vol. 1. Edinburgh: T & T Clark, 1906.

Special Bibliography on the Good Shepherd

This bibliography includes books and articles authored by Middle Easterners who themselves at some time lived among or became shepherds in the Middle East. This section also includes descriptions of Middle Eastern shepherding, written by authors (Eastern or Western) who closely observed Middle Eastern shepherds caring for their sheep.

Freeman, James M. *Handbook of Bible Manners and Customs.* New York: Nelson & Phillips, 1874.

Haboush, Stephen A. *My Shepherd Life in Galilee: With an Exegesis of the Shepherd Psalm.* New York: Harper, 1927.

Krikorian, M. P. *The Spirit of the Shepherd: An Interpretation of the Psalm Immortal.* Grand Rapids: Zondervan, 1939.

Lamsa, George M. *The Shepherd of All: The Twenty-Third Psalm.* Philadelphia: A. J. Holman, 1939.

Moghabghab, Faddoul. *The Shepherd Song on the Hills of Lebanon: The Twenty-Third Psalm Illustrated and Explained.* New York: E. P. Dutton, 1907.

Porter, J. L. *The Giant Cities of Bashan and Syria's Holy Places.* New York: n.p., 1866.

Rihbany, Abraham Mitrie. *The Syrian Christ.* 1916. Reprint, New York: Houghton Mifflin, 1926.

Scherer, George H. *The Eastern Colour of the Bible.* London: National Sunday School Union, n.d.

Primary Jewish Sources

The Babylonian Talmud (Hebrew-English Edition). Edited by I. Epstine. 32 vols. London: Soncino Press, 1980.

The Tosefta. Edited by Jacob Neusner. 6 vols. Hoboken: KTAV, 1977–1986.

The Mishnah. Translated by Herbert Danby. 1933. Reprint, Oxford: Oxford University Press, 1980.

Midrash Rabbah. Edited by H. Freedman. 10 vols. New York: Soncino Press, 1983.

Full List of Middle Eastern Bible Translations and Commentaries

Syriac

Syriac Bible (Peshitta). Geneva: United Bible Societies, 1979.

The Holy Bible from Ancient Eastern Manuscripts: Containing the Old and New Testaments Translated from the Peshitta, the Authorized Bible of the Church of the East. Translated by George M. Lamsa. Philadelphia: A. J. Holman, 1957.

Evangeleion Da-Mepharreshe. The Curetonian Version of the Four Gospels, with the readings of the Sinai Palimpsest and the Early Syriac Patristic

Evidence Edited, Collected, and Arranged, by F. Crawford Burkitt. 2 vols. Cambridge: Cambridge University Press, 1904.

Arabic

The Holy Bible Containing the Old and New Testaments, in the Arabic Language. Newcastle-upon-Tyne: Sarah Hodgson, 1811. The text is taken from the Arabic of the London Polyglot (1657) and revised by J. D. Carlyle of Cambridge University.

Al-Kitab al-Muqaddas [The Holy Bible]. Beirut: The Bible Society of the Near East, 1980. This is the Bustani-Vandyke version, c. 1865.

Al-Kitab al-Muqaddas [The Holy Bible]. 1880. Reprint, Beirut: Catholic Press, 1960.

Al-Kitab al-Muqaddas [The Holy Bible]. Beirut: The Bible Society In Lebanon, 1993. This is the ecumenical version of the Middle East

Ibn al-Salibi, Dionesius. *Kitab al-Durr al-Farid fi Tafsir al-'Ahd al-Jadid* [The Book of Precious Pearls in the Interpretation of the New Testament]. 2 vols. Cairo: 'Abd al-Masih Al-Dawlayani, 1914. Ibn al-Salibi wrote in Syriac and died in A.D. 1164. This commentary was translated into Arabic in the Monastery of Za'farani (Southeast Turkey) in 1728.

Ibn al-Tayyib, Abdallah. *Tafsir al-Mishriqi* [The One from the East]. 2 vols. Cairo: Tawfiq Press, 1910. A commentary on the four Gospels. Ibn an-Tayyib was a Syriac scholar of the Church of the East (Nestorian).

Matta al-Miskin. *The Gospel According to Luke* (Arabic). Cairo: Monastery of Saint Maqar, 1998.

———. *The Gospel According to Saint Matthew* (Arabic). Cairo: Monastery of Saint Maqar, 1999.

Sa'id, Ibrahim. *Sharh Bisharit Luqa* [Commentary on the Gospel of Luke]. Cairo: Middle East Council of Churches, 1980.

———. *Sharh Bisharit Yuhanna* [Interpretation of the Gospel of John]. Cairo: Dar al-Thaqafa, n.d., c. 1965.

Armenian

Nerses the Graceful of Lambron. *On Psalm 23 [22].* In *Commentary on the Psalms. Manuscript 1526* (Classical Armenian). The Mesot Nashotots Institute of Ancient Manuscripts, Yerevan, Armenia, twelfth century.

This was translated for me by His Grace Anoushavan Tanielian, bishop of the Armenian Orthodox Church of North America, New York. Bishop Tanielian is also the author of a detailed and informative introduction to the life and ministry of Archbishop Nerses Lambronac'i. See Anoushavan Tanielian, "Biographical Introduction," in *Archbishop Nerses Lambronac'i: Commentary on Wisdom of Solomon.*

Modern Authors and Texts Index

Ancient Authors and Texts Index

Middle Eastern New Testament Versions Index (with Septuagint)

Scripture Index